THE PERSONAL EFFICIENCY PROGRAM

THE PERSONAL EFFICIENCY PROGRAM

THIRD EDITION

How to Get Organized to Do More Work in Less Time

KERRY GLEESON

WILEY

JOHN WILEY & SONS, INC.

For general information on our other products and services please contact our Customer Care Department within the United States at (800) 762-2974, outside the United States at (317) 572-3993 or fax (317) 572-4002.

Wiley also publishes its books in a variety of electronic formats. Some content that appears in print may not be available in electronic books. For more information about Wiley products, visit our web site at www.Wiley.com.

ISBN 0-471-46321-3

Printed in the United States of America.

10 9 8 7 6 5 4 3 2 1

PREFACE

When Larry Alexander, my publisher at John Wiley and Sons, suggested the time was right for a new edition to this book, I had to give serious thought to the question, "Do I have anything more of value to say about personal efficiency?" After all, earlier editions of the book covered how to get work done more effectively in a low-tech environment. Later editions covered many of the technical advances affecting how we get things done. At the time it seemed there was only so much you could say about people's personal efficiency, but it didn't take me long to discover what I was missing. You told me.

There is much to be gained improving how you personally process your work. That is what *The Personal Efficiency Program (PEP)— How to Get Organized to Do More Work in Less Time* has been all about. There is still much more to be gained when improving how your *team* processes its work.

How effective we are depends on two factors: (1) how well we as individuals are organized including our personal work habits and (2) how well others we work and collaborate with are organized including how we work together. So the question for me became, "How can we work more effectively and efficiently as a team?" This *Third Edition* not only provides you with the know-how to help you multiply your personal productivity, but it provides the know-how to help you get more from your team.

Is purchasing and reading this book worth the cost and effort? *The Personal Efficiency Program (PEP)—How to Get Organized to Do More Work in Less Time* with nearly one million copies in print in 17 languages proves the book subject holds broad interest.

Having worked with so many people from so many continents

and cultures, I realize that the world of business is converging. Businesspeople throughout the world are faced with similar challenges. We feel we have too much to do and too little time to do it in. Why? Maybe it is because we have a crushing mortgage, so we need to make more money, or maybe your company decided to eliminate assistants in the business, and you must do all of your own administration. Or you run your own small business, and if you do not do it, it doesn't get done!

Whatever the reason, most of us feel pressured to produce more and often with less. I try to not get too philosophical about the reasons why this may be so and instead have devoted my energy to figuring out how we can get done the things we need to get done in the most effective and efficient way possible.

Since the publication of the first edition of this book nearly 10 years ago, there have been huge advances in technology that impact how we get things done. Computer chips power electronic devices that enable us to work virtually anywhere and at any time. The Internet is profoundly changing how we conduct business. Businesses are embracing more flexible work environments, work from home, virtual work—all taking advantage of new technology.

The personal computer, personal digital assistant, flexible office architecture, e-mail, voice mail, and intranets certainly make today's work environment complex. But for all this complexity, many people have managed to master these new tools, effectively work in this virtual office environment, *and still have plenty of time!* There is much to learn from these highly effective and successful people.

This book is the culmination of experiences gleaned from the many highly effective people that we at the Institute for Business Technology have coached and trained over the past 20 years. The focus of our work has been on the *process of personal productivity.* What do these highly productive people do? How do they do it? Can their work behaviors be boiled down to principles we all can apply? The book is a near-complete set of the timesaving ideas and behaviors of these highly successful people. The book also includes proven strategies we have developed to help our clients embrace these productivity ideas and make them part of their behaviors.

Charles Dickens once said: "I never could have done what I have done without the habits of punctuality, order and diligence, without the determination to concentrate myself on one subject at a time." This quote conveys many critical ingredients to success in work and life: habits of punctuality, order, diligence, determination, and concentration.

Tools were different in Dickens's time. Time was perceived differently. But successful behaviors appear timeless.

KERRY GLEESON

Boca Raton, Florida
Spring 2003

ACKNOWLEDGMENTS

My thanks go to the many people who directly and indirectly made this book possible.

To my agent/editors from Executive Excellence, Ken Shelton, Trent Price, and Meg McKay.

To Paula Sinnott, editor; Linda Indig, senior production editor; and my earlier editors, Renana Meyers, John Mahaney, and senior production editor Mary Daniello.

Many thanks to Bary and Lynn Sherman for their hard work and contribution of Chapter 8. Their years of experience helping customers transition into Next Generation Workplace environments have enriched this book and will, no doubt, help many people struggling to work in highly technical virtual offices.

To the staff at Cape Cod Compositors, Inc., for their production management.

To the many clients and friends who devoted time and effort to share their experiences. I had the opportunity to visit a number of our clients this year to see how they have addressed their team and personal organization issues. All willingly shared their experiences and insights and enriched this book. My appreciation goes to Hans Schmied, Marie Gollungberg, Magnus Ericson, Anders Noaksson, Jonus Adolfsson, Patrik Olsson, Eric Raaymakers, Blain Pardowe, Christof Hager, Alex Sulkowski, Viviane Harnois, Rosaleen Hayes, Nancy Fredericks, Mikael Sander, Wim Sijstermans, Frank Spreuwers, Yvonne Mellstrand, Dagfinn Lunde, John Birch, Frans Henrik Kockum, Kirk Stromberg, Mike Gallico and Mike Jurcy, whose input vastly improved the book. I thank you.

To Ira Chaleff, whose time and care made the book possible and whose concepts and words can be found throughout.

To all of the Institute for Business Technology staff whose experiences and refinement of the PEP process have greatly enhanced its results and are the basis for this book.

To Lena Holmberg, Jay Hurwitz, Ron Hopkins, Eric Magnusson, Menno van der Haven, Peter Diurson, Johan Chr. Holst, Randi Bough Holst, Bruno Savoyat, Denis Healy, Ann Searles, Bouke Bouma, Sharon McGann, Benno Jangeborg, Tanya Seldomridge, Megan Skubal, Margareta Norell, Catharina Bivar, Loes Nooij, Sonja Strich, Katharina Dietze, Niklas Lindberg, Susanne Lundberg, Mickael Kongsted, Doug Stewart, and Tony D'Arcy for all their hard work and dedication.

To Jim Robinson, whose assistance with the development of the IBT software applications and techniques of organizing a computer were invaluable.

To Brita Norberg and Janita Thomer from Svenska Handelsbanken Sweden for giving me the opportunity to design the original Personal Efficiency Program.

To all of my many client friends who have taught me most of what you find in this book.

To my wife Jill for her love and my children Brooke, Mackenzie, and Quinn for the joy they bring.

To all of you, many thanks.

K.G.

CONTENTS

CHAPTER 4

Plan It Now!   93

CHAPTER 5

Follow-Up and Follow-Through!   123

CHAPTER 6

Do It *Right*, Now!   143

CHAPTER 7

Do It Now!—From Wherever You Are!   157

CHAPTER 8

Be a *Do It Now* Manager   205

CHAPTER 9

Organizing the Team to Act Now!   219

Chapter 10

Maintain It Now 239

Epilogue

Just One New Habit 253

Appendix A

Meeting Improvements Checklist 254

Appendix B

Time Stealers 256

INTRODUCTION
Personal Efficiency Program: The Missing Link

Perhaps the most valuable result of all education is the ability to make yourself do the thing you have to do, when it ought to be done, whether you like it or not.
—THOMAS HUXLEY

- Do you feel that you are always short of time?
- Do you feel that you have too much to do?
- Do you feel overwhelmed by everything you face at the office?
- Do you have a hard time coping with your e-mail?
- Do you feel buried under mounds of paperwork most of the time?
- Would you like more time to do what you want?
- Do you often work overtime, into the evening, or on weekends to catch up on things you don't get done during regular working hours?
- Do you get stressed out because of what you don't get done?
- Do you find it difficult to say "no" to work?
- Do you waste time in meetings?
- Do your teammates' inefficiences affect you?
- Are you unable to focus on the long-term improvement of your life and your work because you face continual crisis or overload?
- Do you wonder if you really are accomplishing what you want in your work and in your life?

1

- Would you like better results for the time and effort you invest in your work?
- Would you like to relax or vacation more often?

When asked these questions, most people answer with a resounding "yes." If your answer is also "yes," you're in for a pleasant surprise: You can overcome these problems. You can accomplish what is most important to your work and to you and still find time for yourself, for your family, and for the things you'd like to do.

SOURCE OF THE PROBLEM

Why do people feel they never have enough time? Why do they feel both overworked and unproductive? The answer is quite simple. Although most of us have been formally educated to work in our professions, few of us, especially white-collar workers, have been taught *how* to work efficiently and effectively. Too many white-collar professionals have no idea how to organize themselves or how best to process their work. They may understand how to draw an architectural plan, write a clever ad, or negotiate a deal, but they can't effectively organize their week or cope well with interruptions and unexpected new opportunities and priorities.

A friend and coworker from the United Kingdom describes the situation this way:

> *You go to the university, get educated in your profession, and get a job. You start your job, and all of a sudden the paper starts coming. No one ever mentioned the paper! What do you keep? Where do you put it? How do you find it again?*

In my work I've met many bright and clever people who know their professions. They easily solve complex problems that boggle my mind. They build buildings, move cargo, develop products, sell services, even heal the sick. But for all their demonstrated capability and all their education, many of these people live stressful lives simply trying to keep up with all they must do. Why? Because, like you and me, these professionals were never taught the nuts and bolts of working in an office environment.

How you process your own personal work is just one example of a missing element in education. The Personal Efficiency Program (PEP) supplies the missing link.

It is only very recently a fascinating program was being tried at various universities around the country: The program is designed to teach professors how to teach. Imagine—teaching a teacher how to teach! Traditionally, professors haven't been trained in this one vital aspect of their profession: They are only required to demonstrate a conceptual mastery of their specialty. But as many university students could tell you, mastery of an academic discipline does not a great teacher make.

Parenting is another area that lacks basic training. How many couples receive any training in the fine art of parenting before they have children? Likewise, few business managers receive any basic training in how to manage their own business!

HOW DO WE COPE?

Well, we're clever people. We know we could be more efficient and effective at work. How do we deal with this lack of education? We may see a colleague with some sort of organizer or calendar, so we get one. We learn from trial and error how to deal with our work as best we can. And most of the time we're pretty successful. We soon become comfortable with these tools. But, because the routines we establish to address our work are not necessarily based on the principles of work organization, they may not be as effective as they could be. The work habits we have may serve us well in one work environment, but when our job changes or the company merges or downsizes, it may take twice as much effort to achieve the same results. Our earlier ways of coping with the workload may not fit this new, more demanding work environment.

Because we are creatures of habit, making the change is always difficult even if we think a change in behavior would be good. So what *are* the most effective ways of processing your work? How can you successfully change your behavior? How can you become more effective? These questions are answered in this book. And the book shows you how to address these issues efficiently. In the end you will work less, and it will be easier to do what you must do.

DOWN TO DETAILS

I once asked a very wealthy and successful man the secret of his success. He told me in two words: "Detail, detail." We all know our professional success comes from attention to detail, but we may not see how this attention to detail relates to how we personally work. The details of how to work have been defined in our PEP. The knowledge and experiences in this book come from the PEP process. Whether you modestly improve how you do your work or aggressively reengineer the whole process, you will be focused on the details of your work. By concentrating on these details, you will alter your behavior for the better. You will realize many more benefits than you can imagine.

Western manufacturing firms have spent a great deal of time and money analyzing, refining, and perfecting each step in the manufacturing process, especially since receiving their wake-up call from the competition. The effort shows. Productivity and quality have increased dramatically in manufacturing. But in white-collar work, from services to information processing to management, business processes are more difficult to analyze or reengineer. Personal work processes are rarely even considered part of the management business process, let alone analyzed and perfected.

NO LONGER A MISSING LINK

Because the knowledge of how to process your personal work to achieve both quality and quantity is missing in the white-collar world, we have a missing link in the quality and productivity chain, even in those companies that aggressively tackle these issues. Because it's missing, we often don't notice it: It's hard to see something that's missing. Still, this missing link is the cause of endless frustration for many white-collar workers in today's workplace.

The PEP process can supply that missing link in the productivity chain. It will help anyone who has a heavy workload. In the past 20 years, PEP has helped 500,000 people get more done in the 168 hours of the week. PEP teaches you how to:

- Gain more control of your work.
- Make your job easier.
- Save time.
- Determine what is most important to you.
- Accomplish what is important to you.

The Personal Efficiency Program (PEP) is a different way to process your own work that can multiply your personal productivity. I truly believe that it's possible for most people to double, if not triple, their current productivity, primarily because the vast majority of people don't produce all that much. This isn't to say people don't work hard. In fact, working with people in hundreds of companies and a dozen countries has taught me the opposite. People work very hard. And the vast majority of people want to do a good job. They try very hard to do exactly that. But most of us, for all of our hard work, just don't get all that much done. By working right, on the right things, there is hardly a limit to one's production capability. PEP provides the know-how to do things right and to work on the right things.

Using PEP will simplify your work. With it, you will exert less effort in work than you do now.

WORKING WITH OTHERS

No matter how efficient you are, you still have to work with others, and their inefficiences are certain to have an impact on you. How do you cope with inefficient coworkers? How can you apply the principles of PEP to improve team efficiences? It is difficult enough to change your own behavior—changing others' is that much harder! So what can you do about this? The hard truth: a lot!

You will learn to apply proven techniques we at the Institute for Business Technology (IBT) use to help our clients establish and operate with common work and organizational standards, take advantage of technology to communicate and coordinate in the most effective way, and influence how your team works together to get done the things that need to be done in the most effective way possible.

IT WILL NOT BE EASY, BUT IT WILL BE WORTH IT

No matter what your motives are—whether you wish to become a millionaire or a couch potato, to get more done or to leave work on time—the fundamentals and basics covered in this book will help make those wishes happen.

This how-to book attempts to parallel the simplicity of the Personal Efficiency Program as it's delivered in person, one-on-one, by the 250 or more trainers who work with the Institute for Business Technology (IBT). It's the codification of the experiences of those trainers, all of whom have succeeded in getting people to adopt better working habits. It's the input of 500,000 people on how they've developed systems, routines, and solutions that have allowed them to overcome their efficiency problems. All of this will help you get into a better working routine, which will, in turn, make you feel better about your performance and yourself.

It's one thing to have the information, another to act on it, and another still to change your behavior. There is no easy method to change, but we've developed tools that do work. When you completely purge your office, you'll recognize the principle: If you want to change your behavior, it's easier to do it completely. The concept of *Do It Now* will be drummed into you. It will both enable you to get more done and help you to overcome procrastination, a major block to behavioral change. You will begin to substitute good habits for bad. If we must be creatures of habit, let's at least make our habits good ones! Since our time and peace of mind are at stake, we ought to want to change.

PEP is like an exercise program: You have to do each step if you're to benefit. You can't just read about it. So if you don't plan to follow the program, don't read this book. Throw it away right now, and save yourself some time. Or follow the program, and save yourself a lot of time. The choice is yours. Personally, I hope you'll read the book. I hope you'll follow the program. I guarantee it will make a big difference in the quality of your life.

CHAPTER 1

Do It Now!

Lose this day loitering—'twill be the same story
Tomorrow—and the next more dilatory;
Each indecision brings its own delays,
And days are lost lamenting o'er lost days.
Are you earnest? seize this very minute—
Boldness has genius, power and magic in it.
Only engage, and then the mind grows heated—
Begin it, and the work will be completed!
—JOHANN WOLFGANG VON GOETHE

Chapter 1 Preview

In this chapter, you will learn how to:

- Get more done by doing it *now*.
- Overcome procrastination by getting in the habit of acting.
- Reduce your workload by doing the work once.
- Become more decisive by looking at the worst possible consequence of your action and then getting on with it if you could live with that consequence.
- Stop using priorities as an excuse not to do things.
- Start thinking: It is either important enough to do or it isn't; if it's important, then I'll act on it; if it's not important, I won't do it.
- Be as clever about completing things as you are about putting things off.

*N*ow! No doubt you hear the word all the time. If not from your boss, your spouse, or your child, you hear it from advertisers and salespeople. Some days it seems everyone and everything is demanding something *now*. A manager or coworker tells you someone didn't show up for work and what she was doing needs to be done by you, now. Or someone from home calls to tell you a pipe is leaking now. Or the telephone rings and demands to be picked up, now. An advertisement tells you to buy it, now. People and things demand our time and attention now, this moment, immediately. And so we find ourselves buried in our work, in spite of all the nice time management theories and tools.

Some time management gurus tell us we should ignore all the things that clamor for our urgent attention, including the telephone. They tell us we shouldn't react to circumstances and people around us; instead, we should organize, prioritize, and gain control of our lives by putting off some tasks and focusing our attention on those activities that are "most important," or "first things," or "top priorities."

Planning, setting goals, and priorities have a place. But too often when we set priorities, we don't get around to everything on our lists. "Less important" activities get shoved into the closet by "more urgent" activities. Eventually the "less important" things rot there. Not surprisingly, when they start to stink, they become very high priorities. And guess who has to clean up the mess? You do, of course, *now!*

WHY THE PERSONAL EFFICIENCY PROGRAM WORKS

The only method I've found that really produces the results people want (the method you're going to learn here) is to gain the advantage by getting the "now" on your side. I call it the *Do It Now* approach to personal efficiency.

By *choosing* to *Do It Now,* you make *now* your ally, not your enemy. So, what do you do about the mess that accumulates on your desk? You *Do It Now.* Doing it now enables you to be better organized; to exercise greater control over the when, where, and how of what you're doing; and to feel better about yourself and your performance. Not surprisingly, *Do It Now* is the first tenet of the Personal Efficiency Program (PEP).

The beginning is the half of every action.
—GREEK PROVERB

Does the following scenario sound familiar?

You arrive at the office, sit down, turn on your computer and open your e-mail. You have 50 messages in the box—many of them there for days or weeks. The subject line of one from Mary reminds you, "Oh, I have to call Mary." Dutifully, you start a To Do list somewhere on your desk. You look at the next e-mail and this one is a complaint by a customer. You think, "I must answer this." You go to the next mail, you see it represents a problem, and you think, "I must talk to my boss about this," and onto the To Do list it goes. You look at the next mail and say, "This isn't important; I can do it later." And so it goes—on and on. You end up shuffling through your scores of e-mail and possibly stacks of paper representing your things to do and by the time you go back to your e-mail and read each one you plan to actually do, you have wasted time reading everything twice! In effect, you've done the work twice, doubling your time commitment but accomplishing little.

This procedure would almost be okay if we only went through it twice! But too many of us look at our mail three, four, or five times before we ever act on them. It takes a lot longer to do something five times than it does to do it once.

The first rule for improving personal efficiency is:

Act on an item the first time you read or touch it.

I'm not talking about those things that you can't do now or even those things you shouldn't do now. I'm talking about all the things that you could and should do, but you don't. I'm talking about routine paperwork and e-mail of the sort you encounter every day. Take care of these things the first time you touch or read them, and you'll save yourself a lot of time in the long run.

Call Mary. Respond to that e-mail message immediately. Answer the customer's letter of complaint. Act on that voice mail as you listen. Talk to the boss about the problem. *Do It Now.* You'll be amazed at how little time it actually takes and amazed at how good you feel when it's done.

If you're not going to act on your paperwork, don't waste time looking at it. If you're not going to return your voice mail messages, don't waste time listening to them. If you're not going to respond to your e-mail messages, don't waste time looking at them. Don't clog up your day with things you *aren't* going to do. Instead, move on to what you *are* going to do, and *Do It Now.*

START WITH YOUR DESK OR WORK SPACE

When people ask for my help in getting organized and putting the Personal Efficiency Program in place in their work and their lives, the first thing I do is put them through a personal desk cleaning. I actually go to the person's desk and go through all the bits and pieces of paper with them. I begin with paper even if electronic communication and documents are quickly taking over as the medium of choice in business. The reason is people can more easily conceptualize with paper than with documents they cannot touch. I'll pick up a paper and ask what it is. They say, "Uh, well, that's something I was supposed to respond to."

"Okay," I say. Then they naturally start to put it somewhere, but I stop them. "Hold it a second. Why are you putting it over there?"

They give me an incredulous look and say, "Well, I have to do it, so I put it over there."

"Well, let's *Do It Now.*"

"You want me to *Do It Now*? It could take some time. . . ."

"I don't mind. I'll sit here while you do it."

And they do it. Usually I clock it. And I say, "How long did that take?"

"One minute," they say, or "three minutes," or whatever.

"Look at that," I tell them. "See?"

"Yeah," they say. "It didn't take much time at all."

And I say, "I was hoping you'd notice that."

When this task is done the first time, it makes people uncomfortable. They do it, but they usually haven't grasped the concept yet, even though we talk about it and ask them to commit themselves to the concept and the work style. What they don't understand is that *Do It Now* is meant to be permanent and ongoing.

Even if they remember *Do It Now* and believe they follow the principle in the beginning, they are often inconsistent in their application of the *Do It Now* concept.

This is evident when I go back for a follow-up visit. Usually, they've cleaned up their office or work space in anticipation of my coming, with everything stacked neatly into piles. They're very proud they've mastered the concept. After all, it's easy enough to talk about *Do It Now* and even to get a person to agree with it. But most people think they *Do It Now* when they don't. Only by working with this concept consistently over time—as I do—do you begin to see more and more evidence of *not* acting the first time and all the reasons people make up for why they can't or shouldn't act now.

A first visit with one client included a thorough desk cleaning. We worked through every item on his desk, one at a time, until everything had been done that could be done. We talked about acting on things the first time—about doing it now—and he was so impressed that he committed himself to *Do It Now* as his new work philosophy.

When I went back for a follow-up visit, I hardly made it through the door before he started telling me that *Do It Now* was the greatest thing that had ever happened to him—it was just marvelous. He was very enthusiastic about the program and about the change it had made in his life.

Then I picked up the papers from his pending basket. The first was a phone message. I said, "Why don't we call him now?"

He frowned just a little. "Now?" he said.

And I said, "Yes."

And so he picked up the phone and returned the call. By the end of our meeting, we'd gone through every single piece of paper in his pending basket.

Why was I able to empty his pending basket when he hadn't been able to? Because his definition of "pending" was something to be done later, and one visit with PEP obviously hadn't changed that.

Let me emphasize then. *Do It Now* means *Do It Now,* regularly and consistently, day after day. Not doing it now is what got you into trouble in the first place. Your pending basket is strictly for things you *can't* do now, for things that are out of your control. For example, you call Mary back on Monday because that's when she's back from vacation, not because Monday seems like a good day to do it. *That's* pending.

Grasp the concept of *Do It Now* and the real meaning of "pending"—and function accordingly each and every day—and these simple words will literally change the way you approach your work and your life. You'll find yourself getting more work done than ever before.

> ***Procrastination is the thief of time.***
> **—Edward Young**

OVERCOMING PROCRASTINATION

Simple procrastination probably eats up more time in the workplace than anything else. If you're a procrastinator, you'll find *Do It Now* is a key element in helping you to identify where procrastination exists in your work habits and helping you to overcome it.

Most people are very clever, even ingenious, about putting things off. "I don't have time" is a common excuse. "I think they said they're not going to be there today, so I didn't bother to call." "This could take forever, so I had better wait until I have a free day to start." "It's not so important." The list of reasons why a task can't be completed is endless.

My approach is this: *Be as clever about completing things as you've been about putting them off.* So Mary's not there. Who else could give you the information? Her assistant? Where else could you get this information? Who could this task be delegated to? How can you get this job done? That is the point, isn't it—how you can get that letter, that folder, or that report out of your in basket and off of your desk so that you never have to look at it again? That's where you should focus your brainpower—not on clever excuses.

How soon not now, becomes never.
—MARTIN LUTHER

This may sound simple, but it's a bitter pill to swallow: Too often the reason you're not getting things done is that you're just not doing them. You can reverse that trend, though, starting now—right now— by learning how to overcome procrastination and to increase your personal productivity. How? The following eight ways to overcome procrastination can benefit you immediately and immensely.

1. *Do It Once.* Sorting through all the papers on your desk and creating To Do and Do Later piles for yourself is a common practice. You have plenty of company if you're a pile creator. One woman I know goes through this creating piles process regularly. The first time through she calls it "reading for familiarity." The second read-through is her "action" read, unless she sets it aside "to do later." Now, this woman is a two-time cum laude graduate of a prestigious university, handling a responsible position in business! By adopting and implementing *Do It Now* she could immediately experience the most immediate benefit of PEP: *Do It Now,* and you do it once.

Needlessly rereading everything on your desk or in your e-mail before acting on it achieves nothing. You know what's required the first time you read a customer's letter of complaint. Reading the letter twice only doubles your reading time and the letter still is not answered. Answer the letter the first time you read through it—*Do It Now*—and you save time, move toward customer satisfaction, and accomplish a task that otherwise prevents you from doing more important things.

2. *Clear Your Mind.* A client once described to me what it was like for him to drive home from work at the end of the day. When he would drive past a gas station, he would think: "I must get a spare tire for my car. I had a flat some time ago and have not gotten around to getting the spare." On he would drive and pass a pharmacy and think: "Vitamin C. We need Vitamin C. Winter is coming, and we need it for the expected sniffles." He would drive past a supermarket and think: "My wife wanted me to pick up bread. Ah, I don't feel like it." By the time he got home, he was exhausted. He told me he would be breathing hard. He needed a drink to calm down. "Everything I looked at reminded me of things I hadn't done!" he said. Mind you, not once did he stop and do any of those things. But he sure felt as if he had worked hard on these things. He was exhausted from procrastination.

Consider how many tasks and projects you have connected with your work. One hundred? Two hundred? Now consider how many tasks, incomplete activities, and wish-list items you have connected with your family. How many tasks or wish-list items could you list that are connected with your hobbies, your friends, as well as civic, church, or other groups you belong to? As you add these up, you'll discover that the outstanding items—the things taking up space in your mind— probably number five hundred to one thousand.

> **Think only what is right there, what is right under your nose to do. It's such a simple thing— that's why people can't do it.**
> **—HENRY MILLER**

Experience tells us that we're limited in how many tasks or activities our minds can juggle at any given time. How does this affect your work? Let's use the example of a customer's letter or e-mail. You look at the first line: "Can you please send me some information about a new product?" Immediately your attention flies off to the information you were supposed to send to someone else, but haven't gotten around to yet. You drag your attention back and read a bit further. "Can you meet with some of my colleagues to discuss a certain project?" Again your attention wanders off to several other meetings you need to prepare for but haven't gotten to yet. Once again you drag your attention back to the task at hand. The sheer volume of incomplete activities in your life distracts you from concentrating on and completing what's in front of you. This is where priorities fit into the picture.

Obviously, prioritizing can be an important part of controlling your work. But prioritizing can also be the best excuse *not* to do something. Prioritizing means that "unimportant" tasks get pushed off until later and may not ever get done at all. The consequence of not doing tasks in a timely way is your inability to focus on the work at hand because of the voices in your head reminding you of uncompleted tasks.

Have you ever kept a list of 10 things to do, only to have the bottom five never change? We tend to focus on top-priority items and neglect lower-priority items. That's why we call them lower priority, yet we still consider these things to be important.

My view is that things either should or should not be done. If deadlines are involved, certainly they must be considered, but if something is important enough to do, do it. Otherwise, don't.

The best way to eliminate task overload is to eliminate these little things that make you feel overloaded and that pull your attention away from your major tasks. Act on these smaller, "less important" tasks. Make a list of all of them, set aside some quiet time, and do them one by one. Or decide not to do one and trash it. Better yet, get yourself organized using the ideas in this book and don't allow tasks to accumulate in the first place.

With this overload eliminated, you're no longer distracted. Your level of concentration increases and, accordingly, you not only finish more tasks, you finish them better and more quickly than before. Komar was reported to have said:

Concentration, in its truest, unadulterated form, means being able to focus the mind on one single solitary thing.

If you can concentrate—focus—on what you are trying to do, you will bring to bear on the task one of the most critical elements of success.

3. *Solve Problems While They're Small.* As you gain experience in a job, you learn to detect those little red flags that tell you something is wrong and will only get worse unless you take action. The question becomes: When and how do I act on these small indicators? Unfortunately, we tend to ignore these red flags too often in the face of more pressing issues.

Sometimes I point out a questionable stack of papers on the corner of someone's desk. Rather sheepishly, the person admits, "It's my problem pile. I figure if they sit there long enough, they'll go away." And sometimes they do.

You've heard of Murphy's Law. In England it's called Sod's Law: If

anything can go wrong, it will. There's a corollary to Murphy's Law:
If 10 things can go wrong with something, you can be sure the thing
that will cause the most damage will be the one that goes wrong!
Maybe most of those items in your problem pile will go away if you
let them sit long enough. But you can be sure the one problem you
don't want to happen will be the one that happens. And how much
longer will it take you to take care of a crisis than to take care of the
warning flag?

Get into the habit of acting on these things now, and you'll catch
problems when they're still small, before they become big, time-
consuming crises. As a result, you'll have more time to concentrate
on the important things.

4. *Reduce Interruptions.* A common complaint I hear is about interruptions. Most people admit they have a hard time avoiding or pre-
venting interruptions. Instead, interruptions are seen as something
beyond the control of mortals and the cause of nearly all our problems.
How often have you heard or said, "Well, I would have gotten it done if
I hadn't been interrupted every time I turned around!"

I remember a time I did some work for a bank in Luxembourg. I delivered my coaching services and sent an invoice. Two months later I had-
n't received payment. I called the managing director, and his response
was, "I did it now!"—with a chuckle—"I signed the invoice and sent it to
the accounts payable department." We both got a laugh out of that and I
suggested I would talk to the accounts payable department. I followed up
with a young lady in the department. By telephone, in my typical American way, I asked, "Where's my money?!" She said, "I am so sorry you
haven't been paid. But I have been so busy explaining to people why
they haven't been paid that I haven't had the time to pay the bills!"

All too often, the interruptions people complain about are the result
of their not having done something in the first place. Consequently,
they not only have the work itself to do, but they also have to deal with
those people who depended on that work being done, which only creates more work! Furthermore, most of us don't relish having to explain
why we haven't done something. Even if you have a perfectly good
reason, and the person on the other end of the phone sympathizes
with you, you'll be left with a bad taste in your mouth just because you
had to beg off one more time with an excuse and an explanation.

If you want to avoid interruptions, do the tasks related to them. You
can then spend more time on your work and less time explaining why
you haven't done it. Gain a reputation for completing work on time,

and you'll reduce interruptions further by eliminating those bothersome requests for interim project status reports.

Mind you, some interruptions are desirable. If a sale depends on immediate feedback, of course the sales manager wants to be interrupted. Eliminating unnecessary interruptions and not aggravating the situation by creating reasons for others to interrupt you is what I'm referring to. Other benefits to eliminating these self-created interruptions are the improved quality of your work when you're free to concentrate on it fully and your ability to complete more work in the same amount of time because you're able to work undisturbed.

5. *Clean Up Backlogs.* If you have to keep up with an ongoing heavy work flow and, at the same time, you have an accumulation of backlogs, you must address the backlogs if you're to get your work flow under control. Remember, backlogs create their own additional work, so eliminating them cuts down your workload more than you may imagine at first. There are five essential steps for handling backlogs:

1. Identify the backlogs.
2. Prioritize what backlogs to clean up first.
3. Schedule time each day to take a piece of a backlog and clean it up.
4. Identify the cause of the backlog.
5. Take steps to remedy the cause to prevent the backlog from happening again and to prevent any further buildup of backlogs.

Once we clean up old backlogs and prevent logjams from happening, we'll be better able to look to the future.

6. *Start Operating toward the Future instead of the Past.* Figure 1.1 illustrates what occurs mentally when you have lots of past due, incomplete, or old tasks yet to be done. The Xs on the diagram symbolize all of the tasks that should have been done then. Your focus is clouded by being dragged back into the past. Psychologists say that one indication of a person's mental health is the degree to which they operate in the past as opposed to operating in the present and future. Operating from the present toward the future is considered healthy. No wonder we can feel a bit crazy when we are overwhelmed with so many overdue tasks.

When you are operating in the past, you tend to focus on what might have been, on lost opportunities. Anything that directs you from the present toward the future is healthier than that which drags you back in time.

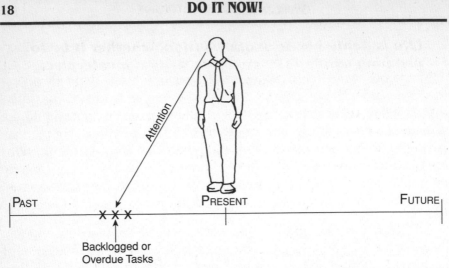

Figure 1.1 Attention focuses to the past, not the future, with a backlog of tasks.

Suppose you are running a race in which the starting line is Present and the finish line is Future. If rather than starting the race at Present you start from the Past, you have that much more to run just to get to the starting line!

Figure 1.2 illustrates how as we clean up these tasks that attract our attention to the past we free up attention capacity for the present. This is important because we all have limited attention capacity—much less capacity than we might imagine. Attention is critical to getting to the meat of the matter and pushing things through to completion.

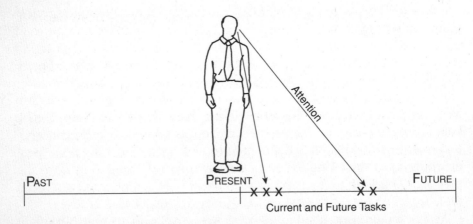

Figure 1.2 When backlogs are cleaned up it is much easier to concentrate on current and future tasks.

Life is denied by lack of attention, whether it be to cleaning windows or trying to write a masterpiece.
—NADIA BOULANGER

7. *Stop Worrying about It.* It's one thing to waste time doing things over again or dealing with added interruptions or bigger fires, but the real harm of putting things off is how it affects you mentally and emotionally.

Almost everyone tends to put off unpleasant tasks. Facing up to your unpleasant tasks and completing them isn't easy, but the consequences of *not* doing them can be much worse than simply dealing with the unpleasantness early.

The greatest amount of wasted time is the time not getting started.
—DAWSON TROTMAN

To compound the problem, most people who procrastinate not only don't do the task, they also tend to dwell on the unfinished or undone task and worry about not having done it. This worry consumes far more time than people may realize. And it makes it harder to take causative action to solve the problem.

Think of some of the problems you've had to face in the past. Did dwelling on them get you anywhere? No. It was only when you finally initiated some action that the problem began to be resolved. If you face up to the big problems and unpleasant tasks and do something about them, they usually vanish rather quickly.

I once worked with a group of highly educated, bright, young service technicians from a large company in Denmark. I noticed a large machine on the corner of one of their desks and asked about it. The technician replied, "That's a bit of bad conscience. I received it from a customer a month ago to repair and I haven't repaired it yet."

I said, "That's terrible!"

He said, "I know. I've thought about it a lot, but I'm so busy that I haven't had the time to repair it. It could take me two days to fix it, and my schedule is so tight I haven't been able to devote the time to it." He went on to say, "As a matter of fact, you could help me."

"How?" I asked.

He said, "You could tell my boss how busy I am."

Well, my help took a little different direction. I said, *"Do It Now."*

"I can't *Do It Now,*" he argued. "I have a meeting at two o'clock, and. . . ."

"Okay. Just *Do It Now,* and let's see how far you get," I suggested.

Well, off he went into the repair area with the machine, muttering to himself. Fifteen minutes later he came back.

"Oh, no," I thought. "This could be trouble."

He looked at me and said, "It's done."

"Done?" I echoed.

"Yes, done," he said. "But it could have taken two days."

Of course, we don't always get so lucky. It could have taken two days to repair. But how often have similar things happened to all of us? When you finally get down to the business of doing something you've been putting off, it isn't nearly as bad as you thought it might be.

The shortest answer is doing.
—GEORGE HERBERT

Most of us tend to exaggerate how long an unpleasant task will take or how unpleasant it really is. We dread doing it, so we put it off. Here was a man who had put off a job for a month, with the machine sitting there on his desk as a reminder of the thing he dreaded. He'd let it become a sore spot in his conscience and a sore spot between him and his boss. And rather than giving the task the 15 minutes it actually required, he'd been blaming his boss for his being too busy. In fact, of course, he'd been procrastinating, but regardless of the cause, the customer hadn't received service and had been without the machine for a month.

The trick? Face up to the unpleasant tasks and *act* on them *now.*

M. Scott Peck, in his book *The Road Less Traveled* (Simon & Schuster, 1978), calls acting on unpleasant tasks "delaying gratification." Peck points out that life is difficult. People who procrastinate tend to want immediate gratification. Peck says:

Delaying gratification is a process of scheduling the pain and pleasure of life in such a way as to enhance the pleasure by meeting and experiencing the pain first and getting it over with. It is the only decent way to live.

What tasks in your own work would you treat on a "worst first" basis? Committing to a *Do It Now* mentality will help you overcome your resistance to dealing with unpleasant tasks. It will help you tackle the things you don't relish doing with a determination to have them over and done with. Some people take an almost perverse pride in being able to deal with the ugliest, meanest, most difficult things first. Most of us can improve our ability to handle the difficult head-on. Remember what Mark Twain said: "If you have to swallow two frogs, swallow the big one first, and don't look at it too long." So, if you can choose the sequence of your work each day, choose the task you enjoy least and do it first. Not only will the second task of the day be not quite so bad compared to the first, but completing the worst first tends to give your self-confidence a boost.

8. *Now, Feel Better about Yourself.* Dr. Linda Sapadin in her book *It's about Time* (Penguin Books, 1997) says:

> *Procrastination inevitably diminishes one's self-esteem, which results in a loss of optimism, happiness, and creative energy. People who suffer from chronic procrastination and do nothing about it find it increasingly difficult to strive toward personal goals or, often, even to formulate them.*

Procrastination and attendant cover-ups create a buildup of negative emotions not always evident on the surface. In one PEP course, a newly married young woman began to laugh almost uncontrollably when the subject of procrastination was brought up. When asked what prompted this reaction she said:

> *Oh, I was thinking about my husband's ruffled shirt. You see, I hate ironing, particularly my husband's shirt with the ruffled front. I would pull all the other items in the ironing basket out from under this shirt and do them first.*

When asked, "What happens when this shirt is the only thing left?" her response was, "Oh, I throw it back in the washing machine! My husband can't ever figure out where his favorite shirt has gone." A tremendous amount of emotional buildup comes with this habit of procrastination. It has strong impact on one's self-image.

By committing to *Do It Now,* completing the hard jobs first, and handling the big jobs bite-by-bite, you'll trim a tremendous load of stress and anxiety from your work. You'll gain more self-confidence and self-respect. Even after completing only one day of the PEP program, participants have processed and purged all of the papers and documents on and in their desks, their file drawers, and their computers. They discover that they can accomplish much more than they ever realized before. They no longer have a guilty conscience. Almost instantly participants feel better about themselves.

Knowing when not to work hard
is as important as knowing when to.
—HARVEY MACKAY, *Swim with the Sharks*
without Being Eaten Alive

NOT EVERYTHING CAN OR SHOULD BE DONE NOW

Having said a lot about doing things now, let me point out that it isn't always possible or desirable to do everything now. You try to call Mary, but she won't be in until Monday. You're on your way to get coffee when a client calls about business. Clearly priorities do play an important part in productive work and in achieving results. However, ultimately success comes from getting things done. And too often people don't get things done because they don't do them! They do not *act now.*

In fact, priorities can be the best excuse a person has not to do something. Yes, there will be times you can't *Do It Now.* There will be times you shouldn't *Do It Now.* Common sense is a necessity; it should be a given. The way to increase your personal efficiency is not to *Do Something Stupid Now.* However, if your approach toward work is to always choose, always prioritize, always give it some time to ripen, always have an excuse to look at it later, always shuffle through your papers or scan through your e-mail, you are *not* acting. In fact, you are reinforcing the habit of not acting. With *Do It Now* and no more excuses to procrastinate, the end product is a propensity to *act.*

BUILD DECISIVENESS INTO YOUR WORK HABITS

Doubt, of whatever kind, can be ended by action alone.
—THOMAS CARLYLE

Successful people in general take little time to make a decision but take a long time to change a decision once it has been made.

Many people are afraid to be decisive. After all, if you make a decision, you have to live with the consequences. If decisiveness is a weak spot with you, there's an easy way to help you handle the quandary. Simply imagine the worst possible consequences of any decision you can make, and ask yourself if you can live with those consequences. If the answer is "yes," go for it.

You can't expect to be 100% certain of your course of action at all times. I understand, though, that George Patton, the famous World War II American general, worked with the following formula for success: "If you have a plan you're 80% certain of, you should violently execute it."

Then there is the Ben Franklin technique. Ben, the famous inventor, politician, and philosopher of the eighteenth century, had a method to help make decisions. Take a piece of paper and fold it in half to make two columns. On one side, list all the reasons for making the decision. On the other side, list all the reasons against. By comparing these two lists, you can often get clarity on the direction you should go.

I've seen decisive people make the wrong decisions. Interestingly enough, they almost always made the intent of their decisions—that is, their objective—happen anyway. I believe there is some natural law connected with this phenomenon. The act of deciding may, in fact, be more important than the correctness of the actual decision and have more influence on the consequences. Be decisive, take action, and get on with your work and life.

> *A good plan violently executed now is better than a perfect plan executed next week.*
> —**GENERAL GEORGE S. PATTON**

ESTABLISH *DO IT NOW* WORK HABITS

Whether we like it or not, we're all creatures of habit. Most of us fall very easily into established routines. How often do you drive the same route to work, or eat at the same restaurant for lunch, or start each workday the same way, for example? Some of these habits and routines are good; others can work against us, and living totally by habit can be very destructive.

Are there habits worth cultivating? Certainly. Habits such as driving safely or showing courtesy to friends and colleagues should be routine and are definitely beneficial. Cultivating the *Do It Now* habit is intended to reinforce an action-oriented lifestyle: to become more decisive and to start and then to stay in motion. Many tasks we need to complete don't require a great deal of consideration and yet, because that's our way of working, we treat them with the same weight that we assign to very important tasks with grave consequences. It's a habit. Your goal in reading this book is to break your old work habits and to become more efficient, and therefore more productive. Having a decisive and proactive approach toward work will enable you to do exactly that.

Procrastination is itself often only a bad habit.

In his book *Getting Things Done: The ABC's of Time Management* (Scribner, 1976), Edwin Bliss describes procrastination as a habit in this way:

> *When we fail to act as promptly as we should it usually is not because the particular task in question is extremely difficult, but rather because we have formed a habit of procrastinating whenever possible. Procrastination is seldom related to a single item; it is usually an ingrained behavior pattern.*

I couldn't agree more. Learn to *Do It Now* and you'll short-circuit the habit of procrastination. *Do It Now* substitutes an action-oriented behavior for the "do it later" behavior. You act before the mental barriers are activated, so you don't have time to think, "It's too hard; maybe it will go away; maybe someone else will see it; I'm not in the mood; I don't feel like it."

PERFECTION

Some may believe there is an inherent conflict between *Do It Now* and doing things right. Most of us have experience with people who execute their work in a slipshod way. I struggle with this with my kids: a homework project that could be typed on the computer instead of handwritten; that last bit of searching on the Internet to get a photo for the project that would top it all off and produce an A grade instead of a B. It is good and healthy to expect a high standard of performance. But some people mix this up with when to *act*.

Perfectionists often procrastinate. After all, if you believe you cannot execute the work perfectly, why do it? And *Do It Now* may mean you will not be able to do it as well as you would like.

Dr. Sapadin puts it this way:

> *Perfectionists are extreme in their thinking: If they're going to do something, they reason, they should do the best possible job that can be done. There is no acceptable "middle*

ground." . . . *Faced with a demanding task, perfectionists are inevitably torn between two extremes: giving all they've got, or giving up altogether.*

How can one realistically define that "middle ground"? Should we work to produce that Rolls-Royce, as near to a perfect car as one can get? Or a Mercedes? Or a Ford? The Rolls costs $250,000; the Mercedes, $80,000; the Ford, $25,000. All get you where you want to go. Each auto manufacturer serves a special customer market. That market has a threshold of what its customers are prepared to pay for a car. The manufacturer produces an automobile that meets its customers' expectations.

When acting on your work, don't ask the question of yourself: "What is the best possible job I could do on this task?" Instead ask yourself: "What level or degree of quality do our customers expect from us?" If you have perfectionist tendencies, you are likely to procrastinate tasks; often your customers primarily want you to be responsive.

Certainly, *do it right,* but establish what *right* is, and *Do It Now!!*

DISCIPLINE

A common word heard when discussing the subject of changing behavior is *discipline.* "It is a matter of discipline. If I had more of it, I would be able to exercise, . . . stop smoking, . . . diet. . . ." While discipline plays a part, I believe it is a red herring. If you exert discipline enough to establish a routine, you make a new habit. The habit helps you maintain the new routine. Discipline yourself to act now, and it will very soon become a habit. Then the habit will lessen the need for discipline. William James, whose studies of human behavior are well known, suggests that if you do something every day for 30 days, it will become a habit. Try it with *Do It Now.*

To be honest, this is more than dealing with procrastination. It is a philosophy toward work and life. It is the view: I am proactive; I am action-oriented; I am bigger than the problems I face. These characteristics begin (and end) with how you face up to and habitually act on the small details of work and life.

So, what is the first thing you should do now? Go ahead—write it down. Focus on the first things. Get yourself organized to *Do It Now,* and do it better!

FOLLOW-UP FOR CHAPTER 1

1. Get started. Go to your desk—if need be, with this book in hand—and go through every single bit and piece of paper on your desk or anywhere near your working space. Pick up the first piece of paper and determine what it is and what must be done to process it to completion. Do whatever is required to complete that task and get that piece of paper off your desk so you never have to look at it again. If a task is going to take you several hours to complete, schedule a time to do it.

2. Go through any saved e-mails, voice mails, faxes, and so forth one at a time and begin dealing with each of them to completion. Again, if any will require hours of work, schedule them on your calendar for action at a more appropriate time.

3. Determine what tasks ought to be done and decide what must be done to process each task to completion. Take the task as far as you possibly can. If you run into a roadblock, get clever. Ask, "How can I get this done another way?" If you decide to delegate the task or pass it on to someone else, remind yourself to follow-up.

CHAPTER 2

Organize It Now!

Don't agonize. Organize.
—FLORYNCE KENNEDY
(Founder, National Organization
for Women—NOW)

Chapter 2 Preview

In this chapter, you will learn how to:

- Clean up your act and save yourself time.
- Stop wasting your time looking for things. Set up separate file systems for your working papers, reference papers, and archive papers.
- Organize your computer files and set up proper directories for computer files and e-mail.
- Put as much attention to detail in how you are set up to work as you do in the work itself.

You must be well organized to establish the routines that allow you to develop the *Do It Now* habit. You'll be surprised at the time you save just by organizing your work area for maximum efficiency.

A SOLDIER'S STORY

A soldier is a study in attention to detail. When recruits arrive for basic training at boot camp, they are drilled in what some may consider very fundamental skills. Apart from a tough physical regimen, soldiers are taught in the most forceful way how to make their beds, how to polish their shoes, how to organize their toiletries, how to clean and maintain their weapons, and other fundamentals. The sergeant no doubt wants to impress upon them the need to follow orders. But it is more than that. Basic training in the armed services is just that—basic. Attention to the basics constitutes the foundation for a successful soldier.

There is no more serious profession than that of soldiers, especially during war when their lives are on the line. Considerable thought is put into where a weapon is placed on the body. Soldiers are trained to keep their weapons in meticulous condition. When an enemy is approaching the soldier can't afford to have a gun jam because it wasn't kept clean. Undisciplined, disorganized soldiers who don't know where their weapons are and who take no care of them will soon be dead soldiers. That's why sergeants are deadly serious about teaching these basics to new recruits.

How well you are prepared and organized for your work is far more serious than most people recognize. Clutter can be a killer.

> *Clutter and confusion are failures of design, not*
> *attributes of information. There's no such*
> *thing as information overload.*
> —EDWARD TUFTE

CLEANING OUT THE CLUTTER

Clutter is the mess you face every day when you walk into your office. It's your coat flung over the back of your office guest chair because you didn't hang it on the coat tree that morning. It's the half dozen reports perched on the corner of your filing cabinet and buried under the remains of yesterday's in-office lunch. It's the stack of magazines you haven't gotten around to reading yet. It's the mound of outgoing and incoming mail strewn across your desk. It's the unfinished letters you are writing by hand to give them a personal touch. It's the cassette tapes you meant to take home to listen to over the weekend but are now buried under the quarterly budget.

Clutter is the excessive disorganized mess you don't need in your working environment. We may yell at the kids every day to clean up their rooms and then go to a messy office and never even notice anything wrong. But clutter in an office and desk environment prevents us from effectively doing our work.

WHERE DOES CLUTTER COME FROM?

The first culprit is paper. Whatever happened to the idea of a paperless office? At one time, people speculated that technology would produce an office free of the clutter of paper because everything would be electronic. That still may happen, but it hasn't happened yet. The computer prints out more paper than we can get rid of, and copy machines churn out reams of paper very efficiently. In fact, the flow of paper is probably worse now than it ever was.

E-mail may be even worse than paper clutter, if that's possible. Although e-mail is a wonderful invention, it has created electronic clutter. You can now send a memo to 150 people with a single keystroke. Some people are getting up to 200 e-mail messages a day on a full system. Can you imagine? Or maybe you don't have to. If your office is fully computerized, you may not have to imagine it at all.

Then there is stuff. A friend just cleaned out his clothes closet. His wife forced him to do it: She suspected mice were nesting in there. Offices are like clothes closets—places where we accumulate a lot of stuff. The same man and his wife had moved across the street to a new home and taken all their stuff with them. Much of what they moved they had stored months and even years ago in the belief that someday they were going to need it. And they put it all in the storage closet in their new house and haven't looked in there for months.

We laugh about such stories, but they reflect normal behavior. Most people think it is possible they will need all the stuff they keep. Everybody keeps their *National Geographic* magazines, but they never look at them. So why keep them? Why keep them organized? It's like a soldier who would love to carry a tank into battle, but that's just not possible. At some point you have to look realistically at what you're carrying around and make sure you're carrying around things you actually need. If not, get rid of them!

WHY CLUTTER STAYS THERE

Clutter represents the way people approach both work and life. It tells something about those people—they may have a cluttered mind as well. Many people justify clutter by saying it gives them food for thought and adds to the creative process. Others believe creative and artistic people are just born this way. A colleague of mine once told an interesting story. She described the first time she went to a famous artist's home in New York. Before she went, she had an image in her mind of what a real artist's home would look like: avant-garde, very messy, with paintings stacked in the corners, the studio filled with things to stimulate the creative juices.

But when she walked into his house and looked around, she found that it was neat and tidy. She thought perhaps he'd straightened up since he was expecting guests, but when she found her way into his studio during the evening, she saw that the studio, too, was in perfect order. All the paintbrushes were exactly in order, and the paint cans were neatly lined up and labeled. She could hardly believe what she was seeing—it violated her expectations of how an artist works.

When she asked him about his neatness, he said he had learned it in college, when he had studied art. He had been taught to keep his tools in good working order. He knew that paintbrushes would be ruined unless cleaned after each use. He labeled all the different kinds of paint, because if he didn't, he knew that he'd forget what colors he'd mixed.

If you want to operate effectively, like this artist, you must have things operational and organized. It's simply easier to function in a clean and neat environment.

OUT OF SIGHT?

I know people who fear out of sight literally means out of mind. They're afraid they'll forget about a task or an assignment if they don't have some physical reminder of it on their desks or Post-it notes stuck within sight. Keeping everything in sight is their solution.

I agree. Out of sight very often does mean out of mind. When people tell me they have trouble remembering things, I give them a system to remind them. Furthermore, they don't need to be reminded of all the things on their desks that they can't do anything about. Being reminded of what you can't do now only reinforces the bad habit of *Do It Later.*

Although most people who leave assorted paper reminders around the desk and office believe them to be helpful, they are primarily a distraction and mostly just help create stress.

My advice is to create places to put things. Have on your desk only what you are working on, and use a good calendar system to remind yourself to do things when you will, in fact, do them.

DON'T OVERLOOK THE OBVIOUS

Very often we overlook the obvious in trying to improve the work process. We try to solve more complex problems and miss the fundamentals. The fundamentals a white-collar worker deals with every day include his or her desk, staples, pens, tape, paper clips, lights, file systems, binders, chair, computer, computer disks, and much more. It's not uncommon to walk into an office and find these items in disarray—scissors misplaced, stapler jammed, tape dispenser empty, papers scattered randomly. Yet somehow we expect to work effectively in this condition.

Many people never realize that by not having the basics of their own workplace in order, they handicap themselves from dealing effectively with their day-to-day problems.

Trivial? Maybe, but the *Wall Street Journal* once reported that white-collar workers spend an average of six weeks a year looking for things in the office! Incredible? Yes, but in my experience, true.

I once visited a high-ranking bank executive who was responsible for a region employing 2,500 people. He was a clever businessman who had risen through the ranks due to his leadership ability and business sense. But he was very overloaded and wanted my help sorting it out. One day I noticed a stack of paper on his desk and asked about it. He said it needed to be hole-punched, but he hadn't gotten to it yet. I could have questioned why he was doing it in the first place, but I decided to teach him a lesson on *Do It Now,* and so I asked him to hole-punch it now. He said, "Sure," and proceeded to leave the office. I followed him out past his assistants, down the hall, through a door, down a flight of stairs and into a supply closet. He took a hole-puncher and walked back to his office and proceeded to punch the holes. Each time he needed to put holes in the paper he went through this process. I asked, "Why not get your own hole-puncher?" He looked at me and said, "What a good idea." He had simply never thought of it.

The obvious isn't only access to the tools you use. Step back and take a good look at your office environment. Is your desk set up most suitably? Is your office warm enough in winter and cool enough in summer? Is your chair comfortable?

Once I did a Personal Efficiency Program (PEP) for Philips Electronics. While visiting one participant's office, I noticed he was very uncomfortable, sitting there and squirming. I asked what the problem was, and he said, "My back hurts."

I examined his chair and saw that it was broken. So I said, "Why don't you get a new chair?"

When I went back for a follow-up visit, he had a new chair. He said, "This is pretty amazing. I got a new chair and my back pain went away. I'm doing so much better at work just because of my new chair."

Another man increased his productivity dramatically simply by having his desk face the window instead of the door. Because the door was open all the time, people walking by would distract him. If he made eye contact, people felt they could stop, come in and say hello, and spend time visiting. As a result, he was constantly interrupted. When he turned his desk and chair so they faced the opposite wall, people stopped interrupting his work.

Entire sciences have built up around the idea of examining and improving how people interact with their surroundings. A few years ago Digital Equipment Corporation (DEC—now a part of Hewlett-Packard Corporation) designed an office concept in Sweden called "Office of the Future." All aspects of the office environment were taken into consideration—the design of the office layout, the kind of computer hardware and software, the color of the walls, the furniture that provides the best back support, and the production support that comes from being in a comfortable environment.

DEC even considered how cultural differences influence the definition of a comfortable environment. For example, in Sweden the office of the future looked like a typical Swedish country home. Why? Because people felt they could be more productive in the environment of a Swedish country home than in a plain office.

Leading furniture manufacturers such as Steelcase Inc., architectural design firms like Gensler, and software/consulting firms like Cap Gemini have all branched out from their traditional products and services to provide services and advice on the establishment of office environments for the more mobile work force. We, too, at the Institute for Business Technology (IBT) have expanded our role from simply helping people become more productive and better organized to helping people make the transition from traditional office space and tools to new office design that encourages a much more mobile work force to function as a team in executing work.

START WITH THE BASICS

If you want to organize yourself for greater productivity, you must consider some very basic ideas most people never master. Are your tools operational? Is your product easy to produce? These are two of the questions white-collar workers need to ask themselves, although they rarely do.

On an assembly line, if a worker has to bend over and pick up a heavy tool each time the worker puts a tire on a car, the process needs redesigning. Maybe the worker needs a leverage device of some sort to reduce the time and effort required to put on the tire. Similarly, if you have to rummage through several different papers or directories every time you need to make a phone call, you need to redesign the process. The idea is to make it easy to *Do It Now.*

YOUR OFFICE TOOLBOX

Let's get specific about the tools you use in your work. If you're not reading this chapter at your desk, imagine yourself there. Think about the physical layout of your work space. What items are there?

1. *Three Trays.* First there should be in, pending, and out baskets or trays for your day-to-day paper flow (not for storage!). Your tray system should look as shown in Figure 2.1.

2. *Standard Office Supplies.* Then there are the things you use every working day: stapler, pens, pencils, scissors, tape, calculator, blank CDs, floppy disks, PDA, Post-it note paper, paper clips, white out, and so forth—all the tools of white-collar work.

Incoming mail and notes, never before touched. When you pick something up, act on it! If you have an assistant, mail should be screened and sorted into folders that delineate your priorities when you are rushed (e.g., signature, urgent, memos, reading, etc.).

In, pending, and out trays must be within arm's reach for efficiency.

Optional, if you have a lot of reading, filing, and so on. Prevent buildup by reading short items at once, scanning table of contents and clipping articles, sharing reading load across department, and clipping or summarizing, scheduling a time for regular reading. Some jobs require additional, specialized trays to facilitate the work flow.

Short-term pending, for things you have tried to act on and couldn't complete (e.g., awaiting info, awaiting callback, interrupted for more urgent matter). NOT for: procrastination, incomplete projects, or tickler-file items.

Completed items for removal. Remove several times a day when leaving office or have assistant do so.

Figure 2.1 The tray system.

I occasionally meet people who have two or three supposedly broken staplers in or on their desks. They're not really broken, of course—they're just jammed, usually because the staples are stuck in the mechanism and no one got around to unsticking them. Worse, each time a stapler was needed the person would borrow one! As insignificant as a stapler may seem, it's a basic tool for a white-collar professional, and having this and other fundamentals in place allows you to work in the most efficient and effective manner.

Make sure that you have all the tools you need and that all of your tools are operational—no more borrowing a pair of scissors or a stapler every time you need one. Take the time to look at all the tools you have or should have. At the end of this little exercise, you will have a stapler, pens, pencils, a pencil sharpener, pads of paper, tape, business card holder, paper clips, blank CDs, files, file labels, and whatever other items you normally use in the course of a day, and they will all be fully functional. These routine items should be stored in the middle drawer of your desk or in the shallower side drawers of the desk—not on your work surface.

At the same time, be alert to waste. I often hear stories of incredible waste from the accounting departments of companies. People say, "Once we got organized, we found what we had in inventory, what we were using and wasting." When calculated, the amount of waste often boggles the mind.

I once taught PEP to a medium-size brokerage firm. I started going through desks one by one. I told people, "Make sure to gather up any extra supplies you have, so they can be returned to central supply." I do this because people often complain that they go to central supply but can't find what they need or, in small companies, that the supply budget has been spent for the quarter or the year, and there's no money to buy additional supplies. Well, as I went through PEP with about 120 people in the company, I rounded up all the extra supplies people had in their desks. In the end there were enough supplies to last a year without buying a single thing! All that was needed was to organize what we'd retrieved from everyone's desks. And that's typical. If you're up to the challenge, look in, on, and around your own desk. I bet you'll find half a dozen extra pens and other supplies you didn't even know you had.

The same principle that applies to supplies in your desk also applies to information in your files: *You don't use what you don't realize you have.* And without organization and maintenance, you don't realize what you have. You're wasting resources. Think of the survivors of a shipwreck, on the ocean in a rubber raft. The first thing they have to do is account, item by item, for every resource available to them so nothing is wasted. Waste in such a situation could cost them their lives.

3. *Photocopiers.* Another tool millions of workers use Monday through Friday is the office photocopier. I know this sounds petty, but not knowing how to make a copy can cost plenty. A friend of mine once told me this story. He had traveled to California to consult with a client. He was meeting with the CEO and president in the conference room. After my friend presented his one-page overview, the CEO wanted a copy made. The CEO stopped the presentation, called in a copy specialist and then waited. Twenty minutes later the copy specialist came back with a single piece of paper. Later, just out of curiosity, my friend asked why it took so long to get one copy made. An assistant to the CEO took him down a long hall, through several doors, and finally into the copy room. There was a huge copy machine—a monster with many gadgets and dials and dozens of bins for everything. You could launch the space shuttle from that room as easily as you could make a photocopy. Approximately 90% of the office staff didn't know how to use it.

4. *Fax Machines.* You should also know how to use a fax machine, a printer, and all the other tools used in common by staff. The machines should be operational and stocked with supplies and replacement parts. Simple instructions on how to use the machines should be posted. And you should take the time to familiarize yourself with them.

BECOME FAMILIAR WITH TOOLS AS THEY COME ON THE MARKET

Keep up with the best time management systems and tools. Make a habit of browsing through catalogs or at an office supply store periodically to discover new resources and tools. You may be surprised at what you find.

I recall one woman who worked for an insurance company. She was very disorganized and didn't want to follow my suggestions. It so happened she had a unique job and my solutions didn't exactly match her circumstances. But then one day a colleague brought in a time management system that had three-by-five-inch cards and a leather binder with little sleeves to hold the cards. The system required users to write a task on each card, and to slip the card for any task not completed into a sleeve for the next day. Well, the colleague found this system useless but rather than throw it away she gave it to this woman, who loved it and ended up solving many problems by using it.

Many excellent tools can be employed to increase both your effectiveness and your efficiency. One person may find one tool ineffective whereas another person can't live without it. Take advantage of the tools that exist and find tools that are suited to your style and personality.

ORGANIZING FILES—BEGINNING WITH PAPER

To deal better with paperwork, organize your papers and files by frequency of use. The things you use most frequently need to be near at hand. Your desk is a work surface, and the only papers on it should be those you are working with currently.

Figure 2.2, showing paper control points, gives an overview of good office organization.

You should have a three-basket system for handling paper flow. Figure 2.1 illustrates how the tray system might look and how it would be best used. Your in, pending, and out baskets (trays) are for tasks completed over the course of a few days at most. Next set up three types of files: working files, reference files, and archive files. These three files are vital paper control points for managing your work flow.

1. *Working files* are for current projects and routine functions. Usually 80% of your work involves 20% of your files, so these files should be kept within arm's reach, most likely in your desk drawers as hanging files. Working files are for items you're concerned with regularly over several weeks or months and for ongoing projects you're responsible for.

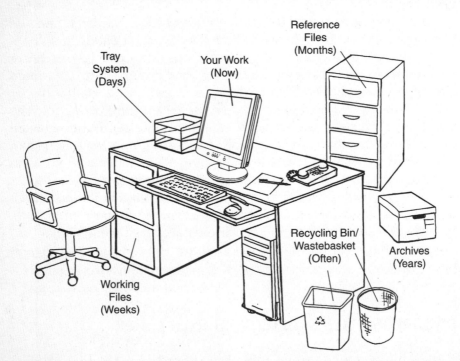

Figure 2.2   Paper control points.

2. *Reference files* contain the bulk of the files in your office. Since you use your reference files regularly they need to be near you, but not necessarily within arm's reach.

3. *Archive files* are kept for statutory reasons and may rarely be needed. They represent the accumulated work of past years and may be stored outside the office.

Working Files

Once a man who kept five tall piles of paper on his desk told me with a straight face that he knew exactly where everything was. I asked, "Then you don't think there's any value in having a system?" He gestured to the mess on his desk and answered: "I have a system. This is my system."

Then the telephone rang. The caller asked him to refer to a memo sent out a few days before. "Yeah, sure, one second," he said in response to this request. He went to a pile and leafed through it; then to another pile and leafed through it; then he looked at me sheepishly, his face turning red, and went to yet another pile. Embarrassed, he told the caller, "I'll have to get back to you."

I just sat there and looked at him. Then he said: "Well, maybe there is a need for a file system, but honestly, that missing paper was right next to the blue piece of paper in that folder."

People think they know where things are, but they waste precious time looking because they really *don't* know. And it would be unreasonable to expect them to remember where every single piece of paper is.

If your boss suggested you should remember the location of each and every piece of paper in your office, you'd probably be outraged.

And that's what your working files are for. As shown in Figure 2.3, working files usually contain several types of information:

1. *Fingertip Information.* These files contain phone lists, address lists, computer codes, company policies, and other information you refer to frequently and want at your fingertips when you need it.

2. *Items "To Be Discussed."* Create a file for routine meetings and a file for each staff member with whom you interact.

3. *Routine Functions.* These files contain information that you need for routine tasks performed daily, weekly, or monthly.

WORKING FILES

Since 80% of your work involves 20% of your files, keep these separate from other files and within arm's reach.

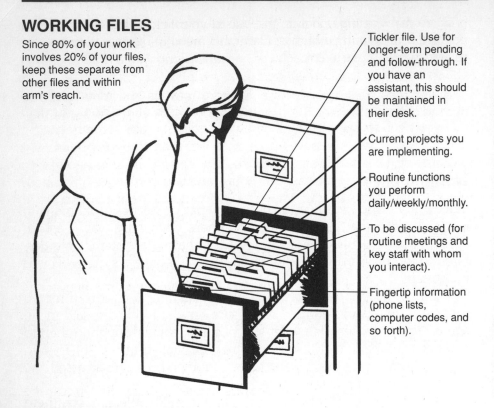

Tickler file. Use for longer-term pending and follow-through. If you have an assistant, this should be maintained in their desk.

Current projects you are implementing.

Routine functions you perform daily/weekly/monthly.

To be discussed (for routine meetings and key staff with whom you interact).

Fingertip information (phone lists, computer codes, and so forth).

Figure 2.3   Working files.

4. *Current Projects.* These are the projects you're working on now. Create a hanging file for each project and include anything necessary for your current work. Clean out these files now and then to move certain less urgent items to your reference files.

5. *A Tickler File.* This file is usually divided in two parts: One is numbered 1 to 12, representing the months of the year; the other part is numbered 1 to 31, for the days of the month. The tickler file is used for longer-term pending and follow-through items.

Tickler System

By creating a tickler file system and checking it daily, you have a fool-proof reminder system. For example, suppose we're scheduled to meet on December 15. You might place the agenda and the papers you will bring to the meeting under 15th. Also in your tickler file at appropriate points throughout the month of December are items such as "Verify flight schedule" and "Check Chicago connection," along with a note to remind you to brief your replacement before your trip.

The tickler file can be used for storage in a way that avoids clogging up your pending basket. For instance, suppose you have an agreement that you need to write, and you know it's going to take some hours. So you have all sorts of papers—perhaps a first draft to be rewritten by a given deadline. You haven't done this rewrite because you know from experience it will take at least two hours, and you don't have a two-hour block to devote to it until Thursday. So you block out two hours on Thursday's calendar, and you place the rough report in the tickler file for Thursday, the 11th, where you know you'll find it when you're ready to get down to work. Then, because it's your habit to check the tickler file each morning, on the 11th you locate the rough draft in your file and check your calendar. Sure enough, you've blocked out time between 9 and 11 A.M. to work on the report. And when the final draft is completed, you'll place it into your out basket and route it to the next person involved.

Everything I am referring to in a paper tickler system applies equally to an electronic tickler system. It can be a specific personal information manager (PIM) software, or a personal digital assistant (PDA) like the popular Palm Pilot. Such electronic tickler systems often exist as part of an e-mail system. For those of us without administrative support, electronic systems are often more effective and easier to use than paper-based systems.

You can see why it's essential to check the tickler file daily. This is the essence of the *Do It Now* philosophy. After checking the tickler file for the day, you know exactly what you must do to keep on schedule and accomplish the tasks that will move you further along in your work.

Setting Up Your Personal Working Files

It is vital to develop a file structure that embraces all your work, is easy to conceptualize, and, most important, facilitates the retrieval of the information you need. When this is done, it is easy to decide where to file a document and where to look for it when you need to retrieve it—whether it is a working, reference, or archive file. You need to create specific files to have a workable system. You do this by mapping out your key responsibilities and the activities and information required to accomplish these tasks. See Figure 2.4 for an idea of the responsibilities a plant manager might list.

This is a simplified job-analysis process. List the broad categories of responsibilities you have as key words. Usually there are about six to eight key responsibilities that comprise your job. Then list subcategories for these broader responsibilities. Use the form found in Figure 2.5 to help identify and label files representing the important parts of your work.

As you set up your own working files, follow these guidelines:

1. *Select your working files drawer,* most likely one of your larger desk drawers. Remember, this is information you want close at hand. Label the drawer appropriately and clearly in big, bold letters.

2. *Remove all nonworking files.* Move them to either reference files or archive files.

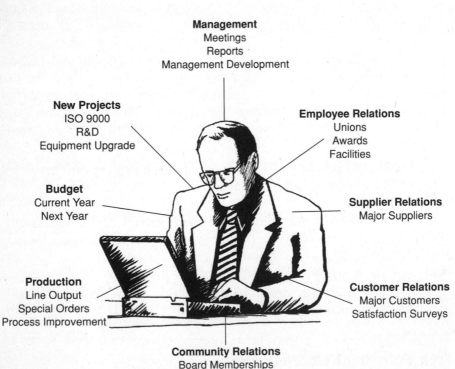

Figure 2.4 Example of a responsibilities map for files structure.

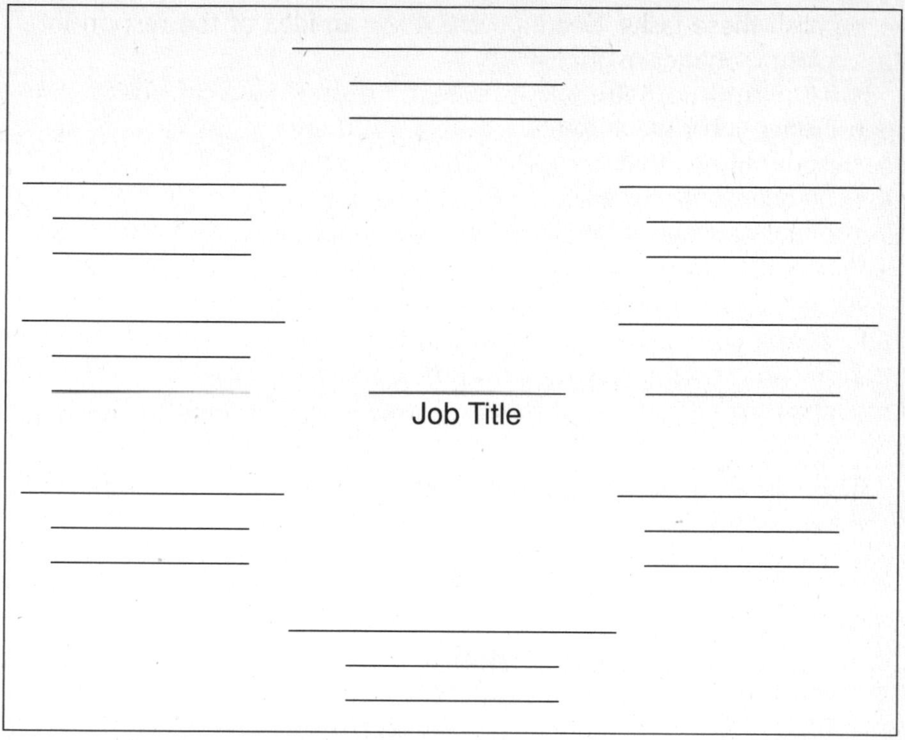

Job Title

Figure 2.5 Sample responsibilities mapping form.

3. *Make sure you have a file folder for each project and activity.* Label each file appropriately and clearly.

4. *Set up a tickler file.* One part is numbered 1 to 12, representing the months of the year, the other part of the tickler file is numbered 1 to 31, for the days of the month.

5. *Remove files that are no longer active.* Move to either reference files or archive files.

Your Personal Reference Files

You're now going to create your own reference files. Your reference files will contain these items:

- Research for your future projects.
- Past projects to which you refer.
- Resource information.
- Personnel information.
- Administrative data.
- Budget information.
- Client account records.

As you set up your reference files, consider these two things:

- What information do you have to keep?
- How can you best organize your reference files for ease of retrieval?

The following ideas might help you to structure your reference files (see Figure 2.6):

REFERENCE FILES STRUCTURE

In order to efficiently locate a file in reference files containing several drawers or cabinets, a simple alphabetical arrangement is usually inadequate, and subject categories must be established. A position can be broken down into key functions, which should be reflected in your file categories.

REFERENCE FILE CABINET

REFERENCE FILE DRAWER

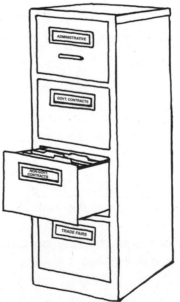

Figure 2.6   Reference files structure.

1. List the key components of your job (e.g., contracts, trade fairs, product development, budget, personnel). These will become the categories in your reference files.

2. Label file folders clearly and appropriately, based on the categories you identified.

3. Cull existing files and throw away useless paper.

4. Using hanging files, organize drawers with one or more categories.

5. Alphabetize files within categories or subcategories.

6. Label file drawers and file folders with large, clear letters to make retrieval and refiling easier and faster.

Archive Files

Archive files are most often set up for common use, so how they are structured and categorized may be different from how you might choose to set up your personal files. There may, in fact, be two systems required: an individual one in your office for archival documents related strictly to your job, and a second system outside your office for common use.

At one company, I found in a file drawer a memo dated 1906. No one had gone through those files since 1906! The memo was on how to clean the office. True. One of our PEP consultants carried a little case with screwdrivers and a hammer because it was so common to go into offices and find that some of the cabinets couldn't even be opened.

Staff members are generally reluctant to use the archive system because they feel they can't trust it. Management's responsibility is to provide a functional archive system; staff's responsibility is to understand the archive system and use it correctly.

The following questions will give you an indication of the state of your archive file system:

- Do you have departmental archives? What about company archives?
- What is the policy on document retention?
- Who is responsible for maintaining archives?
- Does an indexing system exist?
- What are the procedures for retrieving documents from archives?
- Can you rely on documents being recovered if needed?
- Have you tested this system lately?
- Do archive files need to be implemented? If so, who should do this?

I find that no matter how complete a departmental archive system might be, there's almost always a need for some form of personal archive system in the office. The personal archives can reside in the cabinets furthest away from the desk, since they will be the least-referenced files.

TIPS—WHAT TO KEEP, WHERE TO KEEP IT, AND WHAT TO THROW AWAY

For many people, throwing things away is difficult. Just how much information should you retain? Consider the following:

- Do you tend to hold onto things "just in case"?
- Do you keep too much in your reference files?
- When deciding whether to save something, take Stephanie Winston's advice from her book *Getting Organized* (Warner Books, 1991) and ask yourself, "If I needed this again, where can I get it?"
- Can someone else in the organization provide the information? If so, don't duplicate his or her files unless you use this information frequently.
- Should any of these working, reference and archive files be kept in a common departmental reference file system?
- Do you need to coordinate with anyone to determine who will save certain pieces of information?
- Do you need to coordinate with anyone with whom you share reference files on how you will organize files?

TIPS FOR IMPROVING YOUR PAPER FILING SYSTEM

The following suggestions (see also Figure 2.7) will make your filing system more efficient:

- Use hanging files. Hanging files support folders better and facilitate refiling in the correct place. Box-bottom hanging files can hold several manila folders on the same subject.

FILING TIPS

❏ Use hanging files.

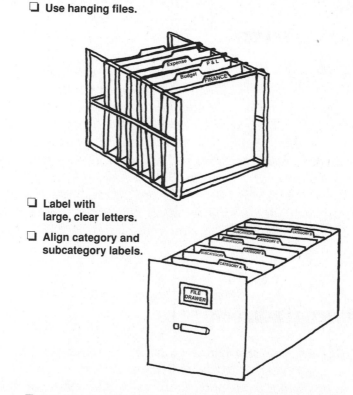

❏ Label with large, clear letters.

❏ Align category and subcategory labels.

❏ Create an index for large reference files for manager's use.

Figure 2.7   Filing tips.

- Label files with large, clear letters. This facilitates retrieval and refiling.
- Align category labels and subcategory labels. Aligning the tabs according to categories and subcategories allows the eye to scan to the correct file more efficiently. Categories can be given colored labels to further aid scanning. (Make sure this step is necessary and useful. I was told of one secretary who spent an entire day color coding her supervisor's files only to discover he was color-blind.)
- Create an index for large reference files. This index enables anyone to retrieve files easily in the secretary's absence. It also minimizes duplicate files and coordinates the use of shared files.

FILING AND LABELING

The main purpose in filing anything is to be able to find it again. The easiest way to do this is to create broad, general categories that will be genuinely useful and easily understood by others. A good rule of thumb is to set up file systems not only so you can find things, but also so anyone else can find them. The reason is twofold: (1) on occasion somebody else may need to find items in your files, and (2) if it's simple enough for someone else to use, it's probably simple enough for you. You can always subcategorize within a broad category, but the main idea is to have bigger categories. Label your drawers as well as the files within them, using lettering that is big, bold, and easy to read.

ORGANIZING ELECTRONIC FILES

Not too long ago you only had to worry about paper (as if that wasn't enough!). Today most of us depend more on the documents in our computers to get our work done than we do the paper on our desks. Digital documents can include letters, e-mail, web pages, spreadsheets, and so on. Because it is so much easier to create digital documents and they are for the most part invisible, they tend to proliferate more than paper. Since electronic storage space is relatively cheap, it is easy to save documents. But the problem isn't storing and saving documents; it's finding them again.

Fortunately, advances in technology are making finding files easier. It wasn't always that way. Those of us who began using computers with MS-DOS (Microsoft Disk Operating System) remember how difficult it was to organize the documents on the hard drive. The biggest single barrier was probably DOS's eight-letter naming convention. As a result of DOS limiting the number of characters one could use in a file name to eight, you would find files named 4Q99cshf.wk3 (which meant, in real life, fourth-quarter cash flow spreadsheet)—hard to decipher and harder yet to remember.

Technology has made it easier to find documents by providing more than one place to easily file (or copy) the same document and more than one way to locate a document.

When you organize your computer documents with the following points in mind, you will waste little time finding what you need to get the job done.

A computer is much like an empty filing cabinet. You can dump your data files into it in a pile, or you can group your applications and files, set up general categories, divide them into drawers, and subcategorize the files in these drawers, much as you would with your paper files. It is possible, and desirable, to organize the hard drive, the desktop (a term used in Windows describing the background where the graphic symbols called objects or icons reside), menus (the list of options and/or instructions to be found by clicking on an icon or object), and files (electronic documents that have been given a name and stored on your computer).

The recommended process for organizing the computer and its electronic files is to:

1. Create a file system for the document files in the computer.
2. Create a file system for retained e-mail messages.
3. Have the system mirror the organization of the rest of your information (paper and electronic).
4. Transfer those documents you wish to retain into their appropriate electronic folders.
5. Create a computer desktop that makes access to files and applications easy.

Where to Begin—The Computer's Operating System

It is through the operating system on the computer (be it DOS, any version of Windows, Mac, or another operating system) that application and document files can be found. Each operating system has its own set of commands or icons that allow you to manipulate files and organize them for easy use. The first step toward organizing your computer information is to get a working knowledge of your operating system file management protocol. Run through the tutorial. Search out file management in the "help" section and study up. If you are like me—lost, slow to learn, and possessing modest skills in only one language (English, nontechnical!)—you might seek out a computer coach (someone technically skilled with a working knowledge of your operating system) to coach you through the learning process. In large organizations seek help from your information systems department or a knowledgeable administrative support person. The rule is: Before you start messing with your computer files, know what you are doing or find someone who does.

Back Up Your Hard Drive

No matter how skilled you may be with file management, it is wise to do a complete backup (make a copy) of your hard drive before you begin deleting and reorganizing your files. In later versions of Windows, it is as simple as going into Microsoft Tools in the Start and Programs menu, selecting Backup, and following the instructions. You no doubt have a method of backing up your computer files. Whether you do it regularly enough is something to consider. If you do not do it at all, you are setting yourself up for big problems in the future. Regardless, be certain to back up your files before you take on the following.

Tip: If possible, consider backing up the whole hard drive, including applications, on an external drive. It is always prudent to back up your data files. But in the case of a crashed and nonrecoverable hard drive, it can be a huge task reinstalling programs.

Naming Electronic Files

The design of your computer file system should mirror your paper file system.

A typical computer user might have the following documents to organize:

- Word processing documents.
- Spreadsheet documents.
- Saved e-mail messages.
- Documents downloaded and saved from the Internet.
- Groupware databases.
- Personal finance files (like Quicken).
- Project planning files.
- Photos.
- Power Point presentation files.
- And so on.

Use your paper system file names to help create your electronic document file categories. The simplest way would be to make a list of the names of your paper files in your working, reference, and archive cabinets/drawers. How to create file names on your computer and how to manipulate these files (move them from one location to another) depend on the operating system you use.

Using the appropriate operating system commands, do the following:

1. Create a My Documents folder (if not already on your C: drive). Create three subfolders (directories) under the My Documents. Name them 1Working, 2Reference, and 3Archive. Working, reference, and archive electronic file categories allow you to store your document files in a system identical to your paper files. Putting the numeral "1" next to the name of your most important file directory (working) will position it at the top of the My Documents tree. The numeral "2" places the reference files below the working directory, and the numeral "3" puts the archive files below the reference directory.

2. Using your prepared list of paper files, create a matching set of subfolders (subdirectories) in the 1Working, 2Reference, and 3Archive electronic directories. (See Figure 2.8.) The end result of

1st Tier	2d Tier	3d Tier	4th Tier
Main file folder/directory structure These folders/ directories are set up using numbers as the first character to ensure their placement at the top of the hard disk tree structure.	**Responsibilities** This folder/ directory tier should be general headings resulting from the responsibility map and will not contain specific files.	**Specific names of subdirectories** The names chosen for subdirectories must be general in nature with each tier giving more information about the files in the grouping. When the number of files in a group becomes excessive, start thinking about creating further subdirectories of the existing group.	**Files** Careful thought is necessary when choosing a file name. Use only abbreviations that are meaningful to you and instantly recognizable. Be consistent with your format and name files so that you will have some idea what it is if you see it away from its home folder/ directory.
Working Files *(folder or folder/ directory)* **1Working**	**Clients Customers Finances Forms People (Personnel) Pending Projects (etc.)**	Actual client/ customer names Expense record, budgets Form names or numbers Actual names of people or personnel records Items awaiting completion Projects currently in progress	
Reference Files *(folder or directory)* **2Reference**	**Graphs/Charts Spreadsheets Completed projects Expense reports Reports Evaluations (etc.)**		
Archive Files *(folder or directory)* **3Archive**	**Previous year's tax returns "Must saves"**		

Figure 2.8 Organizing the hard drive with Windows Explorer.

creating these directories and subdirectories might look like Figure 2.9.

3. Now that you have named your electronic file directories you can go through the electronic document files of each of your software applications and transfer your documents into their appropriate folders (directories). You should have three main objectives in going through document files of your computer. These would be to:

- Purge unnecessary files (if you are uncertain whether to eliminate the document, copy it onto a disk for storage).
- Rename, as may be necessary, any document files you keep.
- Place the document files in the appropriate 1Working, 2Reference, and 3Archive directories.

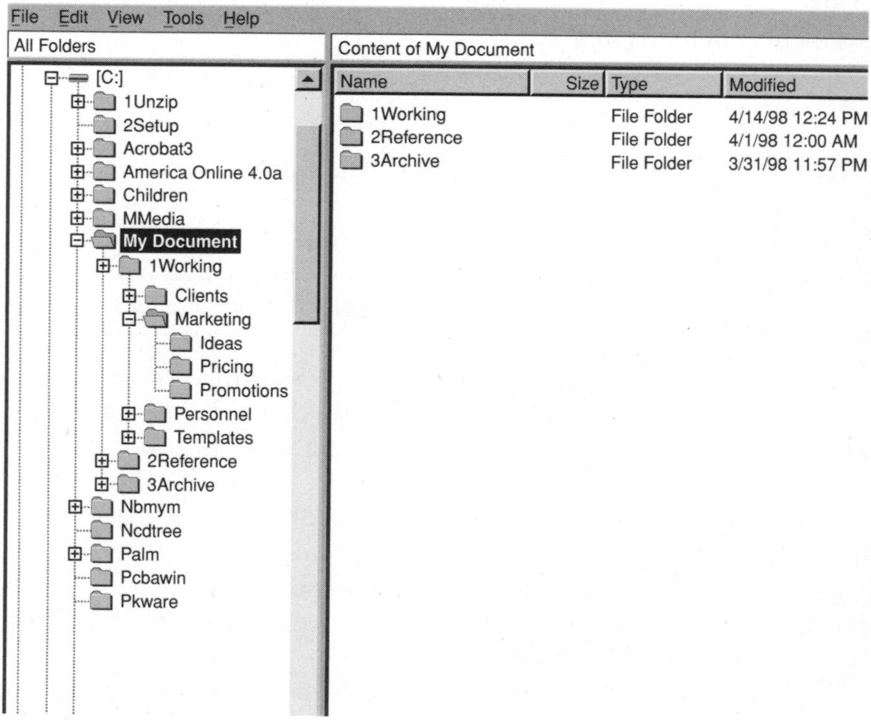

Figure 2.9 How the file directories might look on your computer C: drive.

LET THE COMPUTER FIND YOUR DOCUMENTS FOR YOU

I have given you a rather lengthy way to organize your electronic documents for easier retrieval. I believe it is useful to devote the time to such a process. The process disciplines you in naming protocols, purges out old and useless files, and helps you identify resources you may forget you even have. One such application is Enfish Find (www.enfish.com).

We use Enfish Find in the office. As described in its literature, Enfish Find works like an intelligent assistant, organizing everything on your computer, helping you find exactly what you need when you need it. With the software you type in a subject name, specific phrase, person, company, topic, or whatever, and the software automatically groups and lists all of the files, e-mails, or documents containing the subject. You can view the contents of the files on the list without even having to launch the application. This is one nifty way to access information!

ORGANIZING SHARED ELECTRONIC FILES

The process of organizing your personal documents on your C drive can be simple enough. But many of us are also connected to a network server and have documents we want to quickly access from there.

One of our clients, the human resources department at a large international bank, was having difficulty servicing its customers because it was very hard to find paper documents in other people's work space. Too often, someone would not be in the office when a call came in and another person trying to service a caller would search in vain for information in their missing colleague's work space. The client decided they wanted to reorganize their files to be able to have easier access to materials no matter where they were filed. They hired IBT to help.

IBT first addressed the issue of the paper document within the group. IBT's main role at this stage was to set up standards and categories among all of the personnel in the human resources department so everyone's system was the same.

IBT then tackled the shared common documents within the group.

The human resources department wanted systems set up that made the materials "transparent" and easy to find. They also wanted to eliminate duplicate and parallel filing structures that existed throughout the department.

If your aim is to set up a structure on a network server that allows for transparency and easy retrieval, the first rule of thumb is don't do anything on the server without first consulting your IT (and Legal) department. Information you may need from your IT department might include:

- *What are the company's rules regarding document retention?* What should be kept? How long should it be kept for?
- *How is the server currently organized?* Some companies allow for space on the server where you can store your personal documents. Personal space on the network drive may be a portion of a shared drive that is assigned to an individual. It can have any letter designation depending on how your Local Area Network is set up.
- *Is there a departmental or shared drive?* This is a network drive everyone within a department can access. You can store files on this drive although they are not private. Your IT department will have to tell you what the rules are by which a person can create his or her own private directories or if a directory structure will be offered to the members so they can read, write, or copy documents.
- *Does your firm have a secured drive?* This drive may be a section of secured drive on the server that is restricted and requires security access in order to create or retrieve files. In organizing shared folders we suggest you use terms such as "My Own Personal Reference Files" and "Departmental Reference Files" to distinguish between the two types of file storage.
- *What documents are located in the department or shared drive (the common drive)?* These should have all team related documents.
- *What is allowed on a personal drive?* (Whether part of the server or your C: drive) It should probably only have nonteam/department related information saved.

Once you have established with your IT department what systems you have that they are prepared to support, you can then work out a plan with your team to establish a section on the server drive to place your shared documents. In the case of our banking client, they were able to get a departmental drive secured and devoted to their activities.

Having gone through the Personal Efficiency Program and identified their basic categories within their paper environment, they were able to quickly identify the types of categories and folders they wanted to have established on the shared drive.

This helped them identify the information that belonged on their shared drive. They used the responsibility mapping process as coverage on page 41 to better identify their folder structure. The structure reflected responsibilities of the group, not the names of the members. The created a folder for each area. This process typically ends with between 12 and 15 folders. These folders are created as the primary categories. Subcategories are then created within the primary categories.

It is into these newly created folders that you will be transferring or copying information from your personal drive and any other areas on the server where documents exist that should be accessible by members of your group.

In order to make these new folders more visible within your shared folder directory, you can place an asterisk (*) or any other symbol in front of each newly titled shared folder, and this will place these folders on top of the hierarchy and make them more visible.

Since there are usually many documents involved, IBT has found that the easiest way to make this process successful is to assign individual members of the team the responsibility for specific sections in the old structure. An easy way to identify who is responsible for what sections is by putting the individual's initials in the beginning of the name of the folder(s) they are responsible for, so that all folders they are dealing with will be grouped together under their initials.

It is up to the person responsible for the specific section(s) of the file to go through the old structure folders to identify those they think should be deleted or renamed after bringing them to the group for approval. Once all folders have been deleted and renamed, the responsible person's initials can be removed.

Some rules of thumb that might be valuable to you if you were to run this process within your own department include:

- Group members all have to be well informed of the structure.
- One person has to be made responsible for the structure.
- Clear instructions for deleting, renaming, and storing data must be established.

Organizing and executing such an initiative definitely required an action plan and people assigned responsibility for implementation.

Many of our clients have benefited greatly from this process. Better service is one of the most immediate benefits. Easy access to information has also saved time for all members of the department.

Obviously, organizing the documents on your own C: drive is a simple matter compared to bringing an entire department and the IT group into agreement on how common documents should be filed. Getting people to comply with the rules that have been established also is a process that takes some time. Nevertheless, our clients report to us that the outcome was well worth the effort.

ORGANIZING E-MAIL

It is not uncommon to find people receiving upwards of 200 e-mail messages a day. Obviously, this can be overwhelming. To process this mail in an efficient and effective way is the subject of a later chapter. How to organize the e-mail messages you keep so as to be able to easily find them again is the topic of this section.

Like your paper in basket, the electronic mailbox can fill up quickly. Some systems allow hundreds of messages to accumulate in the in box. This can become unmanageable and cause slowdowns. One of the most important buttons on the keyboard is the delete key. Obviously, the more you delete, the less you need to organize and file. Nevertheless, there will be e-mail messages you will need to keep. Messages you do keep should be stored in the correct computer directory or electronic folder.

Many e-mail applications allow you to create electronic storage folders for those messages you need to keep but do not want to leave in the same location as your incoming e-mail. Which messages you want to keep or delete will depend on the company policy regarding retention of e-mail. Recent developments in which large companies have found themselves in a legal nightmare because they have retained e-mail messages (or haven't for that matter) tell you that this topic is very important. Ninety percent of all major corporations have e-mail and document retention policies. Unfortunately, most staff members have never been trained on these policies, are unaware, and don't follow them. Before you decide to delete anything, make sure that you are in compliance with corporate policy.

Once you have determined what you need to keep and what you don't need to keep, it is a matter of setting up an organizational structure that allows you to easily find e-mail messages that have been stored.

The easiest way to begin this process is to use the responsibility map designed for your paper-based system to create folders of the same name in your e-mail application.

Apart from any other e-mail storage folders you may want to create, I advise you to create a folder called "Pending/Follow-up." In this folder you place e-mail messages received or sent requiring some form of input from elsewhere or needing to be followed through on by you. This is an excellent way to remove and store messages that would otherwise remain in the in box and remain a distraction. The most important thing to remember about this "Pending/Follow-up" folder is to routinely check it to make sure that you do in fact follow-through on messages that have been placed there.

Steps to Organize E-Mail

1. Begin by identifying your e-mail file features. Using the Help function, determine how to set up a folder system within your particular e-mail application.

2. Using your responsibility map and categories created for your paperwork file system, set up a mirrored system of categories within your e-mail application.

3. In the process of going through your e-mail one at a time, identify whether you should:
   - Delete it.
   - File it on either your personal C: drive, personal server drive (should it exist), or shared drive on the server.

4. If transferring the file to your shared drive, verify that the name of the file is intuitive and will make it possible for you to easily find it again.

5. Go through your e-mail messages one by one and follow this process until complete.

6. If you are beginning this process with a large backlog of unorganized e-mail, you may wish simply to set up the folder organization, choose a cutoff date for these earlier documents (like the beginning of the year), create an archive folder, transfer these documents en masse to it, and forget about them. If you need to look up an older message, you can do so by accessing the archive folder and then reclassifying it in the new folder structure. (See Figure 2.10.)

CREATING AND ORGANIZING YOUR E-MAIL ADDRESS BOOK

Your e-mail application memorizes e-mail addresses, and these can be put into an e-mail address book. Most e-mail applications organize the

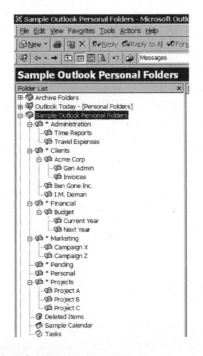

Figure 2.10   E-mail folder organization.

addresses in alphabetical order, but it is possible to create general categories (groupings) within the address book list and file addresses under
these general groupings.

For example, I organize my address book by group according to
those who work in my business, those who are clients, and, under
the grouping/category "Personal," family and friends. The number
of e-mail addresses I have determines how specific I might be in both
organizing and grouping the addresses. I wouldn't organize lots of
groupings if I had only a few e-mail addresses.

Not only does organizing e-mail addresses according to groups
make it easier to find the address I'm looking for, it also allows me to
send specific e-mails more easily to the members of the group.

ORGANIZING THE COMPUTER DESKTOP TO ACCESS APPLICATIONS AND FILES EASILY

The computer desktop is that screen you see when you first turn on
your computer. It is the electronic equivalent of the top surface of the
desk in your office. The computer desktop can be organized much in
the same way you would organize and utilize your office desk. The
documents, electronic files, and ongoing projects that you access most
frequently can be placed and organized on the computer desktop.

For instance, most Windows programs allow you to create categories of and group software applications so you can easily access
these applications on your computer desktop. A group for "Finance
Programs" might include Quicken for personal finance, Lotus 1-2-3
for spreadsheet work, and QuickBooks for business accounts.

Often accessed documents can be grouped and named, and an icon
placed on the desktop. You can simply click the icon, the software program is launched, and up pops the document.

It is worth the effort to study how to organize the desktop for your
operating system and how to set up the desktop for easy access to files
and applications.

ORGANIZING OTHER MEDIA

Other items that might need to be organized include books, shelves,
briefcase, address book, business cards, and floppy disks. See Figure
2.11 for guidance.

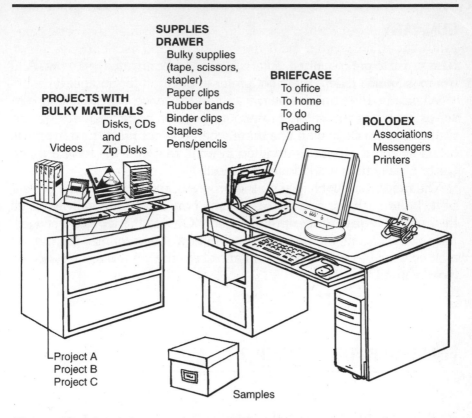

Figure 2.11 Adapting the principles of organizing to other media.

The rules of thumb for organizing these other media are:

- Group similar things together.
- Place them in their own space or container.
- Label them clearly.

Supplies such as paper clips, pens, Post-it notes, thumbtacks, and stamps can be organized in desk drawers using specially designed plastic trays to hold and separate the supplies.

Even the automobile may need to be organized if you spend lots of time traveling to and from customers!

SUMMARY

It isn't easy to get organized. After all, it can be boring, tedious work. And like most boring tasks, you might prefer to put it off for another time.

When our PEP trainers deliver our PEP service we often find ourselves acting as the catalyst—encouraging the participants to get on with it. But we likely won't be there when you get ready to start; it will be up to you to do it. Try to keep in mind that you will have a much easier time getting work done as a result.

The more thoroughly you do the program, the more you will get out of it. I often ask my course participants how much attention to detail they place on, say, a sales presentation. "Oh, lots!" they say. I suggest they give the same attention to detail to how they organize themselves as they would to a special presentation. Do the same! You will not be disappointed.

FOLLOW-UP FOR CHAPTER 2

1. Clear the backlog and organize your work area. Very likely you will require a day or more to do this. If at all possible, schedule this time so you work undisturbed.

2. Get at least three trays and mark them "In," "Pending," and "Out." Your in basket will receive all new material. Your pending basket is for those things you cannot do now, for things that are out of your control. Your out basket is for all those papers you've completed.

3. Empty out onto your desk every piece of paper or document from your drawers, trays, walls, and briefcase. Look everywhere—under the blotter, behind the curtain, under the desk.

4. Pick up the top piece of paper and deal with it *now* in one of the following ways:

- Deal with it until completed.
- Deal with it as completely as you can and then place it in the pending basket if very short-term or the tickler file under the appropriate date while awaiting a response.

- Delegate it.
- Create a pile on the floor for papers needed for ongoing work or projects to file in your working files.
- Create another pile on the floor for papers to file in the reference file, if it's information you need but which requires you to do nothing at the moment.
- Create a pile on the floor for papers to file in the archive file.
- Throw it away! Do this if it's trivial, of no use, already dealt with, or exists elsewhere.

5. Using the responsibility map (see Figure 2.4) begin identifying where the saved documents go.

6. After all this, set up your working files. Create hanging files and labels for each work project and general category. Create files and labels for the reference files and archive files.

7. Create individual follow-up files for each of your subordinates and your boss or peers with whom you have regular contact. Label each file with the person's name, and place in that file notes about things you need to check on regarding ongoing, long-term projects.

8. Create a tickler file. The tickler file is part of your working files. If you have a secretary, the tickler file should be maintained at the secretary's desk.

9. Determine where to file saved electronic files: for example, your C: drive? a shared drive?

10. If your documents are on the C: drive, create 1Working, 2Reference, and 3Archive folders for your saved electronic documents.

11. Using the responsibility map begin creating a set of subfolders that mirror your paper file system and represent the key categories you will set up within your electronic file system.

12. Begin the process of reviewing all of your stored electronic documents. Decide:

- Is this a document you use or will use?
- Can it be accessed elsewhere?
- If you are to keep it, where should it be stored?

- Should the file be renamed?
- Should the file be deleted?

Act on your decisions.

13. Make a list of missing supplies and tools necessary for you to do your job: pen, tape, staples, scissors, envelopes, stamps, extra file folders, labels, formatted disks, and anything else you may need. Make sure you have them all on hand and that everything works.

That's it. Get going. *Do It Now!*

CHAPTER 3

Do It Routinely

We are what we repeatedly do.
Excellence, therefore, is not an act but a habit.
—ARISTOTLE

Chapter 3 Preview

In this chapter, you will learn how to:

- Organize your schedule and work to operate within large blocks of time.
- Batch your work. Schedule time to process mail and memos all at once. Handle telephone calls, e-mail, and so forth the same way.
- Eliminate low-value information and prevent it from coming to you in the first place.
- Stamp out time-consuming and unnecessary interruptions.
- Hold scheduled one-on-one meetings weekly with your direct reports to improve communication and to process work efficiently.

You will increase your efficiency and effectiveness (your productivity) by working smarter on the right things. The simple key to personal productivity is to batch many job-related activities and do them routinely. The idea is to spend a minimum amount of time on the relatively unimportant things so that you can spend a maximum amount of time on important things.

You must determine the important things—what you should be working on first—and then discover ways to do the work you identify as important more efficiently and effectively.

First, you should assess how you currently spend your time. Next, ask yourself, "Would the results be better if I spent my time working on some other activity?" Then ask yourself, "How could I do the high-level activities more frequently and efficiently?"

KEEP A TIME LOG

To identify precisely how you spend your time, keep a time log. In his landmark book *The Effective Executive* (Harper & Row, 1966), Peter Drucker says that we can't hope to control our time until we know where our time goes. No doubt we think we know where our time goes, but most of us don't. Drucker (p. 27) writes:

> *I sometimes ask executives who pride themselves on their memory to put down their guess as to how they spend their own time. Then I lock these guesses away for a few weeks or months. In the meantime, the executives run an actual time record on themselves. There is never much resemblance between the way these men thought they used their time and their actual records.*

Only by keeping a time log will you get an accurate idea of where your time is being spent. I have often used this technique with clients who are especially busy. Their workload is so great that they do not have a clear picture of the nature of their workload to be able to address it effectively. Keeping a record not only tells them what they spend their time on, it also gives insight into who might be dropping the ball in their area, what functions might not be covered, and how they might be wasting the time of others.

To avoid making this time log an administrative burden, you can simply keep a piece of paper on your desk. As you deal with things, you note what it was, how long it took, and who was involved. Figure 3.1 is

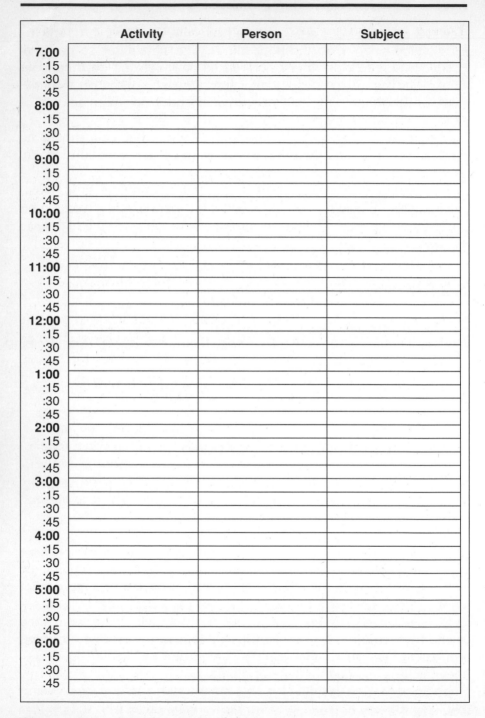

Figure 3.1   Sample time log form.

a sample form of a time log. Soon categories of things begin to become visible.

After a couple of weeks of keeping records, tally it all up. You will have a pretty good idea where your time goes. You can then start addressing the areas of waste and inefficiency.

ELECTRONIC TIME LOG

The computer and modern software make it possible to improve time log accuracy and ease the tabulation and evaluation of results. Not only can you keep better track of your own time, you can do so on a department- or company-wide basis. One such software application is Time Tiger (www.timetiger.com).

The software is useful not only as a diagnostic tool. For accountants or lawyers who track time for billing purposes, the software makes the whole process easier and more accurate.

As a planning tool (see Chapter 4, section on "Project Implementation Planning") the software integrates well with project implementation software like Microsoft Project, allowing for accurate planning of time against tasks.

Once again, the principle is that if you wish to gain control over time you must account for it.

OVERCOME INFORMATION OVERLOAD

We all experience a flood of information. It can be overwhelming and it can blind us to what we should be focused on. Technology has significantly increased the number of ways information and work come our way. There was a time when you only had to cope with the telephone ringing in the office and a mail delivery once a day. Now you have the fax, e-mail, mobile telephones, pagers, and a continuous stream of mail from many postal and delivery services. In this information age, we need to know what information we *don't* need as much as we need to know what information we do need.

The best way to overcome information overload is to stop low-value information and tasks from entering your system. Figure 3.2 shows the different ways to screen information. Nonscreening, meaning allowing all information to arrive unfiltered and sorting through it after the fact, is the least effective way of controlling the flow of information to you. A better method of information control would be to have the information

Nonscreening
(Not Good)

Front-End/Support
Screening
(Better)

Figure 3.2   Three ways to screen information.

screened before it gets to you. Having this done by support staff is better
yet. The ideal solution is to carefully analyze all sources of information
and eliminate at the source the nonessential information by removing
yourself from the distribution list, canceling the subscription, and so forth.

BEYOND THE IN BASKET

Paper in your in basket, voice mail and e-mail messages, telephone
calls, and people all clamor for your attention. Add to this all the meet-

Source
Screening
(Best)

Figure 3.2   *(Continued)*

ings you must attend, and it's no wonder you feel you rarely accomplish anything important.

I've watched people whose idea of a productive day at work is to spend the entire day at their desks going through the items that come into their in baskets. They are fully occupied doing just those things.

Too much of what comes into your in basket daily is the after-the-fact proof of someone else's accomplishment. It's done, over with, and probably 50% of it is for your information and files. Rarely, if ever, does it make the company money. So often what you process is relatively unimportant. That's why I recommend that you dedicate minimum time to it and get on with your real work.

The way to control this often overwhelming flow of information is to categorize and group it and organize an efficient response to it.

BATCH THE ROUTINE WORK

The categorizing and grouping of your work might be called "batching." Each piece of paper, each e-mail message, every telephone call, every interruption, and every item you send out is a form of communication. Process similar communications and tasks in batches, reducing waste and motion. You'll complete each task more efficiently.

Many elements of your work can be reduced to simple routines that will let you complete similar tasks in the shortest possible time. These tasks readily lend themselves to batching. The advantages of approaching your work in this way are numerous.

- It is more efficient to process your e-mail two or three times a day on a scheduled basis. You avoid being distracted by things you're not going to act on anyway and you learn to set time limits and meet those time limits.
- Set aside a time each day to check voice mail and return all phone calls at the same time. Again, this avoids unnecessary interruptions and encourages you to be more effective and efficient in responding to your phone messages.
- Set aside a time in your day for reading. It may be necessary or valuable for you to keep up to date with periodicals and other important reading information. This tends to be assigned lower priority in the face of more urgent demands. But if you set aside a time, for instance, lunchtime, and bring your reading with you, you'll be able to keep up with your reading responsibilities more effectively.
- It is easier to take a batch of completed work from your out basket and distribute it all at the same time than to get up from your desk each time one piece of work is completed.
- It saves time to do all word processing work at once instead of going in and out of the different applications each time you have new word processing to do.
- There is less effort involved in doing all filing at once than filing each paper individually.
- You will find batching like work allows you to prepare and organize yourself for the work one time instead of many times if the work is done randomly.

SCHEDULE AND AVOID HAVING TO DECIDE

It's important to juggle between acting on everything as it comes up and always putting things off to do later. There is a way to deal with this. I refer to it as *Do It Now, Later.* Schedule times to do certain work (such as opening and reading your mail, processing your e-mail, returning telephone calls, etc.) and when the time arrives, *Do It Now!* Don't look at it until you are prepared to act. When you do look at it, act on it. *Do It Now, Later.*

If you want to get something done, schedule it. Since these in-basket tasks rarely represent the most important part of your job, they are seldom considered priority, so they don't get done. Have you ever noticed when you have made a to-do list of open items, the tasks on the bottom of the list never seem to get done? Urgent tasks always seem to delay action on the merely important ones, and both urgent and important tasks will certainly interfere with paperwork and e-mail. If you constantly prioritize you will never get to these often less critical paperwork and e-mail tasks. But if you do not handle your paperwork and e-mail, they will overwhelm you.

The hidden consequence of this clutter and information overload is to slow down the whole process of your important work. If you have to choose between calling the customer and sorting through your in basket, what are you going to do? If you're like most people, you'll choose the customer, right? But the other things don't get done! What you want to do is avoid putting yourself in the position of constantly having to decide between things. It makes your life harder than it has to be. Instead, schedule a time to go through your in basket and do other routine tasks that can be batched. When the time arrives to do that particular task, do it during the time allotted and move on to the work that is important.

Do you brush your teeth in the morning? "Yes," you say. Do you think about brushing your teeth? Do you prioritize it? Do you wonder, "Am I going to brush my teeth now, or am I going to have a cup of coffee?" Probably not. It's part of a nonthinking routine you've established as part of your habits. You don't burden yourself with lots of thought about it. In fact you hardly give it *any* thought. Through force of habit, you eliminated the steps of conscious decision making. You simply do it routinely. And that's the way you want to handle these simple batched tasks.

PARKINSON'S LAW AND THE ALLOCATION OF TIME

Parkinson's law says *work tends to fill up (adjust to) the time available or allotted for it.* If you allocate only one hour to complete a certain task you have a much greater chance of finishing the work in that time. If you set a deadline to complete a project by a certain date you will likely figure out how to do it within the time you set for that deadline.

BLOCKS OF TIME

Working in blocks of time is more efficient and effective than working piecemeal. This applies not only to the batching of similar tasks such as telephone calls or to the handling of incoming mail, but also to project work, sales calls, or a marketing campaign. Peter Drucker suggests that the ideal span of time to work is 90 minutes. You will get more done in a concentrated period of 90 minutes than twice the time in an environment of regular interruptions. Blocking out undisturbed time will greatly increase your productivity. If you manage to get the many little tasks out of the way first, you will be better able to focus during your uninterrupted blocks of time. You'll feel good knowing you've covered all the important issues and organized your time and your work to permit you to do the important things. Giving your mind enough time to get into the heart of the issue is far more productive than being constantly distracted from the work at hand by other tasks that crop up, demanding your attention.

Some of us may not have an office door to close, and so we have to be more creative if we are to enjoy blocks of undisturbed time. One client's company was composed of account officers who worked together in a noisy, open-office environment where the phones rang continuously as clients initiated transactions. In part of the building were several small interview offices. When an account officer needed a block of time to put together a proposal, another officer would cover as he or she used the interview room to peacefully complete the proposal.

Another client would work out of a home office one day per week. This particular client found that working at home afforded him the time he needed for strategic planning and prospecting for new business.

BATCHING TELEPHONE CALLS

Cell phones have made it much easier for us to keep in touch. That may be exactly what is wrong with them! In the not so distant past you could at least avoid the phone on the way home or after hours. This is not the case today. How can you make this tool work for you rather than you working for it?

Decide that you will not accept calls haphazardly throughout the work day; instead, you will return calls (depending on the nature of your job) perhaps once or twice during the day. If you accept calls twice a day, say between 11:30 A.M. and noon and between 4:00 P.M. and 5:00 P.M., simply tell your assistant you will not accept calls at other times. This doesn't mean you want your assistant to hold your calls—it means that you establish a routine: You take phone calls at certain times, except in specific cases. Of course, you then have to define those specific cases. You will probably accept calls from an important client or your immediate supervisor, for example, and you will want to establish clear parameters for emergency calls.

Be sure each office staff member clearly understands the new procedure, who and what the exceptions would be, and how messages for you are to be taken. To return a call you have to understand the message. "Bill called" is not acceptable by itself. Ask assistants to take *complete, correct* messages. Train your assistants in how to find out what Bill wants and when Bill will be available to discuss the subject: "Bill called to schedule an appointment with the sales team in New York. He will be available all afternoon at such-and-such number." This allows you to prepare yourself for the call. You know what the call is all about, and you know when you can reach him. When you reach Bill, you can have your calendar open and suggest several times and alternative days when you're available to meet. You'll impress Bill and wrap up the call in minimal time.

If you have voice mail or an answering service, you could create a message that conveys the same information:

> *"Hello, this is Frank. I'm not available to take your call at the moment. If you would leave a complete message, I will prepare for our conversation and get back to you as soon as I can. I normally return phone calls between 11:30 A.M. and noon, eastern time. Please let me know if that's a convenient time for you. If it isn't, please suggest another time you might be available."*

Now, you have to stick to the new procedure. Stick to the routine of returning all phone calls at a given time in the day, and stick to your procedure of refusing calls at any other time (within the guidelines you establish).

In this way, you'll be prepared to return your calls, and you can organize yourself for them. You can consult files or documents before returning a call. You can have all pertinent material in front of you so you don't waste time. Treat your calls precisely as you treat the items in your in basket—one at a time, working through them to completion. In scheduling these call times allow sufficient flexibility to handle calls that depend on varying time zones, emergencies, and other special circumstances.

ONE MORE THING!

I highly recommend that you turn off your cell phone after 5 P.M. when you leave from work and don't turn it back on until you arrive at work the following morning. I realize that some of you will object strongly to being out of touch. I understand that in some industries, this would be impossible. A doctor must be on call. A real estate agent must be on call. But the vast majority of us have jobs that are supposed to end at a specific time of day. Keeping your cell phone on allows people to be in touch with you at times when you should be taking care of your own private life. You may be surprised to learn if you do turn off your cell phone at the end of your scheduled workday, you will begin to work out ways to figure out how to get the work done within the hours you've allocated for it. Those who would likely want to get in touch with you will also discover that they have to be a bit brighter and sharper about getting in touch during the working hours. The best way to control a cell phone is to turn it off.

E-MAIL

By creating a structure for your electronic documents, you have taken a big step toward controlling the flow of electronic information. The primary source of electronic information for most people comes from the Internet or local area network (LAN) in the form of e-mail. E-mail is a marvelous tool. Most benefits from e-mail are obvious:

- Communication is simplified.
- E-mail is less costly than traditional mail.
- Loss of the message (information) is less likely.
- With a single keystroke, the message can be sent to many people.
- Remote access is possible.
- Receipt of messages can be verified.
- The documents are easier to organize.
- The documents are easier to manipulate, reorganize, and edit.
- It is easier to transfer documents.
- E-mail is speedier than most other forms of communication.
- With e-mail, you can append all previous communications so a complete history moves with the note.
- Some e-mail systems allow you to send yourself a message at a later date, another type of reminder system.
- E-mail makes possible the preprogramming of function keys to set up timesaving keystrokes for tickler system entries (calendar and appointment reminders), delete procedures, and the like.
- With e-mail, you can prepare a group for a meeting. Instead of using meeting time for announcements, prepare and send the announcements beforehand as e-mail.

Along with the good comes the bad:

- Because e-mail makes it easier to communicate, there tends to be more of it. Because there can be so much of it, people tend to ignore messages they deem unimportant.
- E-mail systems are subject to abuse. It is not uncommon to find people using company e-mail for things like advertising kittens they are eager to get adopted.
- E-mail can become the preferred form of documentation, as one of my banking clients put it, "to CYA (cover your [certain anatomy])."
- Some e-mail systems have irritating limitations like having to open an e-mail document and follow a series of instructions simply to delete the message.
- Employees may not have switched from a paper to an electronic mind-set and may end up printing every e-mail message.
- The system can get overloaded. Typically information technology (IT) departments limit the number of messages allowed in any one workstation.

On balance, I consider e-mail to be an excellent tool for improved efficiency. But e-mail will overwhelm you if you are sloppy in dealing with it.

Handling E-Mail the Right Way!

It is vital to apply the *Do It Now* principle when processing e-mail (as well as paper mail, faxes, and voice mail messages). Many of the problems you experience coping with the volumes of correspondence you receive will be resolved by simply doing it now. But *when* to *Do It Now* is important.

Some e-mail applications have a built-in beeper or flashing visual signal alert function, so every time you receive a new message the computer alerts you. The alert prompts you to look at the incoming message, and because you are in the middle of something else or not prepared to spend the time to answer the message your tendency is to do it later. This is not the way to process your e-mail. I suggest you turn off the alert function and instead set up times in your schedule to process your e-mail. Processing e-mail needs to be done more than once a day. E-mail has, to some degree, become a substitute for the telephone and face-to-face meetings and needs to be acted upon promptly, although, in most environments, it should not command the same immediacy as the telephone.

How do you handle this? I suggest you handle your e-mail three or four times a day. Seldom do people expect a response to an e-mail immediately. If you process your e-mail regularly, say first thing in the morning, before lunch, and before leaving for the day, this is normally quite sufficient. Schedule times in your calendar to process the e-mail. Establish time parameters and work to get the e-mail done in those times, if at all possible. If you cannot, then look for ways to cut down on the messages. (More on this later.)

Remember, when I say *process* I do not mean look at and decide to respond later. I mean complete it now. If it is not possible to complete it, take it as far as you possibly can and write a reminder to follow-through on whatever actions may still be needed. If the e-mail represents a large block of work time, schedule it into your calendar and file the message away.

Tip: Our IBT Canadian office advises that people do not start the day by opening their e-mail. Instead start the day doing the most important task. Once done (or progressed as desired) then open your e-mail in box. E-mail can be a distraction from the most vital tasks. So do them first!

Cutting Down on E-Mail

If you have received e-mail, you must handle it. The question you have to ask yourself is, should you be getting it in the first place? Sean Savage of Knight Ridder newspapers covered solutions to this problem in a recently published article. If you have an e-mail address on the Internet and have an Internet service provider (America Online, CompuServe, Prodigy, etc.), chances are you are receiving electronic junk mail (spam). It is common practice for Internet service providers (ISPs), online publications, and other service providers to sell your personal information to marketers. Service providers will take you off their marketing lists if you request it. Here is how:

1. If you receive junk e-mail messages, reply by requesting that the marketer not send you any more messages.

2. If you still receive messages from the offending marketer, you can complain to the postmaster at the site where the messages are originating. To locate the postmaster address, drop the first part of the marketer's e-mail address and replace it with the word "postmaster." If, for example, e-mail is coming from Buynowxxx.net, that firm's postmaster's address is probably postmasterxxx.net. Even if the address is wrong, you'll usually receive a response specifying the postmaster address. Ask the postmaster to see to it that the offender no longer sends you junk e-mail.

3. If the postmaster doesn't stop the unwanted e-mail, there may still be a way to deal with it. Many e-mail software packages allow users to filter out all messages sent from given addresses. If messages from Buynowxxx.net arrive, special software automatically deletes them before you see them.

E-Mail Rules of Thumb

One of our clients, SmithKline Beecham in Philadelphia, was kind enough to share some of their e-mail wisdom with us. I have summarized some of their ideas and added a few of our own. By using these ideas, you will be saving yourself heartache and extra work.

- In composing an e-mail message, ensure the subject matter on the subject line is clearly stated.
- Briefly state the purpose of the e-mail in the beginning of the message.

- Limit yourself to one topic per e-mail message.
- Send messages or replies to only those who need to know. Do not use the Reply All key!
- Use paragraphs and proper grammar. File e-mails in their appropriate folders immediately upon processing. Reread your composed e-mail before you send it. Use a spellchecker.
- When sending a web site address, always type in the full address form including www and so on because there are e-mail programs that allow the user to access the web address directly from the e-mail. List all recipients from which action is required in the "to" area and others under "cc." This will allow multiple recipients to know whether they are part of the action required or just being informed that the action is occurring.
- Number each item if there are multiple actions, questions, or issues in the e-mail.
- If you are part of a local area network, create a link to a document rather than adding the attachment itself to an e-mail message if at all possible.
- If you must send an attachment in an e-mail, try to send it in a format that is likely to be used wherever you're sending it (Microsoft Word would be an example).
- Create distribution lists in your e-mail address book for ease of sending e-mail.
- Check your pending folder within your e-mail files at least once a week, preferably during your weekly planning and organizing time.
- Schedule follow-up items on your calendar.
- Remember that attachments add information and are not the primary message.
- Avoid sending any nonbusiness e-mail.
- Only print e-mails when absolutely necessary. Instead file in the appropriate folder. When you receive e-mail with attachments and the attachments need to be saved, save them on your hard drive or server drive and remove the e-mail from your in box.
- Avoid the use of acronyms and/or jargon specific to the English language.
- If revising or adding to an existing e-mail document, put revisions in bold type so they are obvious to the recipient.
- If someone needs to modify or comment on a document, precede the comments with the author's initials.
- When receiving e-mail, look at the header or subject field of the document before reading the text. Decide whether you want or

need to read the whole message or simply delegate it—or delete it, then and there.

- Turn off the alarm and flash feature. You do not need to be constantly interrupted when an e-mail arrives. Instead, batch e-mail by scheduling two or three times a day to process all e-mail at one time.
- Be courteous and forgiving to those who are not.

Tip: There are Outlook add-on applications to help gain more control of your e-mail. One example is NEO (www.caelo.com). NEO organizes your e-mail in all the ways that you think about e-mails—by date, by sender, and by type—all at the same time. So you don't have to copy or move messages, as they will automatically be available in your (received) Today Folder, your (received) This Week Folder, and with the rest of the e-mails you get and send to an individual correspondent in the (name) Correspondent Folder. You can set up Hot Folders to keep your high impact tasks in front of you.

PAPER-MAIL/MEMOS

Deal with your mail and internal office memos once a day at a set time, perhaps first thing in the morning before the normal meetings and activities begin. Depending on the nature of your work, allow 30 to 60 minutes to process all of the paper that accumulates in your in box during the day. If you have an administrative assistant, have him or her hold all incoming paperwork after you complete your pass at the in box. Ask your assistant to sort the incoming material into logical categories and to use a divider system to organize incoming material and make it easy for you to process. After purging the inevitable junk mail, have your assistant put the incoming papers into your in basket at the end of the day and place items for other people to deal with in their boxes. Then you don't have to go through other people's materials. Included in your incoming papers would be any papers from your tickler file that are scheduled for your attention the next day.

Some managers invite their administrative assistants to sit in with them while they deal with their in basket. In this case, the assistant files as they go along, notes instructions, and generally helps the manager process the work quickly. This, by the way, is how I advise managers to train new administrative assistants. The manager should process the paperwork out loud, so the assistant gets a sense for how the manager deals with things, what is important to the manager, and what the manager wants to see and not see. I find a couple of weeks of this equals a year's worth of experience working together.

Whether you work with an assistant or not, don't just sort through your papers. *Do* each item, one by one, responding, routing, reading, and filing as you go along. If a paper is part of a working project you will be acting on at a scheduled time in the future, file it immediately in your working file. If a paper prompts an origination from you, originate it now. If it's something you need to discuss with a subordinate or your boss and it's not a burning issue, file it in your working file under his or her name for discussion at your scheduled meeting time. If it's something to read, read it.

Make no exceptions to the rule. This is a moment of truth. If a paper represents two or three hours' work, schedule a time to deal with it, and file the paper into the scheduled date in your tickler file. But mainly *Do It Now* and empty your in box of all papers that were there. Some won't be all that important, but deal with them, anyway.

Some might say looking at your papers once a day is not enough. Well, I disagree and so do 500,000 clients. Very important issues normally find their way to you in the form of telephone calls, personal visits, or e-mail. Since most people do not deal with their paper promptly, they don't depend on it for hot issues that need to be dealt with in a matter of minutes. If you *did* process your paper completely every day you would surprise your coworkers with your promptness!

SEARCHING THE INTERNET

If you think you have wasted time in the past finding a paper file, you might be surprised at how much more time you can waste trying to find information on the Internet. Searching the Internet has become so time-consuming that regular users of the Web simply don't do it anymore—instead they have favorite sites they regularly visit for the important information they most often need. Nevertheless, we are expected to use this resource and there are ways to cut down on the time wasted. Some rules of thumb for efficient use of the Internet include:

- Keep a record of interesting/useful web sites. Articles will often refer to a web site and provide the URL (Uniform Resource Locator—the address of the site). It is the easiest and quickest way to access the information on the site.

- Familiarize yourself with the different search engines available on the Web. A search engine is a program that performs a search through most or part of the Internet. Usually it is the best way for you to locate what you want. Different search engines may access different information, so it is best to know which engines are most likely to find the information you need. There are even resources that activate many search engines at once. One such resource is software BullsEye (www.intelliseek.com/prod/bullseye.htm). With BullsEye you type in the subject you wish to search and the software accesses 1,000 search engines, newsgroups, news wires, mailing lists, job boards, electronic commerce sites, and a variety of topic-based web sites.
- Learn to use search engines efficiently. Each engine has a help function which tells you the most efficient ways to use the engine. How you phrase your request plays a big part in how effective the engine will be in locating what you need.
- Lastly, do not be overly curious about the Internet. It can consume lots of time, so you do not want to tempt yourself. If you access the Web, have a specific goal, stick to it, and avoid wasting time chasing something other than what you planned on finding in the first place.

READING

Your reading should be handled in the same way. Set aside a block of time and do it however works best for you. Some of your reading will be done when you process your mail and memos. Remember when you pick up a piece of paper you are going to deal with it then and there. Some people do their reading during the morning commute by bus or train; some do it during plane flights; others take a few minutes at the end of the workday to do their reading and organize for the coming workday. I do my reading during my lunch break. The important thing is to find a time to do it and establish this as a routine. Assign yourself a time, schedule it, and do it.

When you read is one issue; *how* you read is another. Speed reading can cut your reading time in half by training you to look at the material from a concept, sentence, paragraph, or page perspective, instead of word by word, which is how most of us have been taught to read. There is no loss of content comprehension. You simply comprehend more, faster!

WEEKLY ONE-ON-ONE MEETINGS

Weekly one-on-one meetings between the boss and his or her direct reports come under the heading of routine.

One-on-one meetings make for efficient contact time between busy coworkers who have to maintain close contacts in their work.

If the only way colleagues can see you is by sticking their heads in during the day at random, you will be constantly interrupted. They will feel guilty about disturbing you, but they know they must if they are going to get the job done. You won't be prepared for discussion on the subject they disturb you about. Or vice versa if you are the one interrupting.

You may argue that you can't handle another meeting. However, many managers are managers in name only. With downsizing, companies are forcing managers to have many more duties than simply managing. You need an efficient way to keep in touch with those who answer to you and who get the work done.

This is not a team or group meeting. It's one-on-one. Maintain a file for every person you meet with one-on-one, and during the course of the week, collect any nonpriority items you need to discuss. Also, each person who reports to you should maintain a similar folder, covering items they need to talk about with you.

Schedule one-on-one meetings for the same time every week. If it isn't scheduled, people can't depend on it, and they will revert to coming to see you at any odd time. If you travel often or a holiday period makes it difficult to keep to the same schedule, make it a point at the end of your one-to-one to schedule the next one-to-one meeting, taking the holiday into account.

Remember, these meetings cover nonpriority items that crop up and can wait a few days to be resolved or answered, not things that demand an immediate solution.

MORE EFFECTIVE MEETINGS

Our client personnel surveys find meetings typically top the list of time wasters. Meetings are often poorly prepared and run.

It is an extremely worthwhile activity to straighten out meeting protocols in the company. But it is a very difficult thing to do. The PEP program's focus is normally on improvements that can be made within one's own control. Meetings, by their very nature, often involve many other people—including the boss! Changing others' behaviors is arguably more difficult than changing one's own. Even so, we have had success in making meetings effective. Our experiences have taught us several things.

1. *Identify the meeting's purpose.* In one of our client companies the management staff meetings were poorly attended; members did not turn up on time, and some not at all. The feeling was that the meetings were useless.

The management staff had never discussed or determined what the purpose of the regular management meeting was. As part of our effort to make the meetings more effective we cleared with the participants that the purpose of the meeting was to "lead and develop the department." When the group had figured out what the purpose of the meeting was, they began to see this as the most important of all the meetings they had in the department, and attendance rose.

2. *Prepare properly.* Another management group reduced their meeting time by half when they cleared up the purpose of the meeting and identified what information they needed from each other to be able to carry out the meeting effectively. The result was that a large part of the information the members used to bring to and review in weekly meetings could be removed since no one really needed it. Useful information was posted on the company intranet before the meeting so that everyone could review it and the actual meeting time could be used to discuss and form suggestions on how to solve new problems.

3. *Keep the meeting on track.* We have all experienced meetings chaired by people who didn't know what they were doing, who let the meeting be taken over by the most vocal member, or who allowed the meeting to drag on forever. The meeting chairman must lead the meeting, keep it on schedule, control the communication, and see to it that the purpose of the meeting is fulfilled.

4. *Be decisive.* Meetings should result in decisions made and action points assigned. Each decision should identify:

What is to be done.
Who is to do it.
When it is to be done by.

Caution: We often find the *what* is a bit unclear and the *when* is totally lost.

5. *Distribute meeting minutes promptly and stick to the decisions made.* At one company the written notes from the management staff meetings were issued three to five days after the meeting had taken place and the members didn't always recognize the decisions that were stated in the minutes. The head of the client office, who was also the meeting chairman, prepared the meeting minutes and sometimes changed the decisions or made amendments, causing the members to ask why the meeting was held at all. After our training a secretary was appointed to take notes on a laptop during the meeting and the notes were handed out at the end of the meeting. The participants were able to read the notes immediately and voice any need for corrections.

See Appendix A, "Meeting Improvements Checklist," for ways to make your meetings more effective.

But even if you work this subject to the bone, you may run into absurd situations that defy logic. One client asked for my help getting his department personnel home at a reasonable hour.

"Tell me what the problem is," I suggested.

"Well, we have many responsibilities; I have offices in Germany, England, and the United States I must visit. Staff are overseeing two mergers and we are in the process of moving." As an afterthought he mentioned, "And I have 50 hours a week of scheduled meetings." Fifty hours! Hey, that in itself is more than a full workweek! Regardless of whether these meetings were effective, they needed to be trimmed down, and some needed to be eliminated.

Time is the coin of your life. It is the only coin you have,
and only you can determine how it will be spent.
Be careful lest you let others spend it for you.
*—*CARL SANDBURG

DEALING WITH INTERRUPTIONS

Not all interruptions are bad, of course. There are actually some good interruptions. If your associate pokes his head in your doorway and says, "Hey, listen, I had this bright idea about how to get a sale, and I'd like to make a call," that's what I'd call a good interruption.

Still, there are more ways to cut down on unwanted interruptions. Here are some tried-and-true ways that should sound familiar to you:

Do It Now!
- Clean up backlogs so you're not dealing with their consequences.
- Handle things by their due dates to reduce requests for status reports.

Do It "Right" Now
- Handle things completely and correctly to reduce redo requests.
- Give clear and complete instructions to subordinates to reduce their requests for clarification and your own frustrations when things are not done correctly the first time.
- Remember that it is your job to educate your employees in how to complete both routine tasks and larger jobs.

Communicate It "Right" Now
- Give full information when leaving messages to reduce telephone tag.
- Require complete messages be taken when others call you.
- Use communication methods that permit full messages and do not interrupt current work, such as e-mail and voice mail.

"Take a Stand" Now
- Deal with interruptions by stating your time constraints: "Jim, I have 20 minutes to complete this report for a meeting. Let me stop by your office after that meeting and we'll discuss this. Is 2:30 all right with you?"
- Reinforce this by standing up to deal with walk-in interruptions.
- Lend support to creating a culture with fewer interruptions.
- Begin batching your communications.

By batching work you can cut down on interruptions (see Figure 3.3), allowing you to focus better on the work on hand.

FAILURE TO BATCH COMMUNICATIONS

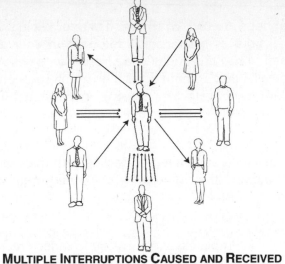

MULTIPLE INTERRUPTIONS CAUSED AND RECEIVED

BATCHED COMMUNICATIONS

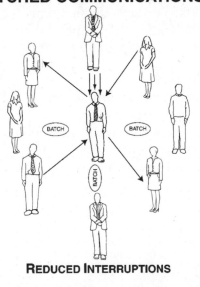

REDUCED INTERRUPTIONS

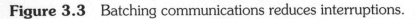

Figure 3.3   Batching communications reduces interruptions.

MAKING IT WORK

You may think: "Hey, I don't want to schedule my life down to the minute," or "This represents an ideal world and my office is far from ideal." These scheduled activities should require no more than 20% of your day. Since all my research shows that you are spending well over *half* of your day on these things now, you can thank me for giving you back at least 25% of your day.

I don't like having my day scheduled to the minute, either. But most of what I'm asking you to do here is to handle the mindless and boring tasks efficiently and routinely. We have to do the mundane if we're to concentrate on what we are truly being paid for. So, why not just face up to it and do it? Get it over with in as painless a fashion as possible. Then the remainder of your day can be made up of blocks of time to concentrate and focus on the meaningful activities of your work.

PITFALLS

One problem people sometimes face early on in learning to work this way is that they sometimes choose the wrong time to do certain things. You may decide to return all your phone calls at 4:00 P.M. every day, regardless of circumstances, when in fact, because you're on the West Coast, it's impossible for you to reach anyone east of Denver at that time. The logical thing to do is to allow a few moments between 8:00 A.M. and 9:00 A.M. for any calls you have to place to the East Coast; there's no reason you can't take care of this business before moving on to your in basket, for example.

Or you may decide to answer your mail and memos once a day at 10:00 A.M. without fail. Of course, that's exactly the time the new staff meeting is scheduled or, for reasons known only to themselves, the Postal Service readjusts its schedule and your daily mail is delivered at 3:00 P.M. For whatever reason, after just one day it's quite possible for your new schedule to fail. And since it fails, you assume it has failed completely, and you give up the effort, instead of examining what happened and trying to reschedule your planned activities to fit reality. You may discover it's more feasible to draft memos between 11:45 A.M. and 12:15 P.M., or even noon to 12:30 P.M. since you seldom get out the door to lunch until then anyway, and schedule 3:30 P.M. to 4:00 P.M. to respond to the day's mail. The point is, you may have to try several times before you find the schedule that works best for you.

Trial and error is often required in getting the job done and in learning new ways to get jobs done. For example, you may have to have people cover for you while you do some of the batched work we talked about. If you have a customer service job, for example, you may not be able to turn off your phone. Or your work may depend on walk-in customers, and you may never know when a customer is going to arrive. Certainly, when customers do walk in, you want to see them and answer their needs.

I had a client who had five employees to deal with 3,000 customers, mostly by telephone and e-mail. But every day they could expect 10 or so unannounced customers to arrive to see their account representatives. The visits were mainly social and considered more or less a waste of time. The employees wanted to treat the customers well. They wanted to give good service, but the unannounced arrivals created havoc with their schedules and work. This problem existed for years and nothing seemed to make it go away until the department was reorganized so each account rep was on duty to see all unannounced customers one day per week, leaving four days per week when each rep was able to get on with his or her work. I can't tell you how many other solutions were tried, though, before they used this rather simple one and found that it worked.

As you attempt to put some of these principles into practice, you'll find some trial and error is required, too. Persistence counts. If you work on the problem, you'll come up with not only a solution, but a solution that works for you.

We all know how difficult it is to overcome habits and years of conditioning. Habitual behaviors usually don't change on the first attempt. Your first 14 tries may appear to be failures. But then something clicks on the 15th try, and you find everything falling into place. Even when you do finally get into the new habit, it isn't necessarily easier to do unpleasant or boring tasks. Every time I wake at 5:30 A.M. to go running, I find it is tough. But, scheduling the routine behavior helps me to do it. If the running were not a habit, I would surely find it even tougher and I would likely not do it at all.

Let scheduling and simple habits make life easier for you.

FOLLOW-UP FOR CHAPTER 3

1. Work smarter. You can increase your efficiency and effectiveness (productivity) by working smarter. Only you can determine what requires and deserves your attention. Regardless of what those things are, you can make more time for them by working smarter on everything. Simple routines to handle the mundane tasks can help you do exactly that.

2. Analyze your time. If you've never analyzed how and where you spend your time, this can be very useful. Use a time log to keep track of what you do and how long it takes. You'll be amazed at how much time you spend on certain items and how little time you spend on others. Once you know what you're doing, you can work on how you do it.

3. Don't allow low-value tasks or low-value information to enter your system. Both clog your ability to produce. Screen them out entirely. Delegate tasks appropriately. Direct information you don't use to someone else's attention. Dedicate minimal time to routine work, such as the incoming mail. Take care of it promptly and routinely, and move on to high-value work.

4. Learn how to batch work. Return phone calls once or twice daily, rather than allowing them to constantly interrupt your work. Do the same with your incoming mail. Set aside a time each day to work through each item to completion, or schedule items to work on at appropriate times in the short-term future. If you batch work instead of letting unimportant tasks dominate your day, you'll find you have about 25% more time to dedicate to important work. Answering phone messages, responding to memos, and handling your e-mail are all tasks you should handle by batching.

5. *Do It Now, Later* means sticking to a schedule. If you're in the middle of a report when your mail is delivered, continue to work on the report. Schedule 30 minutes daily to handle your mail and do it then. Don't break off in the middle of one task to take on another. If you do, both are likely to end up unfinished as the second task is interrupted by a third task.

6. Schedule tasks (and you have less to worry about). If scheduled, you simply do them and move on. If you allot an hour for a particular task, you will likely complete it within an hour. If you allot a day for the same task, you will likely take all day to complete it.

7. Schedule weekly one-on-one meetings for routine items concerning your direct reports. This will eliminate most interruptions and will allow you regular time periods to touch base with one another regarding ongoing projects and personal items. You should maintain a file for each of your people and make a habit of dropping reminders into it to prompt your meeting agendas. Your direct reports should keep a similar file for you, to prompt their discussion during these meetings. Remember, these meetings are for nonpriority items that can wait up to a week to be resolved, and not for emergencies.

8. Make copies of the "Meeting Improvements Checklist" in Appendix A and pass them out to those with whom you attend meetings. (If you have access to the Internet you can download an electronic copy of this checklist for free from our IBT web site (www.ibt-pep.com). Begin a campaign with the chairman and other meeting members to implement the most appropriate improvements.

9. Review the steps you can use to eliminate interruptions and then put them into practice.

CHAPTER 4

Plan It Now!

*There is a law in psychology that if you form
a picture in your mind of what you would like
to be, and you keep and hold that picture
there long enough, you will soon become
exactly as you have been thinking.*
—WILLIAM JAMES

Chapter 4 Preview

In this chapter, you will learn:

- That time flies by when you are in a state of preoccupation. Thinking about what you are supposed to do instead of planning efficiently is a major cause of wasted time.
- That action follows clarity of picture. If you have a clear picture of what you are to do, you will act on it. If the picture is fuzzy, you will hesitate. Planning gives clarity of picture.
- How to establish what is important to you.
- How to write down your goals (those that will define what you value).
- How to establish an efficient planning process by setting aside time each week to organize yourself, review your goals and plans, and plan out the new week.

*The important thing is to start—to create a plan
and then follow it step by step no matter how
small or large each one by itself might seem.*
—CHARLES LINDBERGH

This may surprise you, but the motto for the planning step of the Personal Efficiency Program (PEP) is *Plan It Now!*

One purpose of planning is to get *clarity,* to know what you ought to be doing on a day-to-day basis as well as on a long-term basis. Too many people do very little planning, particularly when their own work is involved. One reason why the personal calendar, planner, or organizer (Day-Timer, Franklin/Covey Planner, etc.) has been so popular is that people see it as a tool to help them get organized, to plan things in advance, and to keep track of work done.

Some mistakenly consider the mental activities they engage in when they're driving to work or when they're taking a shower to be "planning" for work. Although you may be thinking about work, I would hardly call it planning. Instead, it's an inefficient form of thinking that provides little or no real clarity.

Some people feel that any and all planning is a waste of time. They say the time spent in planning doesn't produce that many benefits. If you plan inefficiently, that can be true. If what you plan is not what you do, it is wasteful. A set plan is good only if it is being implemented and accomplished. If what you do is what you plan, then planning is meaningful.

If you feel that you're under stress at work; that you have too much to do, and too little time to do it; that you're out of control; or that you're simply not accomplishing the things most important to you, the cause is often poor planning or the lack of planning. In that case, you'll find that the products you produce bear a resemblance to the bumper sticker "Plan Ahead," where the word "Ahead" is all crunched up on the right side.

That's typical, primarily because people don't connect planning to what they do personally. They think of planning in terms of the huge project their department is undertaking during this fiscal quarter—a project so huge that they'll all get together for a meeting and figure out what to do. But when it comes to their daily work, they don't attach a proper importance to planning.

PURPOSE OF PLANNING

The purpose of the planning process is to get a clear idea—a clear mental picture—of what you need to do. A planning process can be considered effective only if it provides you with a clear picture, because you can't act without a picture. In his book *The Management of Time* (Prentice-Hall, Inc., 1959), James T. McCay writes:

> *The pictures in your mind control your actions. If you have no picture; if you can't make out what is going on, you don't act. If your pictures are cloudy and confused, you act hesitantly. If your pictures are clear and accurate, you act definitely and effectively.*

Planning enables you to get these clear pictures. Planning that fails to provide such images falls short of the mark and isn't true planning.

When doing PEP with a large group, we start out with an orientation, usually in a conference room with everyone seated around a table. I often ask: "How many people in here do a daily action plan?" Perhaps half the people raise their hands. The rest don't even commit themselves to daily action plans. Too often these daily To Do lists have failed for them in the past, and they're reluctant to try them again.

Have you ever started the day with a list of things to do and come to the end of the day with none of the tasks done? If so, you know how many of these people feel. Daily action plans can weigh one down: They're the evidence of unfinished business. There are several reasons for unfinished lists: You might have tried to do too much. You may not have considered the unexpected and the time that would be consumed. The daily list may have been far too general. Proper planning successfully deals with these and many other issues that can make a daily plan a disappointment rather than a useful work tool. What is proper planning?

To give an example, let's look at what it takes to make a movie. Three distinct steps are involved in the production of a movie: preproduction, production, and postproduction. Of the three, the most time-consuming element of making the movie is preproduction. The script is only the starting point. The most essential planning document in the preproduction phase is known as the storyboard, a detailed, artistic representation of every single scene that will make up the movie.

Picture a sheet of paper filled only with empty boxes; sometimes, you'll even find them in the familiar shape of a television screen. These boxes make up the frames for each scene. Artists sketch in rough outlines to represent what is seen at every point of filming: how many people and who are in a particular scene; what they say; whether a scene is shot in close-up or with a long lens; where the lights are; the step-by-step progression from one shot to the next; the combination of shots adding up to a single scene. These are all part of the much larger whole—a motion picture.

Why spend so much time and effort on a storyboard? Because one of the most expensive parts of moviemaking is the on-location shooting. Once production is underway, with two hundred cast and crew members standing around, you want to waste little time and effort, not to mention money, telling people where they stand and what they do next. That's what preproduction is for, not production. With millions of dollars invested, you simply don't waste time when adequate planning and preparation will save you that time and effort.

In the motion picture industry, the need for planning is obvious and the technique of planning has been refined to meet that industry's particular needs. Yet in business and industry in general, there is little formal planning, especially the planning of day-to-day activities.

Take a mental step back from your own company, and you'll see that most of the people you work with every day don't have any formal planning in their work. We see people showing up for work without any script or preproduction planning, merely hoping to handle the fallout for eight or more hours. In motion picture terms they're on the set every day of the workweek, the cameras are rolling, and they don't know what to say, where to stand, or what to do.

PLANNING PRINCIPLES

Planning has three components: prioritizing tasks, managing time, and being well enough organized to execute the plans easily. By the time you have reached this chapter, you should be well enough organized to execute your plans easily. Let's examine the other components.

Prioritizing—Task Management

You cannot discuss planning without also discussing priorities. You have, no doubt, detected my wariness about prioritizing. Priorities are too often used as an excuse not to act. And priorities can create a mess when you are faced with urgent versus important matters. Nevertheless, if you neglect priorities, especially with the volume of work expected of us and the extreme time pressure many of us are under, you are likely to fail.

My friend and colleague from the Netherlands describes it like this: Planning is the activity of determining your priorities and then managing the time to deal with those priorities. To determine priorities one must have a clear picture of one's goals or objectives and then compare tasks against them. You must determine if the tasks expected of you align with the steps necessary to achieve your goals/objectives. Decide whether you are the one to execute these priority tasks or they can or should be delegated to another. If you delegate them, then follow-through to see that they are completed.

Task management can be an especially useful tool for those who have little discretionary time. Call center or help desk employees and bank tellers are examples of those whose tasks are dictated by those contacting them. The less control you have of your own time the more you need to distinguish between very valuable and less valuable issues.

Time Management

Time management could be described as the art of making the best use of time. Once you know what you need to do and how best to do it (task management), you need to make the best use of time to get it done. When planning your day, week, month, or year, you consider the tasks to be done and the time elements involved. Proper management of time includes:

- Routines being established and scheduled into different periods of the day (daily batched work like responding to e-mail, weekly routines like batched meetings with direct reports, monthly routine for end-of-month close-out processes, etc.).
- Open- and closed-door policies scheduled into the day. When do you need uninterrupted time to concentrate?
- Considering your biorhythm when scheduling creative work. When in the day are you most energetic (good for work requiring creative juices)? When are you least energetic (good for boring tasks requiring less concentrated thought—filing, for example)?
- Setting aside periods for planning, both short and long term. Daily planning might require a few minutes; weekly and monthly planning might take an hour; and yearly long-term planning may take a few days to complete.

- The type of calendar system you use—paper for your personal use or electronic, which may be accessible and possibly added to by others. The more other people have access to your time planning, the more you have to schedule time for your own priorities. Does your secretary schedule your meetings? How well does he or she know your preferences for planning meetings, quiet time, routine tasks, and so on? The type of calendar (daily view, weekly view, or monthly view) determines the way you perceive time.
- Lastly, a critical part of time management is protecting your time! Avoid the Time Stealers found in Appendix B.

> *If you spend half your time planning,*
> *you will get it done twice as fast.*
> **—GERMAN PROVERB**

The Time It Takes to Plan: Is It Worth It?

If you increase your planning time, you will be able to reduce time spent in "administrivia" and running around playing "catch up."

Most of us work long hours and work hard. Why do we complain about being lost in "administrivia"? For one thing, no matter how clever we get, we find "administrivia" will take from 10% to 25% of your working time, depending on your job. The average person in industry, before PEP, typically spends less than two hours per week planning his or her own work. If you do the math, that's about 18 minutes a day—the equivalent of the time you spend in the shower! That's fine; don't stop that daily planning exercise (or shower for that matter!). But take it further to reduce time spent in "administrivia" and interruptions. Spend more time planning! The proof? We find when people plan time—at least 30 to 60 more minutes of quiet, thoughtful, scheduled planning time per week (to get about 2.5 hours per week), they see dramatic drops in overtime, meeting attendance, interruptions, and tasks done by them that should have been delegated.

PEP PLANNING PROCESS

Six general categories of planning are taught in PEP:

1. Daily plan.
2. Weekly plan.
3. Project implementation plan.

4. Strategic plan.
5. Goal setting.
6. Values.

DAILY PLANNING

I've already mentioned a common complaint about daily plans. Too often, due to the unexpected, the daily plan is only partially done before it turns into a major disappointment. For some people, it seems, daily plans are only a mocking reminder of what didn't get done.

In the meantime, it's vital that you understand the importance of spending some time each day to plan your activities. Some prefer to do this at day's end, before going home; some prefer the morning, before other things get in the way. Whenever you choose to do this planning, you can use your calendar ("diary," as the British say) to write down the day's tasks.

To make daily planning an efficient and quick process, I suggest you create your daily plan from a weekly plan. With the larger document in front of you, you can then divide the week's work into manageable chunks to be accomplished each day, knowing every day that you're working toward a larger goal.

WEEKLY PLANNING

Once a week you should examine all of your sources of work as shown in Figure 4.1. By "sources of work" I mean all of your working files, including your projects; your calendar for deadlines, scheduled activities, and reminders; your tickler file system for the things that will be showing up during the upcoming week; your pending matters (pending basket and pending files—including electronic files like an e-mail folder for any e-mail awaiting feedback before you can complete it); and any logbook you may use to keep a record of the things you must do.

For example, let's assume you're currently handling eight projects. Perhaps two of these projects are taking up the majority of your time, and the other six are moving along to one degree or another. You have other items in your pending box as well, including plans for a business trip, and your calendar shows six meetings this week with various de-

WHY WEEKLY PLANNING?

Events change rapidly and it is not feasible for most people to plan a month in advance in detail. On the other hand, if one plans only a day in advance, there is insufficient lead time to get critical things done. For most people, weekly planning is the most effective planning interval.

CREATING YOUR WEEKLY ACTION PLAN

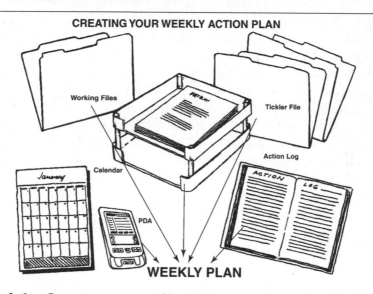

Figure 4.1 Creating your weekly plan.

partment heads and customers. Your tickler file contains items you have to check on at various dates to guarantee they'll be finished on time. You're also surrounded by a lot of little pieces of paper with various reminders of tasks that you need to do. (Or better yet, you may have a computer program or logbook you use to consolidate these reminders in one place, instead of having lots of little pieces of paper.) In other words, to keep up with everything you have to do, you really have to consult half a dozen sources. I suggest you go through all of these sources once a week. During that time, prioritize these various items and plan out your week.

Take the time to look back through your calendar to determine how much of your time is consumed by unexpected, unplanned-for work. Some of this will be boss-imposed time, when you catch the fallout from some higher-up who seems, without fail, to delegate in your direction at the most inopportune time of the day (or week, or month). Some of this will simply be unforeseen work that requires your attention, eating up time you had intended to devote to other work. Whatever the source, it's inevitable that at least some portion of your day and week—perhaps 25%, perhaps as much as 50%—will be given to this type of work.

Whatever the amount, plan your workweek based on the average amount of time left to you. If half of your time is used unexpectedly, you can reasonably plan for only the other 50% of your time to be filled with genuinely productive work of your own planning. By allowing time for the unexpected—actually the unidentified—you maintain your flexibility, you allow time for the things you know are going to crop up (even if you don't know in advance what they are), and you don't overload yourself to the point that you're actually scheduling your week for work that would really take one and a half weeks. You've *planned for the unplanned,* and you can define the rest of your week with clarity and purpose.

By identifying and prioritizing the actions to be done in the next week, you simplify daily planning. Prioritizing is easier, too. If it's important, it will be on your weekly plan. If it isn't important, it won't be there. You only have to decide your priorities once, during your weekly planning. The advantage to this planning is that you see things in a broader context, so you can make a realistic judgment of how much time you have available to devote to various projects. You don't have to go through the whole decision-making process each time you complete a task, and that in itself takes a lot of the stress out of your work. Choosing what to do any particular day is easier. All you do is look at your calendar and note the reminders you've written down, the meetings that are scheduled, and the work you may have taken on for the coming week. You then take from your weekly plan list those tasks you will do that day. Figure 4.2 shows a sample weekly plan.

Setting aside time at the end of the week to do a plan for the new week makes for efficient planning time. This is the time to figure out not only what you should do but how to do it. Take time during this planning stage to think the whole thing through, to see the bigger picture. After all, most tasks are done with some larger end result in mind. With that end result in mind, you can analyze what you need to do (to have, to know) to accomplish the task.

Deciding what should be done first, second, or third takes only a moment. If you schedule tasks across the workweek and do your daily planning based on the larger picture you create, you don't have to spend time thinking about what you need to do day to day or how you're going to do it. You have already done that as part of your weekly plan. Instead, you can focus on the work to be done, and as

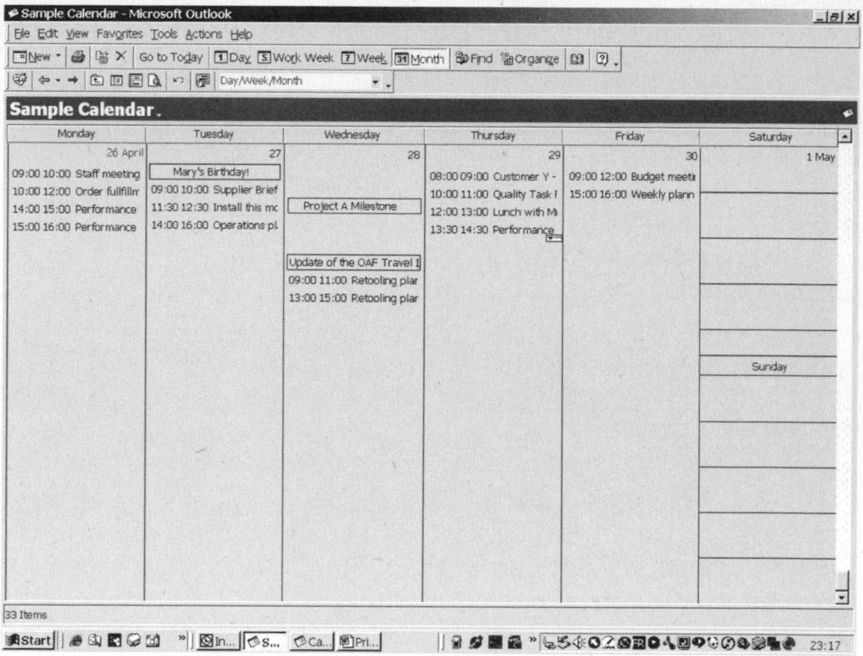

Figure 4.2 Sample weekly plan in calendar.

you complete a task simply get on with doing (not just thinking about) the next one.

Whatever calendar or scheduling tool you prefer, look for one with a week-at-a-glance function. To name just a few of the options available today, you might use a paper calendar system, any of several types of software for desktop computers, or a handheld electronic organizer. If all the tasks for your weekly plan will actually fit in the weekly calendar view, all the better—there's far less likelihood of important things being overlooked. Figure 4.3 shows a sample weekly planning form.

It is often useful to use your electronic calendar functionality to view your work from a broader time frame than a week. With tools like Microsoft Outlook and Lotus Notes you can very easily move from one view of the future (calendar) to another view, which enables you to make the best possible decisions on your planning process and implementation.

Often decisions regarding even a weekly plan are influenced by the monthly view and perhaps the daily view. Looking at these various views is probably needed to best make planning decisions. The

WEEKLY PLANNING FORM

Name:_____

Week Beginning:_____

Monday	Weekly Plan (Consult working files, pending tray, calendar, tickler system)
	1.
	2.
Tuesday	3.
	4.
	5.
	6.
	7.
Wednesday	8.
	9.
	10.
	11.
	12.
Thursday	13.
	14.
	15.
	Unplanned Activities Added during Week
Friday	1.
	2.
	3.
Sat/Sun	4.
	5.
	6.
	7.

Figure 4.3   Sample weekly planning form.

flexibility of viewing, with whatever degree of detail one needs to make the best planning decisions by moving between views should be reinforced regardless of whether the planning is daily, weekly, or monthly. Figure 4.4 shows a sample monthly planning format.

So, what's the point of this whole weekly planning process? This is the time for you to get an overview of your job. This is the time for you to organize yourself and prepare for the new week. It's a time for you to maintain your organized state. It's a time for you to take your objectives, goals, and dreams and put them into action steps.

In his book *How I Raised Myself from Failure to Success in Selling* (Simon & Schuster, 1947), Frank Bettger, one of the most influen-

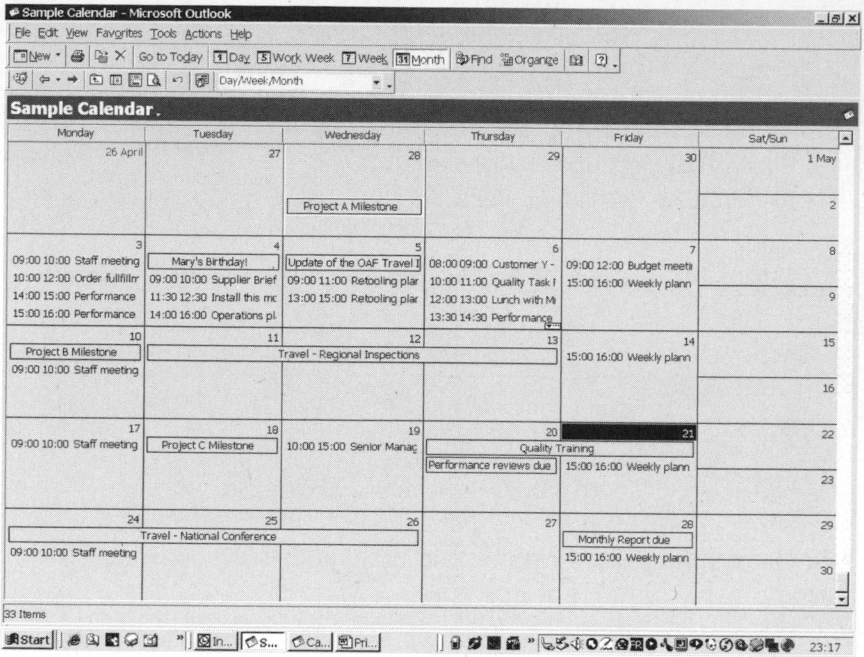

Figure 4.4   Sample monthly planning.

tial salesmen of this century, called his weekly planning time his "self-organization day." He said:

> It is surprising how much I can get done when I take enough time for planning, and it is perfectly amazing how little I get done without it. I prefer to work on a tight schedule four and a half days a week and get somewhere than be working all the time and never get anywhere (p. 25).

SHAPING THE DIARY—A MONTHLY PLANNING PROCESS FOR SENIOR EXECUTIVES

My friend and partner from the United Kingdom, Jay Hurwitz, has been working with top-level executives of the UK's largest corporations and has designed a highly successful planning process he calls Shaping the Diary. As part of their planning routines Jay gets the executives to shape their calendars once a month, usually at mid-month for the subsequent month. Monthly planning is more appropriate for high-level executives as they tend to book important meetings further ahead in the calendar and are involved a bit less in day-to-day operational issues that pop up unexpectedly.

This is what he has each executive do:

1. Take a blank sheet of paper and create the following format:

Actions	Now	Future

2. List no more than eight broad actions that account for 100% of your time expenditure. For example:

- Management team meeting.
- Managing direct reports.
- Personnel matters.
- Budgets.
- Walkabouts, branch visits, customer visits.
- In tray.
- Project work.
- Other.

3. Once the broad actions are listed, estimate what percentage of your time is currently being spent in each category. Note the percentages in the Now column. Don't worry about your estimates adding up to 100% on the first go. Just take your gut feelings. After you have noted a gut feeling percentage beside each action, adjust them if they do not total 100%.

4. Ask yourself if there is some aspect of your job that you are not doing, that you feel you ought to be doing, and that is not on your list (e.g., think time, review time, or planning time). Add it to the list.

5. Consider how you would like to ideally spend your time in the future. For example:

- If there was an item that was added in step 4, start with that. What percentage of your time would you like to spend on that action? Note it under the Future column.
- Consider each of the other actions and your percentages and note those down in the Future column.
- Be realistic. If you are currently spending 25% of your time in management team meetings and note 0% for that item in the future, you're not being realistic. Attendance at management team meetings is probably beyond your control.

6. Block out chunks of time in your calendar over the next month (or the month after if you are already fully scheduled for the next month) just for those actions showing a larger percentage in the Future column than the Now column. This will likely ensure that you *make* the time for these items and actually bring about the change.

Do not block out chunks of time for all of your actions. This would make the diary too rigid and would not allow for responsiveness to developing events.

> *The secret of getting ahead is getting started.*
> *The secret of getting started is breaking your complex*
> *and overwhelming tasks into small manageable*
> *tasks and then starting on the first one.*
> **—MARK TWAIN**

PROJECT IMPLEMENTATION PLANNING

In addition to the weekly planning process we've discussed, we're going to look closely at another type of planning called project planning.

We've already touched on creating your working files and how these files should represent the basic objectives and projects you're working on. Each file may represent hundreds of hours of work over a long period of time and can be pretty overwhelming.

Have you ever heard the question, "How do you eat an elephant?" One fellow told me, "With lots of ketchup!" The answer, though, is one bite at a time, and this is one secret to increased productivity. If you take the time to break down larger, more complex activities into manageable and detailed tasks—as with strategic and tactical planning—you will increase your personal productivity, whether you're discussing long- or short-term goals, or multitask objectives. I cannot stress too strongly the importance of this concept when it comes to productivity and the accomplishment of work and life goals.

Little by little does the trick.
—AESOP

Most of us know in general terms what we need to do. In fact, in my experience too much of our time is consumed in considering what we need to do, thinking about how to do it, and becoming preoccupied with the details of the work involved—none of which actually accomplish anything.

Project planning, however, is the process of creating storyboards for each of your life and work goals. All of us are familiar with project planning in the broad sense. An example would be the yearly budget for the company or division and the goals set to achieve the budget. The preproduction phase of making a motion picture can be considered a project plan. In fact, the preproduction phase, or the budget process, is made up of many individual project plans. All of the goals and objectives, both professional and personal, we work on daily and the individual actions to accomplish these goals can be called project plans. My favorite definition (from a colleague in the United Kingdom, Ron Hopkins) of a project is:

> [T]hat series of connected action points, which, when each and all are completed, bring into being a specific, visualized objective or result.

Each of your objectives and goals should have its own project plan.

The storyboard (project plan) is a set of clear mental pictures of each specific action required to move you step-by-step toward the accomplishment of the goal. Devising the project plan prompts you to explore how best to do it, in what sequence, with what resources, in how much time, with whom, and in concert with what other projects or activities that need to be done.

If complete, your working files will represent each of your work objectives. A project plan should be drawn up and placed in each of your working files. Deadlines for the tasks should be noted, along with the person responsible for the task. The project plan prompts you to do things to accomplish your goals because you've visualized them clearly and analyzed the work required to accomplish them. If the tasks are defined in detail, each one can be done in short time, and accomplishing each task will result in continuous progress toward the larger objective.

When you do your weekly plan, you review each working file project plan and choose the tasks to do in the new week. You don't have to figure out over and over again what needs to be done on the project, because that part of your planning has already been done. You'll have turned your weekly planning into an efficient and speedy process that actually accomplishes what it's intended to do.

A sample project plan is shown in Figure 4.5.

CRITERIA FOR PROJECT PLANNING

Some criteria you can use to determine if work you need to do falls into the category of project planning are:

- It is complex.
- It seems difficult.
- It involves several staff.
- It is a new activity.
- There are critical deadlines.
- You are coping with changes.

IMPLEMENTATION MAPPING

At times you will need to give thought to the design of a project plan before you can work out the implementation steps. Implementation mapping (Figure 4.6) helps identify the critical elements in the project plan, generating pertinent ideas in a free-flowing process, triggering thoughts that otherwise might lie hidden.

The key elements of implementation mapping are:

- Brainstorm about all elements of the task.
- Identify the critical elements to success.
- Group ideas into categories.
- Incorporate these into an implementation plan.

PROJECT IMPLEMENTATION PLANNING

SAMPLE PROJECT IMPLEMENTATION PLAN

Project Title: Office Procedures Manual

Objective: To develop office procedures that have the support of management and staff by the first half of this year.

Actions	Estimated Hours	People Involved	Target Date	Actual Completion Date
1. Collect current procedures.	2	Assistant	1/15	
2. Establish task forces to review current procedures and needed changes.	4	Self	1/20	
3. Task forces review procedures and submit recommendations.*	1	Task Force	2/5	
4. Read and synthesize recommendations.	3	Self	2/15	
5. Review by legal counsel.		Counsel	2/20	
6. Circulate draft for comment by managers.		Readers	3/1	
7. Make final edits.	3	Self	3/5	
8. Oversee production.*	1	Assistant	3/15	
9. Write project plan for internal PR campaign to encourage use.	1	Self	3/20	
10. Distribute manual.	2	Assistant	4/20	
DUE DATE: 5/1				

*Those assigned task should each develop their own project implementation plan to break this task down.

Figure 4.5 Sample project implementation plan.

Planning in Microsoft Outlook—Lotus Notes

Both Outlook and Notes provide the possibility to do project planning within the Outlook and/or Notes environment.

You can easily create a task list within Outlook that integrates with the calendar. By creating a new category with the name of the project

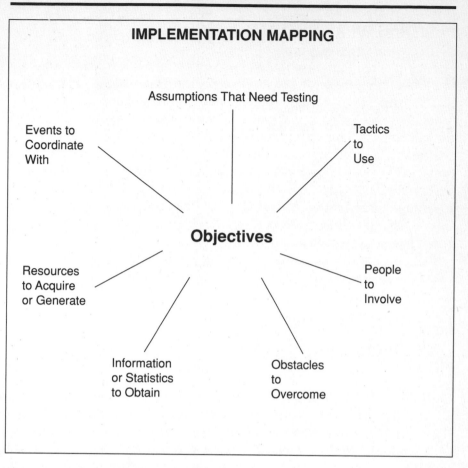

Figure 4.6 Implementation mapping.

and following this, a list of tasks with deadlines scheduled into the calendar, you have a wonderful tool to use to keep track of your project plans.

You are able to look at these tasks through the calendar view if scheduled as well as look at all open tasks by viewing through the category.

The advantage is obvious. Integration with the calendar and being able to link to e-mail messages as well as documents regarding the plan make it much easier to execute the tasks when the time arrives.

PLANNING ON A COMPUTER

I do my planning on a computer. I use a personal information software application that makes it easy to do a project plan. All the forms I need and the structure or format I prefer have been created in a macro command that requires only a few simple keystrokes to see my tasks and all the information I need from many different points of view.

I can add a task into the project plan, along with a due date and the name of the person responsible for the task completion, and this information automatically shows up in my calendar. This way, I only have to write the information down once, yet I can retrieve it several ways—by due date, by project plan designation, by the name of the person responsible, or whatever way is most convenient for me at the moment.

I can do my weekly plans quickly, and a computer function lets me highlight the project plan tasks I want to accomplish during the coming week. As I write this, for example, my computer is tracking 1,568 tasks I have to do. I know that because the computer tells me that's how many tasks I have to do.

Already some of you are digging your heels in, ready to resist the idea of using a computer for planning and managing your work and your group's work. I can honestly tell you, though, that in the years ahead you'll either make the maximum use of computers or die professionally. We really have very little choice in the matter. People have to learn to see a computer as a tool (just as a pen or pencil is a tool) and realize that they can control and monitor and produce much better with a computer than without. No doubt, you would agree that technology is having a profound effect on our personal and professional lives and will continue to do so. You cannot expect to see the possibilities technology might bring to you and your business unless you *use* technology. You will find that using technology to plan will not only encourage more and better planning, it will also enable you to see more ways to incorporate technology into your business.

Again, why all this trouble? Because we all want to succeed. In the book *Think and Grow Rich* (Fawcett Crest, 1960), Napoleon Hill studied Andrew Carnegie, Henry Ford, and others. One of the common denominators shared by these successful people was that they were meticulous planners. They each knew what they wanted to accomplish, took the time to figure out how to accomplish their goals, and then worked until they did exactly that. It's a model we all need to follow.

*What can be done at anytime
will be done at no time.*
—OLD SCOTTISH PROVERB

Microsoft Outlook—Lotus Notes Calendaring

Microsoft Outlook and Lotus Notes calendaring functions are very robust. The calendaring functionality allows for the scheduling of routine tasks and repeated work, providing a better overall view of planning because of the ability to view planning in many different ways. These applications provide for audible appointment reminders.

You can link tasks as well as attachments to the calendars. What's more, it is possible to view other people's calendars through both applications, which would obviously be impossible with a paper calendaring system. This is especially helpful when you are trying to set up meetings among various individuals.

How to employ both Outlook and Notes as a calendaring, task management, and planning tool will be covered in more detail in Chapter 10.

STRATEGIC PLANNING

With a daily, weekly, and project plan we have identified the tactical steps necessary to get things done. But the question remains, are you getting the things done you should be getting done? Have you chosen the right projects to do? Do you have the long-term view in mind? Are the projects based on a sound assessment of where you should be headed? Are they the efforts that will get you where you want to go in the most effective and efficient way? Do you have the resources to carry out these grand plans or could the resources be used more wisely?

Strategy is all wrapped up in goals and, finally, what is important to the business or you. Without a clear long-term vision, whatever you may be able to get done in a day or week, a year, or a lifetime may not get you very far or be all that valuable.

You must be working on the right thing. I have worked with hundreds of companies over the years and although some may have developed strategies for their business or division, few of the staff have any clue to what these strategies are. Defining the strategies to be followed and making them known allow all staff members to better align their own individual actions with the important objectives of the group.

How do you develop a strategy? This is easily the subject of a book on its own. First you must establish the goals you wish to attain. These goals will be driven by your vision and your customers' needs. (More on this later in this chapter under "Goals" and "Values.") Where are you now in respect to these goals? How do you get from where you are now to where you want to go? What resources do you have to work with (finances, people, time, knowledge, experience, contacts who have solved the problems you face in accomplishing your goals, and so forth)? What is the best use of existing resources to get you to where you want to go? Give yourself a direction. Consider the variables. Think your strategy through as far as you possibly can.

In some companies, the development of the strategy is part of the yearly budget process. This may be too narrow a focus. Yes, finances are a critical resource (and restraint). But financial goals and the strategic planning for achieving them comprise only one part of the process. Linking strategic review so closely to the budget process review may prevent you from seeing the value and relation of the strategic planning process to other areas of the business.

Strategic planning, as I view it, is a tool for any job level. Any objective or goal should have a strategy developed for its accomplishment. The overall strategy of the activity should be used to guide the individual in the development of his or her own strategies. With a good strategy in place, establishing the priorities to be worked on is easy. Establishing the ingredients—what working files need to be created and which of these working files requires a project—is also much easier. The question now becomes, what to strategize?

> *If you don't know where you are going,*
> *any road will get you there.*
> **—UNKNOWN**

GOALS

Strategies are built around goals. If you have not set final objectives (goals) how could you know what would even be an appropriate strategy?

Goals could be defined as broad objectives or aims, to which end efforts and actions are directed.

There are qualitative differences between goals. To try out for and make the high school tennis team is a goal but doesn't hold quite the same significance as an ultimate goal to help others by contributing to the discovery of the cause of cancer and be remembered for it for all time. Ultimate goals—those lifetime objectives that define purpose and provide meaning—will be covered in subsequent sections.

Goals are important because once they are established they focus attention and increase concentration. Focused attention and concentration result in more productivity—more of the important things being done.

Goals must be well defined, preferably worked out in writing. Writing forces you to clarify your thoughts.

Identifying and setting goals is a critical part of the PEP planning process. As a salesperson you may have financial goals such as to make so much in commissions during the year. You may have other goals as well: to become a sales manager, to reach the top 1% of all sales personnel, and so on. Each would have to be identified, have a strategy designed, have project plans written, and be followed through on a weekly and daily basis.

You likely will have a number of roles you play in your work. Marketing manager, chairman of the credit committee, XYZ board member, team leader—these can all be considered staff roles you play. Each role may have its own set of goals. When you see how many goals come into play, it isn't hard to see why people may have difficulty achieving them, particularly if they lack a process or system to accomplish their goals.

Identify the various roles you play in your job and work out your goals for each role (clear these goals with those you work with and for).

> *The greater danger*
> *for most of us*
> *is not that our aim is*
> *too high and we miss it*
> *but that it is*
> *too low*
> *and we reach it.*
> **—MICHELANGELO**

PERSONAL GOALS

We've all known someone who talked on and on about some fantasy, such as giving it all up and moving to Tahiti. Suppose a person fanta- sizes for years about moving to Tahiti, but it isn't meant to be. It is too expensive; the individual never has the time or money; or a job and/or personal responsibilities eat up every moment of his or her life. It's sad that so many people live their lives without realizing their dreams.

At least in this example, the person had a dream, but the dreamer didn't know how to achieve it. Maybe it was too overwhelming. Or maybe the dream was too dreamlike—it never became a clearly defined goal where objectives could be identified and set against real time.

Personal happiness is in no small part wrapped around setting and working on personal goals.

In my work I find that people more often set professional goals, ei- ther because they are imposed by the boss or because life has taught them that if they do not have a pretty clear idea of what they need to accomplish in their job they will fail to perform what they are being paid to do. The same discipline is not generally applied to one's per- sonal life. That's a shame because, obviously, there is more to life than work.

To get clarity on your personal goals, use Stephen Covey's sugges- tion in *The Seven Habits of Highly Effective People* (Simon & Schuster, 1989) and define your private roles: mother, sister, wife, head of the Parent-Teacher Association, artist, best friend, and so on. It is likely that each of these roles will have one or more inherent goals. Some goals will be more important than others. Some are short-range; some are lifetime goals. Once you begin this process you see that life is rather complex. Just keeping track of your goals is a major accom- plishment! We are not even talking about the hundreds of details in- volved in reaching them.

Whether personal or professional, goals function like directional lights. They shed light on overriding objectives and provide us a reason to develop strategies. Still, we need to know that our goals are impor- tant and meaningful. What your goals are depends on what you value.

VALUES

While most business is conducted to create profit, long-term success requires more than achieving that one goal. For example, you might improve current profit by eliminating investment toward the future or by cutting costs to the detriment of customer service, but either activity could mean the death of the business.

It is the responsibility of the top executives to define what is truly important to the business. This is not some public relations (PR) exercise. It is a serious strategic step. What is the reason for the existence of your business? What principles does the business live by? What is your organizational vision? What are the governing values of the business?

Often a company defines its purpose and principles in a one-page mission statement and invites employees to develop goals and objectives in alignment with it.

As a manager you might call together your management team to delineate the most important issues your department, group, or business is facing, where you want the business to be in the next several years, and what might prevent you from being there. You might involve all of your staff in the process. The end result would be agreement on the most important issues to deal with so business and professional goals can be met.

VALUES ON A PERSONAL LEVEL

One of the most important questions you need to answer for yourself is, "What truly matters to me?" If you have not identified the principles you value and wish to live by, it will be very hard to work out your purpose in life. But if you do determine what your principles are—those ideals that you value above all else— your purpose or mission in life becomes all the more clear. If you know what is important to you, you can then establish goals to realize it. These goals will be meaningful, because achieving them will give you what you truly value.

There is tremendous strength in this approach. Charles R. Hobbs, the author of the book *Time Power* (Harper & Row, 1987), calls this self-unification:

> *When what you do is in congruity with what you believe, and what you believe is the highest of truths, you achieve the most gratifying form of personal productivity and experience the most satisfying form of self-esteem.* (p. 21)

By establishing your most vital priorities in life you can achieve what Hobbs describes as a concentration of power: "the ability to focus on and accomplish your most vital priorities."

Establishing your values isn't a glib exercise. You're reading this book because you appreciate how valuable time is. You no doubt want more control of it. You want to be able to make better use of it. It would be a shame to come to the end of your life and realize you had not done and been what you wanted to do and be.

Dr. Wayne Dyer, in his audiotape series *Real Magic,* talks of his experiences working in a hospital with terminally ill patients. He noticed that no one ever regretted not having spent more time in the office. The regrets were about the handling of relationships or time with loved ones.

Don't wait until it's too late to realize you have spent the bulk of the time of your life on things that were not the most important to you. It's far better to analyze your goals, your beliefs, and your guiding principles and to make sure your work is in alignment with them.

Most of us want happiness in life. But what brings it about? Happiness is a by-product of working and living with meaning and purpose. Establishing goals based on one's values provides that meaning and a purpose for living. The beauty of working toward the accomplishment of a goal is that it almost doesn't matter whether you achieve the goal—the fact that you are working toward things that matter to you is enough to bring you happiness. Even the most mundane of actions becomes tolerable, even enjoyable, because you know it's leading you closer to the accomplishment of your goals.

If you're to do the things that are most important to you in life, you will need to manage your time wisely:

- Decide what you value above all else.
- Decide what principles you wish to live by.
- Identify your mission in life.

The purpose of life
is a life of purpose.
—ROBERT BYRNE

VISUALIZATION—WHAT YOU SEE IS WHAT YOU GET

You're most likely familiar with the concept of visualizing desired results before the actual performance. Athletes have employed the technique for years. Visualization means crossing the finish line in your mind's eye or imagining the perfect dive. Everything slows down, and you're aware of all that is happening. You see yourself making that three-point basket in the final game of the NBA championship playoffs just as the buzzer sounds to win the game. Charles Garfield, a research psychologist, has spent many years studying hundreds of world-class athletes. In his book *Peak Performance: Mental Training Techniques of the World's Greatest Athletes* (Warner Books, 1984), he says:

> *All peak performers I have interviewed report that they use some form of mental rehearsal in both training and competition.*

How important is organizational vision? Jim Clemmer, in his book *Firing on All Cylinders* (Irwin Professional Publishers, 1992), writes:

> *Your organizational vision acts as a magnet. It attracts people, events, and circumstances to it. Another way of looking at visioning is as a self-fulfilling prophecy. What your people believe will happen, they will make happen, often unconsciously.*

We've spoken of action following clarity of picture. The planning process described in this chapter allows you to get that clarity of picture. There is a difference between dreaming about having something in the future and *visualizing* having it in the future. Visualizing implies a more structured and disciplined view of what you are trying to accomplish. By visualizing, you look at your goal from many different viewpoints. By examining your work from all of the viewpoints described here, you get clarity and act on the things that are the most important and will result in the greatest payback.

By dreaming and visualizing (prompted by a good planning process), you create more reasons to want what you are looking at and you increase your desire for it. Want and desire, in no small part, determine whether you accomplish what you set out to do.

The Japanese are known for the speed by which they can bring a new product to the market. Yet they also have a reputation for taking a long time to decide. This has been incorrectly labeled as a Japanese process of consensus building. Yes, they build consensus. But they also make sure that every angle has been thoroughly looked at before they begin. And once they begin, they act with blinding speed.

You must go through this thorough process if you are to act in the most effective way. The planning process prompts you to examine your work from many points of view. You identify the objects that comprise the objective—the work. The work is categorized in many additional ways it might not otherwise be if you neglected thorough planning.

You must be well organized to execute this all-essential planning process efficiently. You don't necessarily want to spend a lot of time on it. You want to spend the majority of time getting the actions done. But the time and effort are worth it. When you learn to plan most effectively, you'll discover that you are spending some part of every day visualizing and, better yet, *actualizing* your goals with this process.

FOLLOW-UP FOR CHAPTER 4

1. Commit to a daily and weekly action plan. With practice, an analysis of your work for the coming week should take you two to four hours on Friday and probably less if you computerize the process. Devote 10 minutes or so to a daily action plan each morning of the workweek and track your progress through the workday. Your daily planning will be much simplified if you work backward from the larger picture of a weekly plan and derive your daily To Do lists from a series of tasks designed to move you closer to a larger goal.

2. As part of your weekly action plan, go through all of your sources of work. Prioritize these various items and plan out your week. Eliminate multiple sources by combining any stray notes into one list.

Use these current notations, along with items in your pending box and tickler file, to create your weekly list.

3. Remember to allow sufficient time in your planning for unplanned or unidentified work.

4. Remember to define the key objectives to be accomplished. Break down these objectives into smaller tasks. Once a week, review these activities and use them to help create a weekly action plan for yourself. These projects should be counted among your sources of work identified in step 2.

5. Define what is important to the business in the long term. Where do you want the business (or your portion or area of responsibility) to be in the years ahead? You may invite your staff to participate in this process. From this process define specifically (and in writing) what goals you will work on over a defined period of time.

6. Create a working file for each goal.

7. Establish a strategy for the accomplishment of each goal.

8. Write project plans covering the tactical steps necessary to accomplish the strategies.

9. Do some soul-searching. Consider those values you hold to be most important to you. Stephen Covey cleverly suggests you imagine attending your own funeral. What would you hope would be said in a eulogy? In your life, what have you done that you are most proud of? And at the end, what would you hope to have accomplished with your life?

10. Remember, having a purpose in life provides meaning. What is your purpose in life? If you do not know, or it is unclear, work to identify it. Some call identifying it their mission statement.

11. Work out the immediate goals that contribute most to your purpose or mission in life.

12. Apply the PEP planning process to these goals:

Strategy.
Project plans.
Weekly/monthly planning time.
Daily plans.

Good luck!

Follow-Up and Follow-Through!

When you get right down to the root of the meaning of the word succeed, you find that it simply means to follow-through.
—F. W. Nichol

Chapter 5 Preview

In this chapter, you will learn how to:

- Persevere; persistence is the most vital ingredient of success in life and work.
- Put the right systems in place to allow you to remember details.
- Use a calendar and other tools to follow-up and follow-through.
- Practice effective delegation. Unlimited growth is possible only through eliciting the support of others.

In Chapter 4 we covered how essential it is to have an efficient planning process in place if you are to realize your goals and objectives. Planning gives clarity, and with clarity you act. But how successful and effective you are will depend most on how well you stick to what you are trying to accomplish—in other words, how well you follow-up and follow-through.

> *Let me tell you the secret that has led me to my goal:*
> *my strength lies solely in my tenacity.*
> **—LOUIS PASTEUR**

PERSISTENCE

When I say stick to it, I almost literally mean it. Things get done, objectives are met, goals are achieved most often because the person who wanted them possessed the stick-to-itiveness to make them happen. Calvin Coolidge, 30th president of the United States, said:

> *Nothing in the world can take the place of persistence. Talent will not; nothing is more common than unsuccessful men with talent. Genius will not; unrewarded genius is almost a proverb. Education will not; the world is full of educated derelicts. Persistence and determination alone are omnipotent.*

I suspect that your experience tells you this is true. Things happen because you make them happen, and/or persist until they do. Planning's relationship to persistence can best be summed up in a quote of Napoleon Hill in his book, *Think and Grow Rich* (Fawcett Crest, 1960). He says:

> *The majority of men meet with failure because of their lack of persistence in creating new plans to take the place of those which fail.*

This is the essence of the work process. Know what you want. Plan how to get it. Act on the plans. Follow-up until it happens, or develop new plans to make it happen. Follow-up on the new plans over and over until you achieve what you want. How well you do it is determined by how well you are organized.

By following the steps of the Personal Efficiency Program (PEP), you've become action oriented. You *Do It Now*. You've organized your work space and you have systems in place to keep it that way. You know how to set goals and plan to achieve them. These same principles must be applied to how you follow-up and follow-through.

> *That what we persist in doing becomes easier—*
> *not that the nature of the task has changed,*
> *but our ability to do it has increased.*
> —RALPH WALDO EMERSON

FORGET REMEMBERING

Most people I speak with take a certain degree of pride in their ability to remember "everything" that needs to be done. It is a mental game they play. While that may have been okay at one time, the pace of today's work and home life has accelerated and the volume of activities we could or should keep up with has grown so much that it is impractical to expect to keep on top of 1,000 things to do. No doubt you do remember these things to do, but it may not be at the time it's most convenient or effective, such as at three o'clock in the morning, when you sit up in bed and think, "Oh, I have to take care of. . . ." This constant thinking about, planning out, tracking everything you need to do—remembering everything you need to follow-up on—simply overwhelms people.

I don't believe that you necessarily want to reinforce this ability to remember the many hundreds of details that make up your workload. Executives and managers should be more interested in forgetting about all these things they need to do. Yes, I said forgetting. What people need is the right system in place, to allow them to remember this myriad of details when, and only when, it's necessary for them to remember.

Sounds crazy? Not really.

It has been said that Albert Einstein couldn't tell you his own telephone number. When asked why, he was reported to have replied, "Why should I know it? I can always find it in the directory."

PREOCCUPATION AND TIME

Have you ever noticed the first time you drive someplace it seems to take longer to get there than the second or third time? Have you ever considered why? The first time you drive somewhere you tend to be alert to where you are and where you are going. You are on the look-out for landmarks. "Three blocks past the pharmacy on Hilton Street" forces you to keep an eye out for the pharmacy and count the blocks. Once you have been there a few times, you can drive there hardly noticing the familiar landmarks. You get in the car and the next thing you know you are there! The sense of time has little to do with how fast you are driving. It has much more to do with where your attention is focused. Anyone driving today can agree that too many people driving are in their own mental world. They are preoccupied.

When you are preoccupied time flies by. You will have experienced starting the workday only to discover it is time for lunch and you wonder where the morning went and what you accomplished. Too often the cause of this preoccupation is our attempt to make sense of and keep up with the thousands of things we must do. It is the result of a poor planning process. It is our attempt to keep on top of all the things we must track and do, *mentally*.

I am convinced that this constant, unproductive preoccupation with all the things we have to do is the single largest consumer of time and energy, the biggest barrier to individual productivity, and the one thing we can all do something about to materially allow us to take control of our time and our work, and therefore our lives.

ORGANIZE EFFICIENT FOLLOW-UP SYSTEMS

All too often when I arrive at someone's desk, I find it scattered with reminders of things to do, perhaps in the form of Post-it notes spread out around the computer screen and over every imaginable surface. Even if you have a strong *Do It Now* habit, there are normally many things you can't complete at the moment for one reason or another. Accordingly, people leave themselves reminders.

However, having those reminders constantly staring you in the face isn't necessarily conducive to concentration, focus, and productivity. If these little reminders linger long enough one eventually becomes blind to them. Regularly looking at all of these reminders and consciously deciding not to do any one of them reinforces a *Don't Do It Now* habit.

Having simple and easy reminder systems (tools) in place enables you to overcome these problems and move on to your most important work.

Paper Follow-Up

Since paper is so abundant and is one of the biggest nuisances around, let's begin by discussing how to handle paper. You know it's possible to get the papers off of your desk and "forwarded" to an appropriate time to do them. You can do this with a tickler file system that lets you schedule materials by the days of the month (1 through 31), or by months (1 through 12), according to due dates.

As we discussed in Chapter 2, simply make a reminder for yourself in your calendar, and then block out time to do the work. Put the reminder—the piece of paper you'll actually be working on—into the tickler system on the same date you scheduled in your calendar, so it will pop up on the day you scheduled for it. Put papers that are awaiting someone else's input into the tickler system. For example, if you send a letter to a customer and expect to hear back within a week, put your copy of the letter into the tickler system. After a week, your copy of the letter pops up, prompting you to get back to the customer for more follow-up. If a response has been received, the response will dictate your next step. Either way, the reminder prompts you to follow-up and follow-through.

One clever and successful man ran a medium-size bank using just this system. He had a tickler system numbered 1 to 31 and 1 to 12. This one follow-up tool was used and the whole management of the bank could be traced. He would assign duties and tasks to people or write down things to be done and use the tickler system to anticipate when he thought an assignment or a project could reasonably (and efficiently) be completed. When the reminder popped up at a date in the future, he followed up and followed through.

Logbook

Consolidating all the small tasks you need to do in one book eliminates the need for little pieces of paper littering your desk. A logbook of such items makes a useful reminder tool for the odds and ends of work that are part of everyone's day. You can use it when you suddenly remember something you need to do and want a place to write it down. Colleagues may pass by and verbally ask you to check on something and get back to them on it; the logbook gives you a place to write down the request and a means to note your follow-up, all in one.

I recommend a composition notebook, probably about 6 by 9½ inches in size. Use a stitched book so the pages cannot be easily ripped out, not a spiral-bound notebook. In it maintain a chronological diary of activities. You should date each entry. Write big, and put straight lines between entries, so you can easily distinguish between tasks. As you complete a task, cross it out (see Figure 5.1). This lets you see what's been done and what remains to be done.

One manager ran his entire business using this one tool. Everything he needed to remember went into his personal logbook. He took it wherever he went.

Simply using a logbook to organize and remember things to do can be an effective reminder system, especially for secretaries. In fact, nearly all professional secretaries I have worked with have had some form of logbook.

Until you get used to writing everything down in it I recommend you always leave it open on your desk. Otherwise, chances are you will reach for the closest thing to write on and you won't develop the habit of using your logbook.

Calendar Systems

Even if you use a logbook, you will always need some form of calendar system. There are many calendar systems on the market. The Franklin/Covey Planner, Day-Timer organizer system, and Time Manager International calendaring system and course are but a few of the many calendar systems you may have seen. Each of these has a built-in philosophy of time management. These planners are excellent follow-up tools. After all, you can be reasonably sure you'll check your calendar daily, so it makes a good place to jot down items you want to remember. Because calendars are dated, they anticipate future needs, and you can use them as a sort of linear tickler file, if nothing else.

Our Scandinavian offices have designed calendar systems following the planning concepts of PEP. Like others mentioned here, this is a calendar system you can carry around with you (it fits in a small purse or suit pocket for convenience) and use to track your activities and plan your week. It has a week-at-a-glance calendar view and sections for addresses and telephone numbers, as well as other personal information.

One good rule of thumb for any calendar system is this: Whether

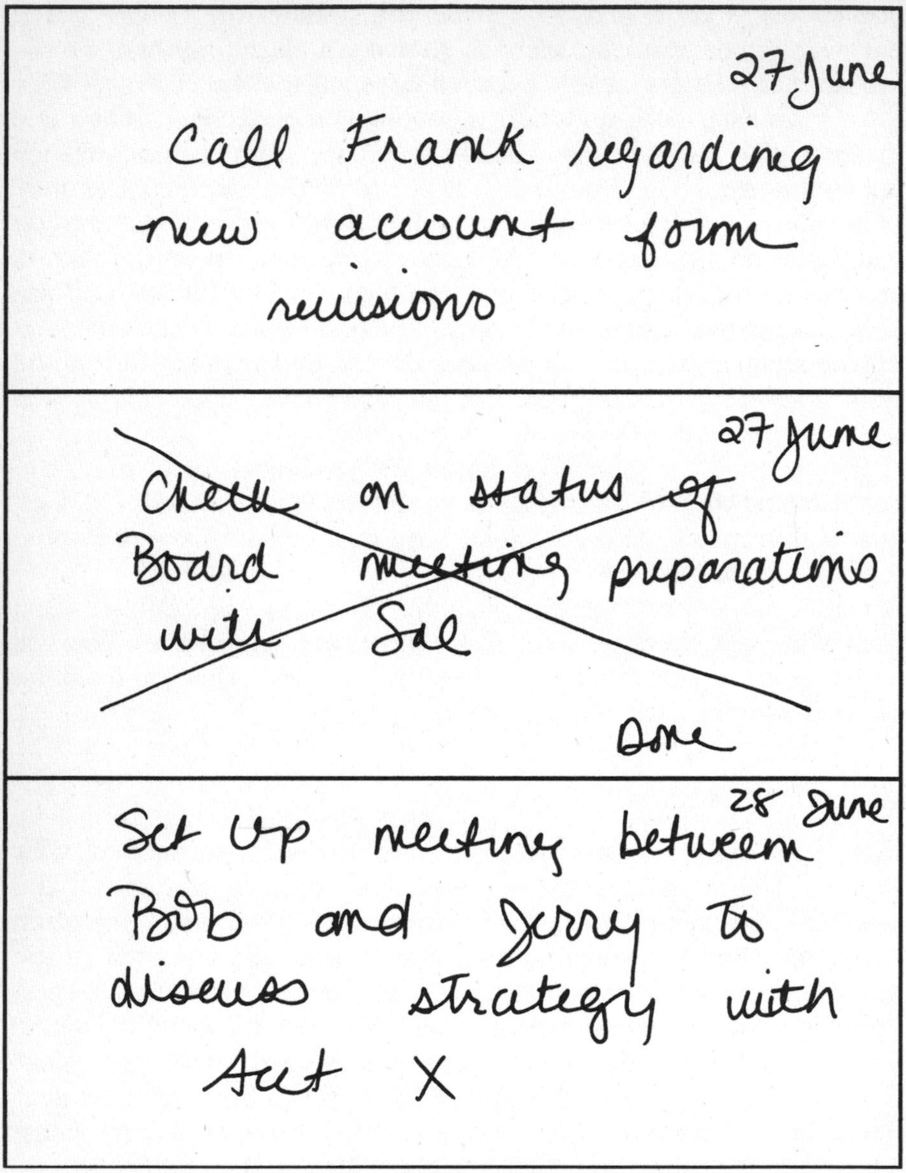

27 June

Call Frank regarding new account form revisions

Check on status of Board meeting preparations with Sal

27 June

Done

Set Up meeting between Bob and Jerry to discuss strategy with Act X

28 June

Figure 5.1 Sample entries in a logbook.

you choose a large, deskbound calendar system with many sections and features or a simple calendar system you carry in your purse or suit pocket, use one with a week-at-a-glance feature. This will reinforce your likelihood to plan on a weekly and a week-long basis and increase your chances of success in both scheduling and accomplishing your work.

If you're inclined to use a bigger and more sophisticated system, you might include subdivisions such as an address book section, a section for your project plans, or a section for notes you take during meetings. Learn to use your calendar system to its full potential. A little imagination, combined with the necessary training and trial and error, will show you follow-up and follow-through capabilities.

An effective calendar system helps you to:

- Remind yourself of future tasks.
- Note appointments.
- Write To Do lists, or plan for the upcoming week.
- Note important deadlines.
- Work back from deadlines and note down milestones.
- Remind yourself of recurring events such as birthdays, holidays, anniversaries, and other special dates in your life.
- Write notes from meetings.
- Keep address and telephone information.
- Provide general information, such as time zones, telephone area codes, and postal zip codes.
- Block out time for your own scheduled work.
- Schedule recurring activities such as time to meet employees on a weekly basis, to process your e-mail, and to do paperwork.
- Store personal information such as insurance policy numbers, driver's license number, automobile registration numbers, and so on.
- Organize activities based on your purposes and goals.

A well-used calendar for scheduling and following through on activities might look as shown in Figure 5.2.

Electronic Solutions to Follow-Up and Follow-Through

Getting more use out of your existing calendar or upgrading to a bigger, more sophisticated calendar is a simple refinement of an existing process that you probably already have in place. Should you wish to

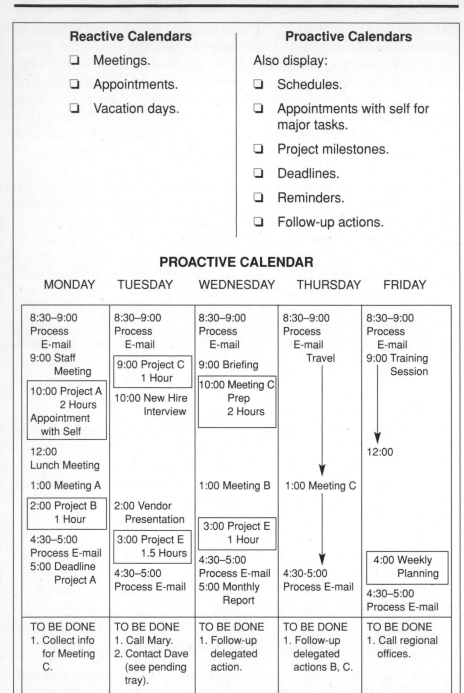

Reactive Calendars
- ❏ Meetings.
- ❏ Appointments.
- ❏ Vacation days.

Proactive Calendars

Also display:
- ❏ Schedules.
- ❏ Appointments with self for major tasks.
- ❏ Project milestones.
- ❏ Deadlines.
- ❏ Reminders.
- ❏ Follow-up actions.

PROACTIVE CALENDAR

MONDAY	TUESDAY	WEDNESDAY	THURSDAY	FRIDAY
8:30–9:00 Process E-mail	8:30–9:00 Process E-mail	8:30–9:00 Process E-mail	8:30–9:00 Process E-mail Travel	8:30–9:00 Process E-mail
9:00 Staff Meeting	9:00 Project C 1 Hour	9:00 Briefing		9:00 Training Session
10:00 Project A 2 Hours Appointment with Self	10:00 New Hire Interview	10:00 Meeting C Prep 2 Hours		
12:00 Lunch Meeting				12:00
1:00 Meeting A		1:00 Meeting B	1:00 Meeting C	
2:00 Project B 1 Hour	2:00 Vendor Presentation			
4:30–5:00 Process E-mail 5:00 Deadline Project A	3:00 Project E 1.5 Hours	3:00 Project E 1 Hour		
	4:30–5:00 Process E-mail	4:30–5:00 Process E-mail 5:00 Monthly Report	4:30-5:00 Process E-mail	4:00 Weekly Planning
				4:30–5:00 Process E-mail
TO BE DONE 1. Collect info for Meeting C.	TO BE DONE 1. Call Mary. 2. Contact Dave (see pending tray).	TO BE DONE 1. Follow-up delegated action.	TO BE DONE 1. Follow-up delegated actions B, C.	TO BE DONE 1. Call regional offices.

Figure 5.2 Sample calendar for scheduling and follow-up.

make a more dramatic change in your working life, you might consider one of the many electronic systems on the market.

Technology is quickly catching up to and matching the needs of virtually every individual. There are handheld electronic calendar systems not much bigger or heavier than Day-Timers or other paper notebook-type calendar systems that can provide us with vast amounts of information. Coming down the scale, the capability we associated with "desktop" 10 years ago is now "palmtop" in the world of computers.

Whatever the size, there are some drawbacks. A palm-size computer/calendar system may have a keyboard that's difficult to work with. But even that question is being addressed now, with devotees using narrow stylus-type instruments to key in their information and requests. These trends indicate that these electronic organizers will increase in popularity and will certainly challenge paper-based systems for superiority (and popularity) in the future.

Organizing yourself with personal information manager software is fast and flexible. Instead of the tedious and sometimes time-consuming effort that goes into planning on paper a good personal information manager and/or groupware program like Lotus Notes lets you use your computer to jot things down quickly and then with just a few keystrokes revise your plans according to your needs. You can see at a glance what you have to do with each project. It is easy to rearrange, add, or delete steps without rewriting each affected item or each plan all over again as you do when you plan on paper.

You can also plan reminders for future dates that will automatically (electronically) pop up at an appropriate time. You can store frequently used information literally at your fingertips, keep track of appointments and meetings, and keep files safely stored in your computer.

Popular personal information managers such as Small Business Tracker Deluxe (info@productivity.software.com) and Lotus Organizer (www.lotus.com) include features to track activities, expenses, appointments, schedules, and tasks. Others such as GoalPro (www.goalpro.com) focus on goal setting and time management.

An electronic solution takes a lot of the work out of planning for you by automatically batching activities and key words. Instead of thumbing through a particular file wondering where you put this or that, you can retrieve all pertinent information about a project with a simple search function. To check your work and to organize yourself, I recommend a personal information manager software application.

Combination Paper and Electronic Calendaring Systems

Although I usually encourage people to embrace technology and computerize their calendaring systems, some may find that computerization doesn't fit their type of work. For example, going to a lunch appointment with a laptop computer may be a bit much. Many people successfully combine paper and electronic calendaring systems, taking advantage of both. Most electronic PIM software packages can print out your calendar in almost any conceivable size. When going to appointments you can use a printout.

Personal Digital Assistants (PDAs), Palmtops, and Handheld PCs

PDAs are fast becoming the tool of choice for calendaring and organizing systems. The success of the Palm Pilot series and other brands has pushed handheld pocket PC/PDA type tools into the forefront of the business world. Brands such as Casio, Palm Pilot, Compaq IPAQ Pocket PC, and Sony Clio are but a few of the many organizer brands on the market.

Technologies are tending to converge in such a way that these small pocket PCs can be used both to keep track of information including a full calendaring system to carry around with you, and a communication tool for voice, text messaging, and e-mail.

Some handhelds serve specific purposes. The Blackberry (www.blackberry.com) handheld device supports wireless e-mail and is a popular communications tool for mobile workers.

Earlier handicaps with these tools including poor memory, poor LCD-screen visibility, a short battery life, a small keyboard, and so on have to a large degree been addressed and improved upon dramatically.

With so much choice it is important for you to identify exactly what it is that you need and expect from a handheld organizer.

- Do you use personal information manager software on your desktop that will need to be synchronized with whatever handheld computer you have?
- What is the purpose of your handheld? Do you want it for the calendaring function and to keep track of telephone numbers? Or will your handheld be used as a communications tool to access the corporate Local Area Network and e-mail?

- Is the handheld something that is easy to put information into? Would you prefer a keyboard or stylus?
- It is possible to get voice recognition software for pocket PCs allowing you to have a voice driven scheduler and even a recorded audio description of a task or activity that will be played back at a specific date or time. Is this practical for you?

Personal digital assistants, pocket PCs, and handheld PCs are the twenty-first century equivalents of a paper-based calendar system. They are excellent tools and highly recommended.

WORK GROUPS

With the advent of network systems it is now possible and even affordable to network nearly any group within an organization. What used to require a million-dollar investment is now within the means of most small groups. The hardware and software needed to network and communicate with each other are affordable to virtually every business.

Follow-up and follow-through are greatly enhanced in a group setting, of course, because groups can develop specific plans for a variety of projects involving any number of different people. These plans can be implemented concurrently, tracked, supervised, or merely viewed by any member of the group.

From the manager's perspective, multiple projects can be tracked with ease. You can view any one or all of the projects your direct reports are responsible for. You can also view the separate tasks and completion deadlines for any of those projects or view the separate (and multiple) tasks for more than one project simultaneously, depending on your software and hardware. This capability lets you keep track of multiple deadlines.

You can get a perspective on the work being done from the viewpoint of any of the people involved and track work that needs to be completed concurrently or prior to the completion of other assignments. You can identify problems you may have been unaware of or merely suspected. For example, if you view the task list of several of your people in columns on a single screen and you see one has an unfair or overly large task load, you may want to look again at how your office delegates.

As changes, modifications, or updates are made, everyone in the network automatically has those updates available. Information can be viewed against time and deadlines. If an individual becomes ill, it's easy to identify his or her responsibilities and tasks, and then redistribute them equitably among the other members of the group. The need for physically meeting to cover issues or plans is greatly reduced, thereby increasing the time available for actual work.

FOLLOW-UP AND DELEGATION

Delegation determines to a large degree your effectiveness as an executive, manager, or supervisor. The quality of your work also depends on your ability to properly delegate. Proper delegation enables you to follow-up and follow-through effectively. If you delegate properly, you will multiply your productivity.

The sooner in your planning process that you detect overload—yours or someone else's—the more effective you will be if you correct the problem. You can't expect to do everything yourself.

You can waste a lot of time trying to master something you are not very good at. Delegating properly, to the right person with the right skills, is one of the most important executive skills. When you delegate, you are assigning another person a task to do and the authority to do it, even though you do not hand over your personal accountability. That stays with you.

One of the best sources of information on the subject of delegation is the book *Don't Do. Delegate!* (Ballantine Books, 1985) by James Jenks and John Kelly. The following two lists, gleaned from this and other sources, contrast effective and ineffective delegation.

The Effective Delegator	**The Ineffective Delegator**
1. Identifies the correct person to do the job.	1. Distributes workload arbitrarily.
2. Delegates now, giving adequate time for completion.	2. Delegates just before deadline, thereby creating crisis.
3. Clearly states the objective.	3. Does not clearly communicate the envisioned outcome.
4. Provides all information needed to complete the task.	4. Issues minimal, hurried instructions.

5. Makes sure staff understands task before taking action.

6. Sets deadline for completion.

7. Encourages written project plan.

8. Regularly monitors progress.

9. Is accessible for clarification and advice.

10. Assumes responsibility, but gives credit to the person who did the job.

11. Helps staff grow by introducing them to new responsibilities.

5. Delegates in a way that creates misunderstandings.

6. Asks for everything as soon as possible.

7. Hopes staff develops an effective approach to task.

8. Establishes no formal review process.

9. Interferes with how job is being done.

10. Assigns blame to others if result not achieved, but takes credit if achieved.

11. Doesn't delegate but instead holds on to the task and acts as a bottleneck.

There is a more important reason to refine your skills of getting others to do the work for you. Eliciting the support of others is the only way you will achieve broad success, both personally and professionally. Only by tapping into the support of others can you multiply your output. There is a limit to any one individual's productive capacity, time, and knowledge. Skillful delegation means limitless production potential.

DELEGATION—USING YOUR ELECTRONIC TOOLS

In some cultures how you delegate can be a sensitive topic. A large Dutch power company client experienced this. There was a negative reaction to how some people would delegate within the concern. Some staff would object to how they were being told what to do.

Our IBT office addressed the issue in this way: The company was a Microsoft Outlook user. They decided to teach all employees how to use the task list in Outlook as a way to keep track of activities without constantly having to nag the employees about the status. IBT's first action was to have the manager concerned go around and see all of the employees and inform them of the new method of tracking delegated tasks through Outlook. He stressed how much easier it would be on the employees by applying this electronic tool to manage their tasks.

Person-responsible categories were created within the Outlook task management. All tasks were assigned to the person responsible.

An additional column was added to the task list form showing the percentage of completion of the task. In this way, the manager could look at the overall list of tasks for the person responsible and the person could make a notation of how far they had progressed on the task, be it 25% complete, 50% complete, 75% complete, and so on.

The managers still had to apply the principles as previously noted but with this tool they were able to keep track of the vast majority of things that were open and outstanding in their department without having to be overly intrusive on the employees.

The employees appreciated the fact that the managers went around and saw them and tried to take up and improve delegation procedures in the department. That in and of itself was worth the effort.

Lotus Notes and many other groupware applications have a similar functionality. Electronic tools exist to improve the delegation process.

EXCEPTIONS TO THE RULE

It can be very frustrating when you have to track down what others have done. On the other hand, if you don't track your subordinates' work, it often means failure. How you pass on things to others to do can affect your results. Effective delegation greatly increases your chances of success. Some people simply will not perform, so don't delegate to them. Give the job to someone else or figure out another way to get the job done.

I use an old rule of thumb. When it comes to getting something done, *give it to a busy person.* Idle people often remain idle when given things to do. Busy people—if they are effective—are busy because they are consistently and regularly working, and that's the person you want to assign tasks to.

> **Next week there can't be any crisis.**
> **My schedule is already full.**
> **—HENRY A. KISSINGER**

BACK UP YOUR SYSTEMS

In a movie entitled *Taking Care of Business* the character played by actor Charles Grodin leaves his calendar system in a phone booth at an airport and it is found by a convict who has escaped from prison. The movie is a comedy and produces lots of laughs about this poor guy's experiences, but it also drives home how much we depend on our follow-up and reminder systems.

The chances of misplacing your calendar system or having your computer malfunction are high. I back up my hard drive on floppy disks each week when I create my weekly plan.

A colleague of mine makes copies of his paper calendar system—not necessarily the entire calendar but all of the personal information, addresses, telephone numbers, and so forth. He was once very grateful for having done so. He misplaced his original but because of the copy, he found it relatively painless to reconstruct the information.

If you are susceptible to forgetting things, you should make sure you regularly back up your reminder system so that it will be there when you need it.

MAKE FOLLOW-UP PART OF THE WORK PROCESS

Your weekly planning process becomes the formal time for you to get an overview of your work, look at all of your objectives and plans, prioritize your upcoming week, and remind yourself of what you need to follow-up on. Scheduling your weekly planning and doing it ensures that no important item gets overlooked.

As an executive, manager, or supervisor, you should use your weekly one-to-one meeting with your direct reports as the time to follow-up on the items you're tracking through to completion. By scheduling and holding these meetings regularly, you let your people know what to expect. They know it is time for progress reports and that progress is expected. It eliminates random checking and disturbing your people in the process. Your staff members, in turn, have the chance to follow-up with you on input you're expected to supply. They know the meeting is predictable, useful time that helps them get their own jobs done better and faster.

If you learn to recognize the tools that exist to facilitate follow-up and follow-through and make these tools an efficient part of the work process, you'll make it much easier to persist to success.

FOLLOW-UP FOR CHAPTER 5

1. How successful and effective you are primarily depends on how well you stick to what you're trying to accomplish—in other words, how well you follow-up and follow-through. Things happen because you make them happen, or you must persist until you do.

2. Adopt simple and easy reminder systems that will enable you to overcome problems and let you move on to your most important work. If you have a stack of papers on your desk that detail tasks to be done, eliminate the clutter by scheduling this work in your calendar, and filing the papers in a tickler file. Then, on the appropriate date, the papers will be there to remind you of a task to be done, and you will have blocked out the time to complete that task.

3. Eliminate the clutter of multiple reminders by consolidating everything into a logbook. Use it every day to reinforce the habit, and you'll keep your desk clear at the same time. Use the logbook when you suddenly remember something you need to do and you want a place to write it down. Use it to keep track of verbal requests to do things. Date each task to be done, and cross off the task when it's completed. A logbook provides a reminder system and a follow-up system all in one by prompting you to do things and verifying tasks that have been completed.

4. Use a calendar system that lets you plan an entire week at a time. This will reinforce your likelihood to plan on a weekly and a week-long basis and increase your chances of success in both scheduling and accomplishing your work.

5. Learn not to limit the use of your calendar system. People almost never use a calendar system to its full potential. A little imagination, combined with the necessary trial and error, will show you follow-up and follow-through capabilities you never anticipated.

6. Do not overlook electronic solutions. If your firm uses Outlook or another group application, consider adopting it as your calendar/task management tool. Most PDAs and pocket PCs support Outlook (and other popular applications) and can be useful tools for when you are out of the office or for mobile workers.

7. Delegation is prime in determining your effectiveness. The quality of your work also depends on your ability to properly delegate. Delegate properly and you'll multiply your productivity. Remember, when you delegate, you are assigning another person a task to do and the authority to do it. You don't hand over control or accountability, though. These stay with you.

8. Make follow-up and follow-through part of the process of work. You can do this by including it as part of the weekly review process as you meet regularly with each of your direct reports. Remember, too, that these weekly meetings are the time for your staff to follow-up with you on input you're expected to supply. If follow-up and follow-through work both ways, these meetings will become dependable, useful times together that will help everyone do their work better and more efficiently.

CHAPTER 6

Do It *Right,* Now!

*You can't escape the responsibility
of tomorrow by evading it today.*
—ABRAHAM LINCOLN

Chapter 6 Preview

In this chapter, you will learn:

- It isn't enough to do what you think is important. Check what the customers' expectations are and fulfill those needs.
- To improve the process of your group's work, you should begin with the process of your personal work.
- To make dramatic improvement, you must abandon your old ways of processing your work and start using new methods to introduce more effective ways of working.

THE ORIGIN OF PEP

In the early 1980s, I was living in Sweden and had a small sales and marketing consulting business. To attract new clients, I devised a compensation plan unique to Sweden at the time: I wouldn't accept a fee unless the client got a measurable result. It had an attractive ring to it, and I found it pretty easy to get companies interested and to be willing to at least see me and listen to what I had to say. If a potential client thought I had something to offer, the first hurdle to overcome was figuring out what constituted a measurable result. Since I specialized in sales and marketing, I often was able to work out a measurable target, usually increased sales and customers.

The next challenge I faced was creating a marketing and sales campaign that would deliver that measurable result. This was easier than I imagined: All I had to do was ask the people who did the work what they would do to increase the desired result. Most of the time they knew what to do.

I would develop a plan based on their input and give it to them. Now this is the interesting part: Almost invariably I would return to find that the plan hadn't been executed. The staff members didn't have time. They had too many other things to do; someone got sick or went on holiday. This posed a problem for me. I had to get them to do the plan or I wasn't going to get paid. The workers were caught up in day-to-day inefficiencies, wasting time looking for things, being disorganized in hundreds of ways, and my main duty became not my help with sales and marketing but getting the principals well organized so they could do the things they had been thinking about doing all along.

I succeeded to build up a client base. One of my clients was a branch of Svenska Handelsbanken, one of the most profitable banks in Sweden. It hired me to increase the amount of money in savings accounts—a measurable target. Along with the management team and staff, I worked out a marketing plan to accomplish this target. Then came the hard part—getting it done.

At Svenska Handelsbanken, several things were keeping the plan from being implemented. For example, as a matter of policy the bank personnel periodically rotated jobs and workstations. As a result, every few months people found themselves at a new workstation without knowing where things were. It took a few weeks to attain some semblance of order. Meanwhile, time was wasted.

Instead of processing each transaction immediately, some cashiers would create huge backlogs by putting aside until later the tasks they thought would take longer. Cashiers who processed each item of work immediately, as it happened, didn't develop backlogs.

Since there were no baskets on the desks, when mail came in, it sat on top of the desk with all the other papers. Sometimes individual items from the day's mail were buried beneath other papers and overlooked entirely.

The branch manager was a competent executive, but she spent most of her time dealing with customers. This gave her little time to devote to the organization of the individual workers.

I started a standard filing system at each desk and purged the place of clutter. That way, if someone had to use a workstation he or she was unfamiliar with, at least he or she knew where to find things. I asked the senior cashier to describe how she processed her work. This became the model for processing transactions in the bank branch, and the other cashiers began following her model. We set up a central mail center with baskets for each worker. Soon the staff were initiating their own solutions to common problems affecting their productivity. Eventually the bank hired me to package for it what I had done in this one branch and train 50 internal trainers to deliver the Personal Efficiency Program to the bank's 500-branch network.

I learned from this experience and from the many other clients in Sweden and a dozen other countries in Europe and North America that the vast majority of people are proficient and technically skilled to do their work but they don't understand the principles of work organization or the application of these principles to their jobs.

Work process improvement is understood by most to be improvement of the computer system or the manufacturing process. Most individuals are only vaguely aware of a personal work process, and they seldom, if ever, address this personal work process.

The greatest success I had in improving group productivity came from focusing on the basics of the personal work process. Most people don't give much thought or assign much importance to the work process. But once they begin to work on *how* they do their work, they often continue without my encouragement because they become much more productive. William James, the famous nineteenth-century psychologist and philosopher, said: "What a person puts their mind to happens."

WHY QUALITY?

The American Society for Quality (www.asq.org) has kindly provided permission to publish their arguments for Quality:

- Quality is not a program; it is an approach to business.
- Quality is a collection of powerful tools and concepts that is proven to work.
- Quality is defined by the customer through his/her satisfaction.
- Quality includes continuous improvement and breakthrough events.
- Quality tools and techniques are applicable in every aspect of the business.
- Quality is aimed at performance excellence; anything less is an improvement opportunity.
- Quality increases customer satisfaction, reduces cycle time and costs, and eliminates errors and rework.
- Quality isn't just for businesses. It works in non-profit organizations like schools, healthcare and social services, and government agencies.
- Results (performance and financial) are the natural consequence of effective quality management.

Copyright © 2003 American Society for Quality. All rights reserved.

If a leader or a manager really wants to improve the performance of his/her team, Quality initiatives are *the* answer. They are simple and effective.

KAIZEN

Kaizen is arguably the single most important management concept to be applied to the manufacturing sector in the past 50 years. *Kaizen* is the Japanese word for "continuous improvement." I like to add the word "incremental"—as I see the need to maintain small consistent improvements to ensure they are lasting. These improvements most directly apply to the processes involved in the work. I would therefore define *kaizen* as "continuous incremental improvement of the process."

The dramatic improvements in manufacturing productivity and quality over recent years can be attributed to *kaizen* in its many applications. TQC (Total Quality Control), TQM (Total Quality Management), hoshin, and 4S are all quality initiatives built on the *kaizen* concept.

Applying *kaizen* to the white-collar environment is a bit trickier than to a visible manufacturing process. Managers and service personnel have processes that are more random and harder to define. This is especially true when it comes to their personal work processes.

Yet, white-collar productivity is often very poor. Our IBT coaches find professional people, on average, waste about 50% of their time. This is not to say professional people do not work hard. They most often do. It is simply that they do not get nearly as much done as they could! How often have you arrived at the end of the day and looked at your To Do list to find few items done, and wondered where the day went?

I ask participants in my workshops how often they include tasks on their daily To Do list that if done would improve how they process their personal work. Seldom do people spend time on the things that would improve their work process! But when it comes to potential productivity improvement, there is no more fruitful potential than examining your own behavior in how you execute your work.

If you were to accept only this one concept from the book, and were to fully apply yourself to this concept, you could throw the rest of the book away and I would have succeeded in helping you become more organized and effective.

PEP—A PRACTICAL TOOL FOR QUALITY IMPROVEMENT

At one division in General Motors, a client said:

> *The quality gurus build awareness here, but PEP makes time management and organizational efficiency workable because it's done on the job, at the desk,* and this is practical.

The act of improving *how* you process your work will give you visible and immediate results. The results encourage you to extend your methods to other processes and give you the fortitude to continually improve these work processes until you achieve success. It also gives you the *time* to focus on improving the broader work processes.

4S

A Japanese approach to the subject of quality only recently coming to the attention of the West is called 4S. 4S is the label for:

Sei-li	Organization
Sei-ton	Orderliness
Sei-kez	Neatness
Sei-sou	Cleanliness

4S actually comes from the Chinese, but has been successfully copied and implemented by the Japanese. As described by Ingrid Abramovitch in an article entitled "Beyond *Kaizen*," in *Success* magazine (January/February 1994, p. 85), 4S goes beyond *kaizen*, the better-known quality concept of continuous improvement. *Kaizen* focuses on manufacturing processes, whereas 4S "takes a grass-roots approach, helping each individual to attain the highest level of personal effectiveness."

4S is a way of thinking and working. 4S is being aware of the need to be efficient, being aware of waste and the need to eliminate it, spending time to get things in order, looking for ways the work could be done better and acting to make it so, and cleaning up after oneself.

The basic philosophy of 4S is: to organize your materials and work space tools neatly; to execute the job in an orderly way; and to clean up afterward. In a company that has adopted 4S, everyone, from the chief executive officer (CEO) to the receptionist, applies 4S to their day-to-day work.

There is a process (how you do what you do) that needs to be addressed and improved if you are to do the right thing, now. You do this by concentrating on the components of 4S and bringing order to your environment and the way you work.

IDENTIFYING YOUR CUSTOMERS AND THEIR NEEDS

I run into an interesting phenomenon in delivering PEP. In conducting before-and-after surveys to establish measurements for success and to get feedback on our own work, I ask PEP participants how they have personally benefited from the program. Typically, 85% to 90% of our clients make excellent personal progress, and the results are more meaningful because they are so personal.

Another question we ask in the surveys concerns participants' perceptions of how their coworkers have done with PEP. At first the answers to this question were much more mixed. People told us, "Well, her desk isn't that clean anymore." "I still don't hear back from Sam fast enough." We found that PEP had made the participants more capable of accomplishing the things that were important to them, but they weren't necessarily meeting the needs of the people around them. Since that time we have asked the participants to find out what their coworkers expect and need and to make the satisfaction of those needs one of their objectives. It is a great success.

The lesson to be taken from this is that it's important not only to produce what you think is important but also to produce what others perceive as important to them. You have to find out from your colleagues, coworkers, all of your "customers," both internal and external, what they consider to be important. Not only does PEP enable you to know what your customers need, being well organized enables you to respond better to those customers' needs.

> *It takes less time to do something right than*
> *it takes to explain why you did it wrong.*
> —ANONYMOUS

BENCHMARKING

Benchmarking, the comparing of what you do with the best of a class, is a critical tool for improving quality. The comparison tells you how well you're doing and, usually, how to improve. The PEP process first defines excellent personal work systems and organizations and then provides that benchmark for individuals to compare how they process their own work.

Like the senior cashier in the Swedish bank, a select few in your group may develop efficient and effective ways to get their work done. Use these people as your own models. They are known as master performers. If there is a gap between your high and average performers, identify how your high performers execute their work and what behaviors allow them to produce better than their average coworkers.

FOCUS ON PREVENTION

PEP moves you from a reactive mode to a proactive mode. Putting good planning processes in place enables you to look into the future and prevent problems. It makes you aware of those red flags and indicators that could become fires in the future. Not only are you aware of them, but with a *Do It Now* frame of mind, you act on these things while they're manageable and you can prevent serious problems from occurring.

PROJECT-BY-PROJECT IMPROVEMENT

Joseph Juran, an American quality consultant who introduced management systems that plan, control, and improve quality, emphasizes the need to improve quality by using project-by-project improvement plans. Dr. Juran stresses that management's role is to provide planning and guidance to improve quality. Translating quality concepts into action at every level is management's job. Management's role is to help improve the skills and knowledge of its staff to plan work and accomplish actions that will improve quality and increase productivity.

CONTINUOUS CHANGE

People have a very difficult time dealing with change. And yet, continuous improvement is all about continuous change. Top executives can dictate but most effective managers prefer to involve their people.

Continuous change is hard to deal with if personal goals and desired end results are not clearly stated and regularly reviewed. Project management, time management, work space organization, follow-up, and follow-through are all components of continuous improvement.

From a PEP perspective, quality improvement has three main ingredients:

1. Identify what needs to be improved.
2. Plan out the actions to improve it.
3. Push the plans through.

QUALITY AND TEAM EFFECTIVENESS

There are a number of work processes that tend to be ignored by leaders trying to improve their teams' efficiency and effectiveness. A leader or manager can make big improvements by examining:

- How easy or difficult it is for the team to retrieve documents.
- The effectiveness of the group's meetings.
- How tasks are managed.
- How projects are run in the department.
- How planning is conducted by the group.
- How the team confronts difficult issues.

Our client experience tells us the place to start is identifying areas of waste and step by step eliminating them. The value of this approach is that team members end up working less, not more and are more inclined to tackle waste problems because it means less effort on their part in the end.

PEP AND REENGINEERING

Depending on the state of your personal organization, it may be necessary to do more than simply improve upon your existing work process. You may consider abandoning your old way of working and, usually with the help of new technology, substitute new ways of doing the work. In their book *Reengineering the Corporation* (HarperCollins Publishers, Inc., 1993), Michael Hammer and James Champy call this process "reengineering." Instead of getting a new paper calendar, you might consider using Outlook so others can access your calendar saving everyone time. Or instead of having a paper To Do list on the top of your desk, make it available to your team on a shared system (along with everyone else's) so all know who is working on what, when.

How do you identify what might be reengineered? Hammer and Champy suggest you must question why certain things are in place and question your assumptions and beliefs if you expect to make dramatic changes. To illustrate what some of your assumptions about personal work management might be, I'll use Hammer and Champy's belief/response/solution format from *Reengineering the Corporation.*

Belief: One has to operate on the basis of priorities.

Response: This is only partially true. I recommend you get rid of the little nagging things periodically and efficiently, since they make it very difficult to focus and concentrate on the real priority items.

Solution: Set up an efficient process to first eliminate the things you get that shouldn't even cross your desk. Secondly, process your day-to-day activities in an efficient and timely manner so you can concentrate the bulk of your time on the important priorities.

Belief: Planning is a waste of time because new things constantly come up and interfere with the plan, anyway.

Response: Without planning, you spin your wheels, have no direction, and do things out of sequence. The result is that things take much longer to do—so long that the time is consumed by other issues that catch up with you. If you are inefficient at the planning process it will take longer than it has to and discourage you from planning.

Solution: Identify key objectives you're responsible for and, with whatever tools you're most comfortable with (preferably a computer or other electronic solution), create specific project plans for each of them. This way, you can monitor and oversee the things you need to get done in an organized way. Make planning an efficient process.

Belief: If a cluttered desk equals a cluttered mind, what does a clean desk equal? The assumption is that to be creative one has to be disorganized and messy.

Response: Creativity does not depend on clutter. To get things done, you have to be well organized and have processes and systems in place to allow you to do that. Create creative time.

Solution: Organize your working environment so you have the time for creativity. Identify creative time and put yourself in an environment that is conducive for you to work creatively.

Belief: I'm too busy trying to get my job done. I can't afford to take the time to write everything down—it gets in the way of my work.

Response: All work has inherent in it a preproduction phase. To the degree that you have a clear picture of what it is that you need to do, you get it done faster and better. Writing things down forces you to articulate and get a clearer picture.

Solution: Schedule a time weekly as your organizing and planning time. Introduce that as part of your work systems and habits and test ways to make it as efficient a process as it could possibly be.

Belief: He went to college, so he should know how to handle his papers efficiently and work effectively in an office.

Response: Because people are educated does not guarantee they know how to work or they have good work habits. People on average waste up to 50% of their time due to poor work habits.

Solution: Place emphasis on the improvement of the personal work process. Put staff through a PEP type of program.

By examining your assumptions, you can begin to identify ways to do what you do differently or not at all.

REENGINEERING AND TECHNOLOGY

As mentioned previously, two of the major complaints I hear repeatedly are first, that too much time is consumed in meetings, and second, that people could finish their work if only *other* people would do their share of the project on time. Few old solutions to these two problems have ever worked. That makes both of these areas prime candidates for the reengineering process.

Imagine reducing meeting time by 75%.

Imagine people dealing with their share of the work concurrently so you didn't have to wait to be able to address your own work.

Technology has come to the rescue on these two very difficult and deep-rooted problems in the white-collar environment. Groupware software and shared databases now exist so people can communicate with each other on issues that previously would have required in-person meetings. Everyone can contribute information from their personal perspective through a personal computer (PC) network, cutting down dramatically on the need for face-to-face meetings and the time they waste.

I'm not saying that meetings will be eliminated completely. This is neither necessary nor desirable. Face-to-face human contact remains essential. But the ability to cut down on this time-consuming contact while substituting other, more efficient (and yet satisfying) ways of sharing this information can eliminate a major source of wasted time.

Another convenience you enjoy through networking and groupware is that you can share information with others at any time and not have to wait for a scheduled meeting or to get the person on the telephone line.

Much of the need for follow-up and the delays you face in completing the things you need to get done are wrapped up in how your work group may be organized. In *Reengineering the Corporation* Hammer and Champy state that the way to eliminate bureaucracy and flatten organizations is to reengineer processes so they are no longer fragmented.

Too often work is done sequentially. As an individual, you might finish one part of a project and have to wait for someone to finish a related part before you can begin working on the next step. Even if you use the parallel design process to overcome this particular problem, this method has its own problems. As described by Hammer and Champy, the parallel design process involves many people working on different parts of a bigger scheme at the same time. "Usually," say Hammer and Champy, "the subsystems will not fit together because, even though all the groups were working from the same basic . . . design, changes—often improvements—occurred along the way but were not communicated to the other groups. Then . . . it's back to square one in design." (p. 45) This dilemma is eliminated by having technology in place that facilitates and makes it possible for people to work concurrently on issues with knowledge about each other. At the same time, via technology, people are able to communicate any changes introduced so the consequences of those changes are immediately known to all involved.

In my experience in delivering PEP to thousands of people, most follow the route of continuous improvement of their existing processes. They are more comfortable introducing incremental changes and improving existing systems. But the dramatic gains available to you through PEP most often come when people take a radical and completely different point of view of how to address their work. These radical approaches almost always depend on the use of technology. The greatest gains from

PEP come to those who embrace the planning process and change how they do what they do and who put organization and planning at the forefront of their work. To really succeed with PEP, you have to put organization and planning into all of your routines in a complete way.

FOLLOW-UP FOR CHAPTER 6

1. PEP has the potential to be a critical success factor for you and for your company. PEP addresses how you process your work. It isn't enough to be proficient and technically skilled to do your work; you have to understand the principles of work organization and the application of these principles to your job.

2. Quality improvement concentrates on continuous incremental improvement of *existing* processes. Reengineering focuses on discovering and implementing completely different and *new* processes. You will find both methods useful in improving your personal productivity and the productivity of larger groups with whom you're associated.

3. PEP has the ability to help you with not only the things that are important to you as an individual but also the things that are important to the people around you. One of the objectives of PEP is to enable you to satisfy those expectations and needs, as well as your own.

4. Select a model you can use as a benchmark in improving your efficiency and effectiveness.

5. Examine your assumptions for misassumptions. You can then make the decision whether reengineering or quality improvement is the next step in improving any given work process.

6. If you lead a team and hope to improve their team performance, begin your own Quality initiative. Start by identifying the obvious areas of waste in the department. Using Juran's Project-by-Project technique act to eliminate these wasteful habits. Don't give up!

Do It Now!— From Wherever You Are!

The office is where you are—not where it is.
Work is something you do—not a place you go.

Chapter 7 Preview

In this chapter you will learn:

- A working definition of the Next Generation Workplace (NGW).
- Major trends of the NGW.
- Common issues companies face when first approaching the NGW.
- *Move* PEP—Information and tips to quickly transition to your NGW.
- Employee issues and solutions on learning to work in your NGW.
- Tips on working effectively in the NGW.

WHAT IS THE NGW?

EVOLVING WORK ENVIRONMENTS

Why Now?

At least since the 1970s, and probably for many years before, the business world has been seeking sound alternatives to what has evolved into Dilbert's Cubicles. Our clients have told us they have known for years that at any given time their office space was often thinly occupied by staff and they were paying fixed overhead, which depleted bottom-line profits. Clients also told us of their concern that employees often got into ruts, restricting their conversations and brainstorming the envelope to a repetitive and limited number of associates.

It now appears wherever you turn in the U.S. business community that alternative offices are being explored, embraced, and adapted. Why now at the beginning of the twenty-first century is this continuing to happen? One word—*technology*.

Technology has brought us portable computing, personal information managers, cell phones, wireless phones, pagers, e-mail, voice mail, instant messaging, satellite phones, both wired and wireless Internet and intranet, text messaging, scanners, and multifunctional devices. Each of these technologies has contributed to the distillation of the office culture or, as Dr. Frank Becker, of Cornell University calls it in his and Fritz Steele's benchmark book *Workplace by Design* (Jossey-Bass Publishers, 1995), the "workplace ecology."

In the 1970s, computers had to be housed in a good-size room, needing a special temperature and a humidity controlled environment. Today's portable computing gives us the ability to store and retrieve information (given that we correctly implement and practice effective organizational principles) from wherever we are, 24/7.

High-speed wireless technology has given us continual connectivity wherever we are. Now, there is an upside and a downside to all this. Just have lunch in any restaurant and you'll hear the ringing—the downside. Conversely, what great customer service it is to be able to respond to an urgent client from your car, an airport, or even when jogging—the upside. Today, you can do business without going to "the office." The cell phone, more than any other device, allows us to say, "The office is where you are—not where it is."

The entry of the wireless communication into the next generation of office space allows all-the-time and real-time accessibility to all employees within the office. Wireless phones work via a transmitter within a building allowing the phone to be with the employee, not requiring the employee to be fixed to where the phone is.

Connect the cell phone to voice mail and e-mail and there is even less necessity for employees to be locked into a specific workstation. Factor in the Internet/intranet coupled with instant messaging and it becomes even clearer how technological advances have changed the office of the 2000s, playing a linchpin role in the Next Generation Workplace (NGW). We can, because of technology, be wherever we need or want to be and still accomplish our work.

What Is a "Next Generation Workplace"?

Although change is a constant, the speed of change in the work environment, granted us by technology, has powered-up to net-speed with a variety of names. Within the United States the most used lexicon for these new work environments is Alternative Office or AO. In Europe the phrase of choice to describe evolving work environment is Flex Office.

Corporations have also identified this process by a wide variety of titles including Hewlett-Packard's Next Generation Workplace (NGW) and Ernst & Young's Workplace 2000. Additional widely used terms are *virtual, hoteling,* and *mobile office.*

We prefer to think of this workplace evolution as continuous generational steps and therefore have selected (our sincere thanks to Hewlett-Packard for allowing us to use it) the phrase "Next Generation Workplace (NGW)" as the one that most correctly describes the various paths of change being traveled by U.S. industry. Regardless of what the NGW is called, there is no doubt it is, and will always remain, a work in progress.

NGW space can be divided into five broad categories: free space, hoteling space, team space, drop-in/short-term space, and home office space. Which specific one or combination is best for an organization should be decided only after careful analysis by internal and/or external expertise.

1. *Free Space* is a first-come, first-served concept. No advance reservation is required, yet there is proactive assistance in stocking the work space with basic, standardized supplies. There are also office services support such as reproduction and mail. Exact attention to the communications and computer systems is, of course, necessary.

2. *Hoteling* is a prearranged, computerized reservation system similar to that of a hotel. Mobile staff can reserve a certain type of space for a specified time period. There are typically restrictions, by job function, as to which type of space can be reserved and for how long the space can be occupied with a single reservation.

3. *Team Space* is an area within the office environment that is to be collectively utilized for project development. Effective space design will build into the plan a variety of team spaces for both long-term and short-term use. Some team space is typically allowed to be reserved and other team space is always left available for impromptu collaboration.

4. *Drop-In/Short-Term Space* is designed to offer a quick visit for mobile staff who will usually not require more than a brief period of office time. This space is small, basically supplied, and easily accessible. Think of it as "just in time" space where no reservation is required.

5. *Home Office* is where staff work from home either routinely or electively. Both are proven concepts that are employed successfully by large and small organizations.

We have been participating in workshops dedicated to home officing since 1989. Although technology has changed, the basic structure of work and e-mail is the accepted norm of communication, and little has changed in the fundamental needs of individuals to home-office effectively.

Home office situations can be broadly divided into three basic types:

1. Small home-based business (easiest).

- Typically few employees.
- All information and decision making are at one source.

2. Entrepreneur (more difficult).

- Consultants, independent sales reps, writers—Lone Eagles.
- Work with few people at a time.
- Gather information from a wide array of sources.
- Used as a base to travel from.

3. Corporate employees (most difficult).

- Managers, administrative, staff consultants, sales.
- Interface with large groups of people.
- Large amount of information routinely exchanged with many.
- Many varied sources of information.
- Strong need to be connected to others.

All three types of home offices have two common denominators that must be addressed in order for them to work effectively. They are:

1. *Making choices with personal issues.* This is both a blessing and a curse. From a blessing side, you don't need to get dressed, put on makeup or shave, and spend time commuting. (See Figure 7.1.) No one can see what you look like when you're in your home. Well, not in most cases—but the widespread use of videoconferencing is on the way within the next few years. The core issue for both those who work in a home office environment and those who supervise home office workers is the *result of work,* not hours worked.

Since most of my associates and I are home office workers, I can tell you from firsthand experience that if anything, most home office workers work too many hours—not too few. "Measuring by results" both for the worker and management is the only thing that counts.

If a home office worker goes to her son's T-ball game for an hour or two—that's a wonderful quality of life improvement that can bring high return to an organization. Go to that game! (See Figure 7.2.) Yet make sure you establish typical working times so you get out of the office on time. I do so, and know that with the application of PEP habits and planning principles discussed throughout this book, other home office workers can also put in a fully productive, yet reasonable, workday.

2. Understanding that organizational systems and the control of information is a critical issue. If you are a corporate worker with a home office an hour or so away from the corporate facility, you can't afford to not have all the information you need to complete your work. Control and organization of both paper- and electronic-based information is critical to the effective accomplishment of work. Although the ability to move files and documents through the Internet as attachments is routine, it is still not easy to get assistance from others to share information. The reality is that there is a good chance the people you're looking

Figure 7.1 All the comforts of the home office.

to for assistance are also working at their home offices or are out of the office and not easily available at the moment you need them. Please note that if your using an instant need is an interruption to others, your lack of planning is not necessarily justification for barging in on them.

More than ever, we must take (read as *invest*) the time to plan, prioritize, and anticipate our future needs.

Go to the Source for NGW Knowledge

For the most complete reference to Next Generation Workplace and its nuances we suggest as mandatory reading Franklin Becker's and Fritz Steele's benchmark book *Workplace by Design*. The beauty of this book is that it was written some years ago and still has much relevance to today's business decisions.

Figure 7.2   Home office mom enjoying kids' sports during normal business hours.

Company Issues

IS YOUR COMPANY CONSIDERING A NEXT GENERATION WORKPLACE?

Having worked with more than 75 companies over the past 15 years helping them plan for and transition to a NGW, we've learned a great deal about what has worked and what hasn't—especially the success factors that must be in place to make the most out of a NGW implementation.

One of the most important points to recognize is "this is not simply a facilities issue." Of course, real estate costs, and the need to lower them, are normally the driving force of a NGW initiative. But there are many more disciplines required to make the most out of such an initiative. These should include IT, Communications, Administration, Human Resources, Personal Efficiency/Productivity, Change Managers, Operations (Management), and others as required. It is not uncommon for a client embarking on a NGW initiative to put together a work team comprised of these disciplines to precisely plan the proposed initiative.

Obviously, identifying what your people do and how they do it, then incorporating this data into your NGW plans is critical. Three groups in particular, Dr. Franklin Becker of Cornell University, and architecture and design firms Gensler and DEGW, specialize in just these kinds of studies providing clients with detailed information on the functions staff carry out and the kinds of NGW facilities best suited for these functions.

Based on our experiences assisting clients in their NGW initiatives, we have found ourselves assuming a number of roles that have tended to otherwise be overlooked. These include the following topics, which are discussed in detail in the balance of this chapter:

- Clarifying, understanding, and supporting the company's goals.
- Ensuring proper furniture selection and function.
- Defining management's role.
- Emphasizing the need for the proper equipment to support the NGW initiative.
- Establishing structural consistency of Information Organization.
- Key elements to a successful move.
- Being the Worker's Advocate.
- Immediate and long-term benefits of the PEP Move Process.
- Rules to help you move.
- Common issues and solutions to segue into and work effectively in the NGW.

Is One of Your Goals to Go Paperless?

For more than a decade we have heard the forecasting of a "paperless" business environment. This claim has been made by dozens of companies in myriad industries involved with the storage and transmission of information. Like the "checkless" society promised in the 1980s and described in *The Myth of the Paperless Office* by Abigail J. Sellen and Richard H. R. Harper (MIT Press, 2001), the paperless office is perhaps myth for the foreseeable future.

We believe the objective of heading toward a paperless society is more of a very slow evolutionary process than a rapid revolutionary event. Clearly it will be years before we become truly paperless and perhaps the better way of thinking about this paperless office is to rethink our goal and to target not at paperless but at PaperSmart.

ALCOA Corporation of Pittsburgh, Pennsylvania, addressed this issue with realistic thinking when they termed their NGW paper objectives as PaperWise. ALCOA has realized that this process is evolutionary and is continually taking steps down the road to become PaperWise not "paperless."

There is no doubt most of us are living with a foot in both worlds—the world of *molecules*, paper-based documents, and the world of *electrons*, computer-based information stored both as hard drive and e-mail documents. Quite frankly, we encourage the process of heading toward PaperSmart because it is much, much easier to manipulate information in the electronic-based world versus the paper-based world.

Let's face it, most information today is generated and stored by someone electronically. Factor into this thinking the scanner or "imaging" and virtually all information can be stored electronically.

Yet we can think of several good reasons to generate paper such as writing marginal comments, flipping back and forth between multiple pages, and sharing information with a group of people at a meeting. Conversely, we can think of very few reasons, mostly couched in legal rules or corporate policy that actually require storage of information in the paper-based format and these are disappearing rapidly.

How Do You Select the Proper Furniture so It Functions Best for Your Needs?

Hardware + Software Combined Properly = Effective Operating System

Companies typically will spend many thousands of dollars per employee for *hardware* (furniture) where people will be positioned to do work in the NGW environment. *This hardware is limited without effective software.* Our Personal Efficiency Program (PEP) is the *software* that will improve the ability of individuals, teams, and organizations to accomplish work in a consistently high-quality manner within a NGW environment.

The application of the PEP principles explained in other chapters in this book will provide you with the necessary skills to increase your productivity and effectiveness in a NGW environment, as well as throughout your entire business careers.

By improving organizational skills and gaining confidence in and control over the electronic-based environment, organizations have the opportunity to solve the problem of achieving a reduced physical volume and usage of paper-based information.

I have come to the realization that *successfully adapting to an alternative work space has as much to do with changing the way human beings work as it has to do with technological capabilities.*

The Architectural and Design Team (A&D). The Architectural and Design (A&D) firms are the teams of people who can best support the move to a NGW environment. Your choice of an A&D firm is the first crucial vendor decision you should make. And this decision, like most others, is a mix of rapport, trust, and intuition. The A&D firm's reputation with businesses of similar size and style to yours should be your primary criterion for selection.

We suggest that you first interview the firm as to its expertise in NGW concepts and designs. Clearly, all A&D firms have a working knowledge to aid in furniture selection. Yet only some are strategically skilled in understanding and implementing proper solutions to meet the immediate and long-range goals of a NGW environment.

After satisfying yourself that an A&D firm has NGW strategic skills, it is time for you to let your intuitive self come through. Keep in mind that you will be spending more hours than you can imagine with your A&D firm's project manager. As the old saying goes: "If it doesn't feel good—don't do it."

Form versus Function. Clearly, there is a need to have an eye-appealing, pleasant space to work within. Yet sometimes there is a tendency among those not working in the space to be overly concerned with the artistic appeal, that is, *form*, of the work environment while sacrificing the core element of an effective work environment, that is, *function*. (See Figure 7.3.)

At one of our technology clients, a member of the design team creating a shared office space environment was so concerned with the publicity photos to be taken of the finished project that he convinced the rest of the team to raise the height of the main work surface table within the office by 3 inches above normal desk height and the height of the other work surfaces to 32 inches high so this table would overlap other work surfaces in the office. Unfortunately, that additional height also made it difficult for many people to work at this table without getting back pain or adjusting the chair height many times throughout the

Figure 7.3   "Looks great! What does it do?"

workday. It also made moving easily from one work surface to another extremely problematic. Modern office chairs have been designed to be adjustable to meet the needs of a large range of people, not to be readjusted by an individual dozens of times in a given day.

Another client situation we encountered was with a manager having to make a choice between high panels, which allowed each worker to have overhead binder storage, and low panels, which would add visibility and eye contact between members of the group. The decision was not cut and dried. There were balancing considerations between the two choices. Yet the needs of the workers for space to store the many binders they had to work with daily should have weighted the decision to a functional choice that would allow for the needed binder storage. Instead, the low-panel height was chosen by management, who would not be working in the space. Now the administrative staff struggles daily with a shortage of storage space and the need to move binders around work surfaces. Both worker satisfaction, concentration, and productivity have been permanently reduced by someone who clearly was just a manager and not a leader.

After the dust settles from a move to a NGW environment, the most important thing to remember is that real people are going to be spending a lot of time doing serious work in this space. Because it is important that the space *works*, it is necessary to have a clear and careful balance between how the space looks (form) and how it works (function). Your NGW is a work space, not a showroom; it is a workplace.

Selecting a Furniture Vendor. For decades the office furniture industry has invested many hundreds of thousands of dollars and huge amounts of organizational time and manpower to move from being furniture (hardware) providers to becoming solution-based organizations who partner with their clients to develop NGW environments that accomplish their clients' needs.

Not all parts of the office furniture manufacturers' distribution channels typically "walk the talk." We continue to find that too often even some of the largest furniture providers' salespeople are still in the "selling desks and cubicles" mind-set. They continue to pay little attention to, or take adequate time to truly understand or offer solutions to their potential client's objectives. They simply offer cookie-cutter proposals.

We participated in meetings with an international client who had requested proposals from various office furniture providers. It was shocking that in the first years of the twenty-first century a team of people from one of the world's top three furniture manufacturers' response to this client was to offer as a proposal an overview of all their product lines and suggest (in the client's mind) that the client pick what they want.

In a similar meeting we saw that another major office furniture vendor had not listened very well. The client's objective was to begin alternative officing for their mobile professionals, with some form of free-space arrangement that would encourage serendipitous opportunities for collaboration. This manufacturer's solution was an arrangement of walled, cubical-type space that was 180 degrees away from the client's clearly stated goals and objectives.

These clients began their journeys toward their NGW with a high-quality, smaller vendor who actually listened to what the client wanted to achieve and proposed a solution that met our client's objectives. This furniture vendor, because they listened to and understood their client's objectives, now receives global business from these clients.

We have been most impressed with the recent progress of both Knoll and Teknion toward a solution-based approach to their clients.

Selecting a Seating Vendor. Purchasing chairs for the NGW should be a separate decision from the rest of the furniture hardware decisions. Chairs are very personal and can directly affect both productivity and quality.

The chair selection process is an excellent time for strong employee involvement. After the financial decision of price range has been made, we recommend that several vendors be requested to bring the chairs, within the decided price range and selected colors, to either the mock-up area (more about this soon) or a special room where employees can "kick the tires" to their hearts' content. (See Figure 7.4.)

Either a vote can be taken for style and vendor or even better, let the staff select their own chairs and forget about uniformity, which actually accomplishes little in the broad scheme of things.

MANAGEMENT'S ROLE IN A SUCCESSFUL MOVE—LEADERSHIP

We have compiled the following list of elements to help ensure success from our over a decade of involvement with hundreds of organizations

Figure 7.4 Let employees "kick the tires."

and thousands of people who have moved to next generation work-places. Most of this list rightfully focuses on management's role in the process. By following these guidelines, you will generate the highest probability of a successful move.

- Management must have visual, vocal, hands-on involvement in the move process. People follow people who lead by example—not talk.
- Move preparation instructions and training must be time-lined into the move plan for both individuals and teams.
- Double bookings for participants in any training/communications program related to the move cannot be allowed. Management at *every* level should be aware of the move schedule and related training activities and should not make other appointments for training participants.
- Senior management must convey, as often as necessary, to their management that they have 100% permission to participate in all training programs to prepare for the NGW.
- All levels of management must convey to their staffs that they have 100% permission to participate in all training to prepare for the NGW.

THE MISSING LINK—PROPER EQUIPMENT TO SUPPORT THE NGW INITIATIVE

Every employee in the NGW needs to have the proper equipment in order to be productive and effective. In most situations, the proper equipment means a reasonably current PC or laptop with current versions of the organization's operating system such as Microsoft's outlook or Lotus' Notes as well as the organization's correct tools for off-line storage, such as read-write CDs, zip drives, jazz drives, printers, fax machine or modem, cell phone, instant messaging systems, and reproduction capabilities. These types of equipment are usually considered normal fare in an office. The move to the NGW requires alignment and upgrading as necessary of this equipment to best support the employees' new work mode. However, the technology tool that was missing when we first wrote about this subject in 1998 and still appears to be *the missing link* to most offices wanting to come closer to being PaperSmart is the *scanner*.

One of the most often heard comments from the people we work with is, "I have to keep this document/information in my files because it's not available electronically." We then ask if scanners are available. Too often, the answer is still "No," "We're thinking about getting them," or "There is one in the next department."

The scanner provides an important component to solving the paper/paperless issue. Virtually all information, including old typewritten letters, pictures, magazine articles, and personal handwritten notes can be converted into electronic data.

We urge organizations and individuals wanting to move toward an electronic environment to make scanner usage an integral part of their process. Scanner technology has come a long way over the past decade and the scanner is now as easy and reliable as the printer. Yet by all means do your due diligence and get the right one for the jobs that need to be accomplished.

Many companies for statutory or other reasons must keep hard copies of selected documents. Even these can be scanned and posted on a secure intranet site (typically requiring special access protected by user name and password) for ease of access.

It is most important to remember that with scanned documents, as with all other electronic documents, the core issue still remains how to organize and store information so it can be quickly retrieved when it is needed.

Moving to the NGW

PEP AND THE MOVE TO THE NGW

IBT has been involved in helping companies move to NGW environments for almost two decades. From this wealth of experience we know how important PEP is as part of the process for moving to NGW. Yet our most critical measurement of the value of PEP as an integral part of the successful move into NGW space comes from client feedback.

One such client was located in the northeastern section of the United States. After reviewing the PEP process and how it approached the move from the individual human viewpoint, this client said, "You are what we have been looking for—*PEP is the missing link in our process!*"

Another client, located in the western United States, after conducting a post-move focus group told us that *"100% of the people who went through the MOVE PEP Program believed it was an absolutely integral"* part of the success of their move process."

PEP AND THE MOVE PROCESS

There are certain core components that must be addressed whether the move is an office of a few people across a hall or that of an entire corporation moving across the country. Most of these components address the Big Picture issues of the move, such as overall floor plans, electronic information systems, and communications systems.

Our work clearly indicates that if equal attention is not paid to the Small Picture, such as how staff members will respond to the move, the seeds of a nightmare will be sown, while the seeds of opportunity are wasted.

The single most neglected Small Picture issue in the NGW move process is the *individual* needs of people. Many times the human factor requirements are not addressed. Attention to helping individuals prepare, pack, and unpack are virtually nonexistent. It is imperative to address these concerns as a proactive, ongoing process before ordering furniture and finalizing move dates.

We were recommended to a large U.S. financial services organization by their A&D firm because after they had moved, the staff could not work in the new office. After meeting with senior managers and staff, we understood that core Small Picture issues had simply not been addressed in advance. Some of the issues causing dysfunction were:

- Managers who were out of the office for many hours of every week occupied the "window space" offices, while administrative staff who were in the office for every minute of every week were placed in the interior of the building with no outside view.
- Filing space was assigned solely by rank with no consideration to job function.
- Left- or right-handedness was given no consideration in either the assigned or unassigned space design. (See Figure 7.5.)
- Consideration as to flexibility of space relating to individuals' physical size was not factored into the planning process.

Figure 7.5   The workplace should be designed to make it easy for the individual to produce.

- Helping the individual staff through the move process was left to chance, with no in-place support or training.
- Speaker phones were still being used in a low-panel, open space environment.

THE KEY TO SUCCESS—STRUCTURAL CONSISTENCY OF INFORMATION ORGANIZATION

One of the important lessons of PEP, which is discussed in detail in Chapter 2 of this book and my book *Hi-Tech PEP*, is the basic premise that the ability to *find* information is one of the most critical factors in beginning to do work. (See Figure 7.6.)

Two elements that need to be thought through as part of preparation for NGW are:

Figure 7.6   "Where is that file?"

1. How do we organize information so we can find it when we need it?
2. How do we keep and organize information in both electronic- and paper-based formats?

In various reports over the years, Accountemps Inc., a California-based temporary agency, reported in a survey of their clients that executives and their assistants spent an average of *4.3 hours per week* looking for information they couldn't find. Our own survey indicated the average PEP participant in the United States reported they were spending, prior to learning the PEP process, 1.8 hours per week looking for information they couldn't find.

Clearly, both of these surveys indicate too much time is being wasted because of the inability to easily find information we believe we have. We work too hard and have too many things, both personal and business, we can do with our valuable time other than to spend it looking for things we can't find. Ask yourself, "What would I do with another 100 hours per year?" After you answer this question, I am sure you will want to seriously improve your organizational system and control of information.

Most of us ask, "Where are we going to *file* this electronic- or paper-based information?" The correct question to ask ourselves, given it will be some time before we will again want a specific piece of information, is "When I next need this, where will I logically go to look for it and easily be able to *find it?*"

REMEMBER: INFORMATION LOSES VALUE IN TIME

A usual key objective in the design of a NGW environment is to reduce the amount of space used for storage of paper-based information. This is both a necessary and realistic goal for segueing to a NGW environment. Our research shows that more than 50% of the paper and electronic information people are keeping has lost all *value* and should be discarded or deleted. The overriding reason we should be keeping information is we have determined it cannot easily be retrieved from any other place.

During the late 1990s and earlier, printed information, primarily because of the cost of producing and distributing paper, kept value for months if not years. Today information can easily and inexpensively be updated and distributed. This speed of information update and distribution often has the effect of rendering valueless what was new and current just days ago. In order to maintain what has value, and discard what has lost its value, we need a process for organizing information that serves us well as a self-sustaining methodology.

To find or not to find—that is the question.

MOLECULES OR ELECTRONS? ONE—NOT BOTH

For centuries, we have become accustomed to having important information documented on paper (molecules). Only recently (primarily through e-mail and electronic documents) has written communication come in the form of electrons. It is easier to manipulate electrons than molecules. And to control and manipulate electrons into a high-powered information retrieval system is the only way to work effectively in the NGW world.

A senior vice president of marketing at one of our clients receives more than 300 e-mails per day. This individual had his administrative support print out all 300 e-mails and then file this paper in file cabinets. (We have heard similar stories dozens of times over the years.) After going through the Move PEP Process, this individual, who understood how electronic *systems worked* but not how to *work the system*, stopped this time-consuming and useless habit of keeping electronically available information in a paper-based world. Not only did he recover a great deal of time for both himself and his support person, but he stopped contributing to a paper buildup of about one inch per day— that's approximately 220 inches (that's about one 42-inch-wide lateral file cabinet) of information per year.

And perhaps more important, after some investigation of his files, we uncovered that he was not only printing and saving e-mails—he was printing and saving *everything* from his computer in a paper-based format. The core issue was that this individual had no confidence that he could *find* anything in his computer. (How to organize your electronic and paper information is explained in Chapter 2 of this book, as well as my *Hi-Tech PEP* book.)

After learning through PEP how to organize information so he could find it in his computer, he made an effective business decision to discard more than 80% of the paper he was keeping.

Most important to our NGW discussion is that this individual (a senior vice president) went from an absolute belief that he could not function in the NGW world to an individual who is now leading his staff and influencing his company through change into a new and more effective way of working.

KEY ELEMENTS FOR A SUCCESSFUL MOVE

Involve the Employees in Much of the Decision Making

The successful move has key elements included in it to assure the expected outcomes. There is, perhaps as a preamble to a successful move to a NGW, the need to establish a linkage between employee expectations and corporate expectations in the NGW.

A process needs to be established where all employees end up having a clear understanding of how the entire facility is going to be equipped and function. No one should expect a gym, a barbecue area, or showers unless their facility will have them.

Another important pre-move process is setting protocols on how people work in an open environment. The Move Team leadership, through role playing and facilitating dialog, can gain group consensus and buy-in from staff that people can no longer eat noisy food such as potato chips or smelly food such as a sardine sandwich, or shout into a speaker phone without negatively affecting the focus and productivity of others in the group.

Critical Facilities Issues

1. An ergonomically time-based paper-management configuration should be in place and operating within the current space before any individual planning or packing for the new office begins. Employees who have effective time-based office processes routinely operating in their current space can easily transfer these efficient processes to the NGW environment.

2. Knowledge of what one's space looks like and where it is located within the new office plan will allow people to *mentally* familiarize themselves before the actual move.

It is important to create drawings that show detailed plans and views of individual types of work space. These drawings, called *typicals*, should be detailed and include every storage unit's dimensions, the number of shelves, the filing format options (front-to-back or side-to-side), and the number of filing inches for the individual components. Each employee should get a typical drawing of their work environment months before the move begins. (See Figure 7.7.)

3. Part of any furniture buying decision should include a provision that the selected vendor will deliver and install one or more *mock-up* models of the new work space for employee examination and understanding. (Manufacturers routinely provide mock-ups. This mock-up should be available until after the move.)

If you are reconfiguring existing furniture, the same rule applies; a "real" mock-up should be constructed and made easily available to all employees.

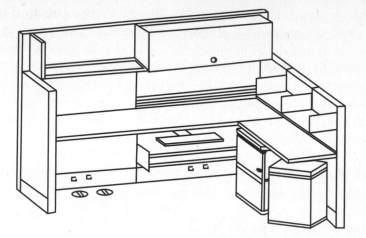

Figure 7.7 Provide a drawing of what their new workspace will look like. Including filing space allocation for all components.

This mock-up will prove to be a valuable asset to the move process. You should insist upon and contractually agree with your furniture provider that all elements of the mock-ups and typicals will be complete and exactly as they will appear in the new office environment. Effective planning requires that mock-ups contain the *exact* components that are *identical* to those of the new office space.

It is recommended that the mock-up be installed in a central position for continuous, easy access by all employees so they visit often before the move. People should sit in the chair and envision where they will position their working files, reference files, binders, manuals, supplies, personal items, and individual mementos. Managers should schedule their teams to visit the mock-ups together so they can collaborate on team storage and filing issues.

Recently, we saw furniture mock-ups at NCR's headquarters' cafeteria in Dayton, Ohio—what a great place for easy mass accessibility!

In ALCOA's move to its Corporate Center, in Pittsburgh, Pennsylvania, their furniture provider, Herman Miller, placed mock-ups of their new furniture system in the lobby of ALCOA's existing building for months before the move. This gave all employees ample time to routinely and casually review and understand what type of furniture they were moving to.

Technion, Hewlett-Packard's furniture provider in their Orlando, Florida, site put complete mock-ups right in the work areas of their current office so all employees could "kick the tires."

Some years ago when Owens-Corning moved to a new campus in Toledo, Ohio, they took an extra step. They had Steelcase, their furniture provider, install mock-ups in the lobby area of their existing building and went a step further by employing Williams Marketing of Grand Rapids, Michigan, to generate a complete communications module, including having the mock-ups displayed so all employee questions or suggestions about the furniture, or any other issue regarding the new environment, could be recorded and answered.

4. Blocking out time, prior to the move, to purge old files is an *investment in success*. This is also the time to update the filing system to one that is time based. There is no value in moving outdated or never-used documents. Eliminating the valueless papers before the move will accelerate the process of getting up and running in the new environment.

This point became apparent to us in early 1993 when we were hired by a major aerospace client in Santa Monica, California. As with so many other client engagements, we simply matched calendars and established a start date for their PEP Program.

During the first day of the typical PEP Program the participants are asked to go back to their workstations and implement the organizational process explained in the classroom portion of the Program. After about an hour they started a usual and expected "*Wow*" response to the pleasure of the clutter-busting and clarity brought about by the PEP organizational system.

We, of course, responded how pleased we were that everyone was grasping PEP so well. The client then told us we didn't understand something. This department had just moved the week before we started their PEP Program. They had the obligatory throw-away pizza party (which really doesn't work very well) and had tossed out a lot of junk. *Now they were throwing away 50%+ of what they had moved only days ago.* (See Figure 7.8.)

We routinely survey all participants of our PEP Program involved with moves to find out their throw-away factor because of the PEP principles they learned. Conservatively, they report discarding 50% of what they were keeping in the paper-based world. We have also found that this discard figure, on average, equaled 84 inches of paper, weighing about 150 pounds.

A specific example of this figure showed itself in our survey of Ernst & Young's Los Angeles office move to their Workplace of the Future in 1999, which indicated a cumulative discard result of

Figure 7.8 Eliminate valueless papers *before* the move.

50.8%. This figure of 50.8% recovered file space is typical of client results even today!

5. Converting from legal-sized filing systems should be done at the time of the move to a NGW. The old paradigm held that certain professions or businesses used legal-sized filing systems because most of their records were in $8\frac{1}{2}$" × 14" format. That's simply not the case today; in recent years there has been a continual movement toward letter-sized, $8\frac{1}{2}$" × 11" documents and almost completely doing away with the legal-sized format. Ironically, this trend is occurring even in the legal community. Letter-sized documents are a good idea because of the cost-savings in filing equipment and supplies. Moving to a NGW is an ideal time for an organization to convert from legal- to letter-sized filing.

6. Although it is important for all employees to be involved in the proactive planning of their personal move (see Figure 7.9), it is of paramount importance for all levels of management to be visibly involved in their own personal move process. We cannot state often enough that visual and vocal involvement of management in the move process will directly affect the outcome of the move of everyone in the organization.

Figure 7.9   Involve all employees in move planning.

We worked with an international firm who was moving to a NGW. One of their more senior managers was unhappy about this change in work space and decided to show his disdain by planning a business trip while the rest of the organization was getting ready to move.

Our input was that this business trip was not a necessity and could have waited until after the move. This manager told his administrative support person to "just move him." As much as he had the authority to tell his support person to do all the packing for him, he perhaps did not have the right to have her do this for him. It was simply a lousy business decision and a prime example of the difference between management and leadership. The administrative person did not know what to keep or what to throw away, where it was going to go in the new office, or what personal files should be packed to go to the manager's home.

As in any other organization, word of this event got around to everyone on the manager's team, thereby prompting comments like, "If he can do this, so can I." And most did in one way or another. The result was that almost every team within this organization, who followed the PEP principles of moving, were up and running in minutes. This was in sharp contrast to this wayward manager's team, which took weeks to get organized. The related lack of productivity and shortfall in client service can never be fully recovered.

ADVANTAGES OF THE PEP MOVE PROCESS

The investment of time, energy, and money in proactive attention to the individual in the move process brings multiple forms of return to organizations.

The *immediate benefits*, which will be experienced within the first day after the move, are:

• The move becomes a nonevent for all those moving. It's over in minutes. (See Figure 7.10.)
• Work and file space footprints are reduced in conforming with organizational goals.
• The NGW is adapted to by all quickly and easily.
• Cultural protocols of the NGW are embraced.
• Information exchange is more frequent and spontaneous.
• Control of information is improved.
• Electronically available information is not kept in paper format.

Figure 7.10   The move became a nonevent.

Many *long-term benefits* will begin to emerge a short time after the move. They are:

- Personal productivity and effectiveness are increased for the balance of all of the employees' careers.
- Organizational productivity and effectiveness are increased for the long-term.
- Information organizational processes are improved on a self-sustaining basis.
- Client service is improved and client expectations are met.
- Stress levels are reduced.
- Time is recovered to do more of the right work.

RULES TO HELP YOU MOVE

1. *Organize* your files before you move.
2. *Review* every file. Look for duplicate copies and outdated files.
3. *Know* why you are keeping something. Ask yourself, "If I need this information, where can I easily get it?" *not* "Will I ever need this again?"
4. *Do Not Keep or Duplicate Files* when you know someone else within your organization can quickly provide you with the information.
5. *Carefully Review* the layout of your work space within the NGW.
6. Put into *one* moving box only what will go into *one* file drawer or storage shelf.
7. *Label* each box to identify into which drawer, shelf, or part of a shelf its contents go in the NGW.
8. *Make a List* of the contents of each packing box. Tape a copy of this list to the moving box.
9. *Identify* critical items you will need the first morning after the move, place them in a Special box or briefcase, and take them home.
10. *Completely Empty* the entire contents of each moving box into the correct preidentified drawer or shelf in the NGW.

WORKING WITHIN THE NGW

WELCOME TO WORKING IN THE NGW WORLD

Working in the NGW is different from working in the traditional world. The issues we encounter and the solutions to these issues can broadly be broken into four separate areas. They are Managerial and Support, Company Office, Home Office, and Mobile Office. Although the following discussion is divided among these four areas, please understand that there is duplication and overlap that may occur between these issues.

MANAGERIAL AND SUPPORT EFFECTIVENESS

Out of Site—Not Out of Mind

Managing staff in the NGW requires a clear understanding that workers are not measured by the amount of time they occupy space within view of their manager. They are, rather, measured by the results of their work.

The true measure is *did the work get done on time in a quality manner? Were the customer needs and expectations met or exceeded? And was the work accomplished in keeping with the company's goals and policies?* If the answer to these three questions is yes, then the work was done correctly and positively.

Feedback for a job well done is in order. This is another difference that separates leadership from management.

This issue of managing and measuring staff productivity and effectiveness has been written about for decades. If you are involved in a situation as either virtual staff or management, you might contact your Human Relations, Organizational Development, or Change Management team for professional guidance.

Help—Where to Go and What to Do

Without question, technological developments have created a new need—Help! Organizations have designed the Help Desk to support staff with the use and fixing of all the electronic tools we use in our high-tech world.

We have worked closely with the Information Technology (IT) groups from dozens of companies. The Help Desk staffs we have worked with are extremely dedicated to helping you, their customer, keep your electronic tools working correctly. These folks all have specific areas of expertise. They can either solve problems over the phone, or in person, or they know where to go to get the information needed to help you.

Universally, the main gripe of the Help Desk team is that *we wait way too long to call them for help.* There is a bad tendency on most of our parts to believe that small technology problems will go away. They will not. If anything, small problems, which could have taken minutes to fix, have exploded into large problems with the resulting grief and aggravation of hours of wasted time and unneeded stress.

If ever the *Do It Now!* principle applied, it is with electronics. So the next time you even suspect you should call the Help Desk for assistance with your electronic tools—*Do It Now!* Do not allow yourself to procrastinate and you will reduce the possibility of small problems, with short time-lines, becoming serious crises with long time-lines.

COMMON ISSUES FACED WORKING IN THE NGW

Individual Issues

1. *Use of electronic calendars.* Years ago when I first entered the working world, I became part of a yearly ritual—choosing a calendar. My choices were typically centered around what size calendar and what format calendar I should buy for the next year.

I used small, pocket-sized calendars that fit into a jacket pocket and large format calendars that only fit into a briefcase. I tried calendars with a major focus on either a daily, weekly, or monthly format. All of these formats had their advantages. The Daily view gives you minute details of the day's events and ample space to write in. The Weekly view gives you a broader look at the workweek and aids in short-term planning, while allowing sufficient room to write. The Monthly view gives a wide view of downstream events and allows effective planning, though it offers very limited space to write in.

Even Steven Covey in his best selling book, *The Seven Habits of*

Highly Effective People (Simon & Schuster, 1989) devotes some pages worrying through what type of calendar is best.

With an electronic calendar all of this daily, weekly, and monthly decision making stuff disappears. An electronic calendar, which at a keystroke, can move between a daily, weekly, and monthly view is the only way to work in the NGW. There is unlimited availability of space to record meetings with others, appointments with yourself to do your own work, and all the space you could ever want to record all reminders, to-dos, follow-ups, thoughts, and notes.

Additionally, in an electronic calendar all actions entered are designated, usually by color, as current, future, and past due. Your noted actions will follow you until you do something with them, such as mark them complete, move them to a future date, or trash them. There is no need to ever again rewrite reminders or to bring them forward to new pages of paper.

Of course, like paper, you have to *Do It Now* to have the correct prompts or cues for future actions on your part.

Electronic calendars, regardless of the brand, also have the capability to store various databases such as tasks or to-dos and contact information. This is most helpful since we know people move residences, work locations, and phone numbers with amazing frequency.

It does not matter if you are working from a PC or notebook. You can always print a paper calendar (there are many formats from which to select) for current use while you travel. Remember, it's okay to print a calendar for this purpose since it's for short-term usage and not for storage.

2. *Use of a PDA.* Personal digital assistants (PDAs) are small, handheld, electronic devices that essentially do everything an electronic calendar does.

The elements that make these palm-sized devices clever is that they sync through a "docking" device so you can transfer information between the PC or notebook and the handheld device. They also allow information, via infrared, to be transferred between devices.

PDAs are certainly the device of choice in the NGW. We applaud and encourage the move toward complete electronic mobility.

3. *Administrative paperwork and less support*—Do It Now! Okay, so you and the rest of us don't like doing paperwork. Never have, never will! It's okay not to like paperwork, but there are some things we need to accept.

First, the world of administrative support has been evolving for years. When we first started working with U.S. companies in the late 1980s, virtually every executive with the title of vice president or higher had a dedicated, excuse the ancient word, secretary. As we entered the early 1990s, we saw this one-to-one support relationship change to one administrative person for multiple executives.

Second, the computer has changed the way we work and the type of work we do. Recently, we were working with a major service industry client. The senior person (with some gray hair) in one group routinely had his administrative support person fill out his expense reports. His second in command (with no gray hair), did her own expense reports on her computer. Different styles, perhaps, but more importantly, continually changing work styles. Today, executives and managers write their own letters and use support staff to perhaps edit and generate final versions for distribution. Quite a change from the ancient days of dictation machines and shorthand stenographers.

Third, we strongly suggest that you always follow the PEP rule "Do the Worst First." Most of us put off things we don't like to do and don't get around to them until there is a crisis. We tend to fill time by taking longer to do the things we like to do to avoid the things we don't like to do. This is tremendously inefficient and adds unneeded stress.

At the beginning of the day ask yourself, "What are the *worst things* I have to do right now?" and then do them. Ask yourself the same question about an hour or two before you close the day and again, *do them!* This a powerful method for quickly getting paperwork and other less-enjoyable tasks out of the way.

4. *Organization and maintenance of paper and electronic files.* In the NGW environment, command of information is paramount. In other parts of this book there are complete models on how to organize your information for rapid retrieval. There is no shortcut; you must make appointments with yourself, placed on your calendar, to complete your organizational system in both the paper and electronic worlds.

After you have organized your information into a system that permits you to know where everything is all the time, it is now necessary to *maintain* the integrity of your information. Moving information to proper parts of your organized system and deleting information that has *lost value* is crucial to managing the rapidly changing world we live in.

Information is the DNA of knowledge! If our information is incomplete, so, too, is the knowledge we generate from that information. Investing in routine maintenance of your information on a scheduled basis is the *key* to maintaining trust in your information retrieval system.

Our advice is to schedule appointments on your calendar at monthly, quarterly, semi-annually, and yearly intervals to perform maintenance and implement improvements to the organizational systems of your paper- and electronic-based information.

5. *Need to keep, maintain, and use more electronic information.* In the NGW we can only predict that we will be in ever changing physical situations. We are best served by having the information we need to do our work stored in a mobile electronic format.

Most people tell us that they keep paper because they are afraid they cannot find information easily in their computers. By following the PEP organizational principles, which are based upon time and predictability of retrieval, coupled with proper maintenance, you will be able to find what you need in your computer all the time.

6. *Printing paper for usage—not for storage.* Do not create paper from your computer system for the purpose of filing it away. I can think of many good reasons to print paper information, most of which centers around sharing information with a group, needing to read many pages, and comparing one page of information to another. These are all excellent reasons to generate paper copies from electronic sources. However, from the generation of this paper routinely comes new knowledge that is created in an electronic format. So there is no need to keep the papers that have been printed, for any significant length of time.

One of our clients decided to measure the value of paper. She was conducting a meeting for a group of 10 people. In order to best share information she printed many copies of letters and reports to distribute to the group. When the meeting was about to end, she advised everyone where the paper information could be found on their network. She then told everyone to leave behind any papers they did not think they would need. More than 80% of the paper she generated was left in the meeting room and then taken to the recycle bin.

Team Issues

1. *Keeping track of where everyone is.* In the NGW many of us will work in a virtual team environment. Team members could be almost anywhere doing work, from anyplace in the country or at their home offices. Sometimes the need to find someone quickly is the difference between winning or losing a sale. We must employ effective techniques to keep track of each other. Keeping track of each other in the NGW demands both common sense and creative thinking.

The most effective overall organizational way of keeping track is to use a network calendar with everyone's schedule available to everyone else. This demands both diligence and responsibility by everyone in the organization. Make it a cultural protocol agreement that everyone will input into their electronic calendar complete information as to their future activities.

On more than one occasion individuals have asked me what to do about very private appointments such as a doctor or job interview. My best advice is that you write into the calendar only general notations of these types of appointments. Also, most current calendar systems allow you to mark appointments as Private. This process keeps your personal life personal, yet allows you to give information to others from which they can make business decisions that affect their ability to continue to do their work.

Another way of keeping track of each other is to have weekly meetings. One of the activities at this meeting is for everyone to give a brief update of their schedule for the coming week. In the NGW this meeting does not have to be face-to-face. It can be a telephone conference call.

When working in Hong Kong with our client Hewlett-Packard, one of the PEP participants told me tomorrow was his late day for getting into the office. He went on to explain that he was part of an international team with members in Asia, Australia, North America, South America, and Europe. This team talked by prearranged weekly conference calls. The meetings began at 11:00 P.M. Hong Kong time because it was determined that everyone around the world could reasonably be awake to participate in the meeting. These meetings lasted two to three hours. If this worldwide team could figure out how to have everyone present, most us who work in closer proximity can also schedule teleconferences to keep in touch.

2. *Organization and maintenance of both paper- and electronic-based team files.* Team information is a little trickier to organize and maintain than are individual records because it requires promises, commitment, follow-through, and feedback from all members of the team.

However, in the NGW, it is clearly necessary for information to be available to all members all the time.

Naming conventions for both paper and electronic files must be established at a team meeting called specifically for that purpose. It may take more than one meeting to iron out what everything will be titled and where it will be stored. This work is not an expense of time; it is an investment in the team's ability to do its work effectively.

Basically, the naming convention process is very similar to the creation of a hierarchical outline. This hierarchical outline is what most of us did when we wrote our first term paper in our junior year in high school. It is a subject-focused outline, which proceeds from macro to micro topics.

We have facilitated client team meetings where these issues have been decided. Once the team gets focused on the issue of *finding*, not filing, the process proceeds quite smoothly.

As the team creates its hierarchical outline, it is also the time for team members to volunteer or be assigned the responsibility for filing and maintaining sections of the files. Everyone in the team must promise to maintain his section of the files on a real-time basis.

If members of the team do not keep their promises, it must be part of the routine of team meetings to give feedback to those who are not doing their file maintenance responsibility that they are hurting the team. This open, honest, nonconfrontational feedback will have great influence in supporting team members to keep their commitments.

Since the NGW is currently a world of both paper- and electronic-based information, the previous discussion applies to both file areas. My view is that the electronic world is actually an easier place in which to maintain information. Drag and drop ability, the rename function, and the Delete key make moving electrons a heck of a lot easier to manipulate than molecules.

3. *Need to be prepared to share and give away knowledge.* In the net-speed world of the NGW it is not possible as well as not necessary for any of us to know everything about what is going on all the time. It is also not possible or necessary for everyone to know everything about how our electronic tools work.

The NGW requires we routinely share information with others. The sharing of information should be continuous and spontaneous. As we acquire information we should, without others asking, advise our peers and team members of what we have learned.

In the NGW we need to be bold and ask questions without fear of showing our lack of knowledge about issues. In my working with teams of people from all segments of the public and private sector I have found it amazing that almost all answers to all the questions everyone has about technology are known—we simply are not asking questions. There are no dumb questions *except* for the ones we do not ask. Ask your question in a room of 20 people and it is probable that your question about information or technology will be answered or someone knows a source for the answer to your question. Ask technology questions, and you will be amazed at how many answers are immediately available.

Voice Mail

1. *Keep it short—one minute.* The real world is that you will get voice mail when you make a phone call, so plan what you are going to say before you make the call, and then say it in the shortest amount of words possible. My feeling is most voice mail messages are twice as long as they need to be.

You also have a responsibility to influence others to improve their message leaving skills because it is not only you who is being left long messages; everyone is being left long messages by these individuals.

One of our clients recently cut their recordable message length from three minutes to two minutes. They repeatedly advised the entire organization of the change before implementing the shortening of the message length to two minutes. They quickly found that messages could easily be left in shorter time.

In the NGW business world of this client where *you are either fast or last* the time savings among 15,000 people receiving 20 messages each per day was phenomenal—somewhere in the area of 500,000 hours of time saved per year for the entire organization.

2. *Hate it or love it—use as appropriate.* People who like to receive information by *listening* tend to love voice mail. People who like to receive information by *reading* tend to hate voice mail and love e-mail.

The best way I know how to determine whether to communicate with an individual via voice mail or e-mail is to *ask them*. They will immediately share with you their preferences and expected response time to your messages. Teams of people must agree how they will communicate as a prerequisite of working effectively. Set information exchange protocols on a *Do It Now* basis upon the formation of the team and you will avoid communication crises.

3. *Proper use of Urgent/Priority—Don't Be Chicken Little.* One of my associates who started his business career as a salesperson for a major hi-tech company told me this story. When he was in training, one of the factory guys told him that every order marked Urgent was ignored and put into the normal production run. The factory felt every order was urgent and without specific justification they could not take any special action.

We essentially hear the same complaints from members of NGW teams. Some team members mark every message Urgent/Priority and they are simply ignored. If you want your true Urgent/Priority notice to be heeded, then use it sparingly and for important reasons.

If a member of your team is using Urgent/Priority incorrectly, it is incumbent on you to advise him of the error of his ways. He's hurting himself and every member of the team.

4. *Got the number?—Leave It Twice.* In the NGW we can never be sure where someone is when they are listening to voice mail. They may be in a car, walking along in an airport corridor, or doing other tasks while perusing voice mail. Help them out by leaving your number twice, one immediately after announcing yourself at the beginning of the message and then again, slowly, at the end of the message.

Oh yes, if you're driving alone and listening to voice mail, please *Do It Now* and *pull over to the side of the road before you start writing notes.*

E-Mail

In just a few short years e-mail has gone from the *promise* of business to the *problem* of business. More has been written about e-mail than any other business tool issue. Most of these articles center around e-mail abuse and misuse. In the NGW we do not have the time to have poor e-mail habits among the teams we work with. Following is a list of the rules we have found most useful from working with NGW clients.

- *Messages*—Process all within one day or establish a response time protocol among team members.

- *Folders/Categories*—Create new ones as necessary to assure effective retrieval.
- *Action/Follow-up Items*—Restricting yourself to one screen (no scroll bar) of your in box as an action/follow-up area works extremely well.
- *Out of Office Notification*—Use it to give information from which team members can make business decisions.
- *Outdated Messages*—Delete those that have lost their value from your in box, sent items, and folders.
- *Proper Paragraphing and Proper Grammar*—Use them so people can quickly understand your message. Remember, no e-mail theoretically *ever* leaves the face of Earth. Make sure you leave the image of yourself you want others to see.
- *One Subject Per E-mail*—Improves response time and the quality of your reply.
- *FYIs*—Don't clog people's in boxes to make sure you're covered if things go awry or to gain visibility in your organization. Always have a good business reason.
- *Distribution Lists*—Keep yours current and use a variety of them for specific purposes.
- *Thank-Yous and Okays*—Stop sending them. Only reply if you cannot meet a request or things are not okay.
- *Carpe Diem*—Seize the day, or even better the moment and *Do It Now!*
- *Joke Lists*—Belong at home.

I see this list as a work in progress and am sure there are items we have not included. If you visit IBT's web site (www.ibt-pep.com) you will find, under the NGW section, an area for your feedback and reply. I would very much appreciate your sharing with me additional e-mail tips you have found effective. I will then post them on our web site so that others might benefit from your experience.

Work Issues in the NGW Office

Clearly, working in a NGW office is not the same as in Dilbert days. Our senses quickly become aware of all that is around us. Because of the interrelationships of more open environments we need to modify our rules of behavior. Among the most important issues I have observed are:

- *Food:* Sounds and smells are invasive and distract from work focus. It may not be okay to eat things like popcorn, pastrami, corn chips, and the like at your workstation. The café or commons area is better suited for lunch or snacks. Besides, there is nothing wrong with taking breaks and having lunch.

- *People Yells:* In the NGW office everyone will hear you when you call "How d'ja like the game last night?" across the room. Private conversations can take place in designated Not Reservable small conference rooms, which are usually scattered around an effective NGW office. If others are practicing this behavior, you owe it to yourself and your team members to advise the shouters, on a *Do It Now!* basis, of the effect of their actions. They're not bad folks. They're good folks with bad habits.

- *Interruptions:* There are usually no doors that can be closed. We must be aware of the consequences of walking in on someone while they are pounding away at their keyboard deeply focused on their work. Most interruptions can wait until a scheduled or more convenient time. Batching is a skill to be embraced in the NGW.

- *Speaker Phones:* They're forbidden for obvious reasons in the open environment of the NGW office. An enclosed conference room equipped with a speaker phone is the place to be if there is a need to have a hands-free or multiple party conversation.

- *Respect for the New Protocols:* New ways of working together in the NGW often take some getting used to. A list of the agreed protocols of how you are going to work together in the NGW should be placed prominently in locations throughout the office.
  We have found that it takes about six months for the NGW office to really come together and for collective habits to become NGW office routine.

- *Staying in Hoteled Assigned Space:* If hoteling is the mode of your NGW office, then staying in the space assigned to you is most important. Space is typically assigned by a first come, first served process, usually electronic, which reserves space for you and directs people and calls to you. If you are not in the assigned space, both people and information cannot get to you. Of course, if you are in the wrong space, you create a snowball effect for others. Like any other reservation system, the earlier you make your reservation, the better are the chances you can have the type of space and location you want.

• *Returning Wireless Phones and Other Tools to the Central Area:* Wireless phones have limited battery life. When you leave the office, return your wireless phone to the central area for recharging. In some cases, returning wireless phones to the central area also triggers a faster voice mail messaging process. Of course, all collectively shared tools and devices should be returned to their central area so others may use them.

• *Special Supply Needs in Hoteling Work Stations:* Only a limited array of papers, pens, clips, and the like can be stocked in nonassigned NGW workstations. If the supplies you like are not stocked in the workstations, I suggest you get some accordion sided, boxed-bottom hanging folders, place them in your file drawers, and put the supplies you like in these folders for easy access when you are in the office.

• *Do Not Disturb Signs:* I've been told that people put up a sign in their NGW workstation saying "Do Not Disturb" and no one pays attention to it. Well, they probably should not pay attention to it. This is because "Do Not Disturb" does not give enough information for people to make business decisions as to whether to interrupt you or not.

For example, a team member has a question she needs to answer for her client at the 2:00 P.M. meeting. You are the only one who has the answer. It's now 9:30 A.M. and you have a sign clearly posted that says "Please Do Not Disturb until 10:00 A.M." There is a pretty good chance that your coworker will make a business decision that she can wait to ask you her question. On the other hand, if your sign reads, "Please Do Not Disturb until 3:00 P.M.," then your coworker will probably make a decision to interrupt you to get her question answered.

Do Not Disturb notices advising *until what time* you need privacy will give people good information from which to make business decisions and will reduce, not eliminate, interruptions.

WORK ISSUES IN THE NGW HOME OFFICE

An effective home office is one that creates an efficient environment to control, maintain, and retrieve information that is used to create and complete work. (See Figure 7.11.) The factors that make it effective are:

• *Dedicated work space*: This is imperative. The dining room or kitchen table does not work. Within a small apartment the dedicated space may be a screened off area of a room. In a modest home or larger apartment, the home office space may be a section of a room. And, of course, in a large home one room can usually be dedicated to the home office.

A word of caution. We have noticed in print some suggestions that the home office space be in a hall alcove. This suggestion goes back to the form versus function issue. People recommending a hall alcove type of space have obviously never done real work in a home office. If at all possible, do not allow the selected home office space to be in a high traffic area of the home. Our experience has shown how important attention and focus are to the accomplishment of knowledge work. Family traffic, even the dog, is unnecessary distraction.

Figure 7.11   An effective home office.

• *Furniture needs to be of high quality:* This is not to say that you need to spend lots of money. Your options include buying new furniture from a major manufacturer who has designed products for the home office worker, and many have, or buying used high-quality products. In almost every town there are businesses selling used office furniture that they have purchased from local businesses who have either remodeled or gone out of business. Buy quality. Our office is comprised of first rate previously owned furniture. Remember, file cabinet drawers will open and close thousands of times per year and you don't need them falling apart.

• *Buy the best chair you can afford:* A folding chair or the dining room chair does not cut it in the day-to-day routine of a home office. If you can afford nothing else, buy an excellent chair. This will make all the difference in your effectiveness over the days you will spend in it.

• *Lighting, glare, and reflection:* They play an important part in the design of a corporate office. So, too, should you invest time making decisions about the position of lighting that makes seeing easier by decreasing glare, thereby reducing fatigue.

• *Sound can either distract or help you focus:* We all respond differently to sound and these differences in our human condition must also be considered when we are making home office decisions. Do you concentrate better with background music? How will you or your clients respond to a dog barking or children playing in the background?

• *Room temperature:* Any factor that affects comfort in turn affects productivity. Watch the position of the sun, the heating and air-conditioning vents, and your proximity to windows and drafts.

• *Planned work hours:* The office is where you are. As such, we need to focus and operate in a businesslike manner. I have found it best to establish regular business hours. Everyone in my family knows and respects that during business hours, although I am just in the next room, I am at work and not to be disturbed unless for very good reason.

If I want to go to a family event during work hours, I approach my decision to attend just as I would if I were working in the company office. I review my business needs well in advance and schedule time on my electronic calendar to attend the event. I do take regular lunch hours and always go out for a run in the morning before normal work hours no matter how busy the day may be. I have found that keeping to the plan and schedule allows me to do my work, pay attention to my family, and end my work day as I have scheduled it.

• *Support needs—outsource or other options:* When working at home in the NGW, we often need to proactively identify resources who can help us or fix things. I keep a complete Help and Fix list in my computer contact list, by categories, with the phone numbers of all the people and organizations I can go to for help or to fix things. I have a computer guru whom I can call and get advice from or who will come to my house and fix my computer or adjust my software. I have a printer repairperson who makes house calls in less than two hours.

My contact list has the telephone numbers of help desks for all my software and electronic tools. If you are a corporate worker you would also include the specific telephone numbers of all the various help desks within your organization.

• *Home alone and lonely:* Working at home does not have to be lonely. I often schedule lunch meetings and invite others to my home office for meetings.

Additionally, in the NGW, home office does not typically mean there is no corporate office. Plan to spend part of your work week in the corporate office. Typically, the 80/20 rule works best. Spend at least one day out of every five in the corporate office. We also heard from our clients that it is best to vary the day of the week you go to the corporate facility. Not all staff are available every day so you tend to see everyone if you stagger your visits.

WORK ISSUES IN THE NGW MOBILE OFFICE

1. *Client, car, hotel, or airport:* The office is where you are and work is something you do no matter where you are in the NGW. I travel the world supporting the various IBT units and have found that effective planning is my key to successfully being able to have everything I need regardless of where I am and what I am doing.

Before any travel, appointment, or meeting schedule a time on your electronic calendar to plan, in detail, where you are going and what you will need to successfully carry out your business purpose.

Plan It Now! This will assure you the success you need to win in the business world.

2. *Proper support/equipment needs:* Remember the Help and Fix contact list I talked about in the section on working at home? I keep this list with me all the time so that I can get in touch with my support network if I should need them.

I also find it best to keep a small amount of stationery, company literature, business cards, and postage stamps in my briefcase. You never know when you will need to send a quick thank-you note or brochure to someone you just met or spoke with.

3. *Getting it all done on time:* Those of us who travel often still need to schedule time to be either in the corporate office or home office to do the work that comes from all this traveling. We have learned that *every one hour meeting typically generates two additional hours of work.* Some of this work is preparation for the meeting and the remainder is the actions and tasks that result from a meeting. While traveling I begin to detail my schedule for when I return to my office. Plan It Now assures that I keep my promises to my clients and associates.

ATTENTION—NOTEBOOK USERS: A WORD OF CAUTION

If you are a notebook user, you must back-up your notebook at least once a week. No if's, and's, or but's about it. Pick a time and day that you will back-up your notebook. Mark this date on your calendar and do not miss this appointment. No excuses! You can't afford the risk! (See Figure 7.12.)

FINAL THOUGHT—THERE ARE NO DUMB QUESTIONS

There are no dumb questions when it comes to technology. All your technology answers are known—probably by someone within 20 feet of you. Regardless of where you are, ask questions. You'll find great solutions from your peers. Scheduling a two-minute technology Q&A time into meetings is an effective way of getting excellent answers and directions to technology questions for all team members.

Figure 7.12 Back-up your computer so you don't lose information or miss important appointments.

FOLLOW-UP FOR CHAPTER 7

Steps toward an Effective NGW

1. Identify what type of NGW works for you and your organization. A superb reference to aid in the decision-making process is *Workplace by Design* (Jossey-Bass, 1995), a Benchmark book by Drs. Franklin Becker and Fritz Steele.

2. Furniture vendors are plentiful in every price range category. Begin the interview process to select a vendor you believe has the knowledge of the NGW alternatives and clear understanding of your

NGW goals. You will be spending more time than you might like with these people. Make sure you completely trust them and you like being with them.

3. Architectural and Design firms are plentiful in every price range category. Begin the interview process to select a vendor you believe has the knowledge of the NGW alternatives and clear understanding of your NGW goals.

4. Carefully review plans to assure a proper balance between *form* and *function*. Ask the people who will work in the space what they think of the various options being considered.

5. Management involvement is the key to success. Get strong support and commitment to the change process and the time necessary for employee involvement to assure meeting goals from the CEO on down.

6. Employee expectations and corporate objectives must be in alignment to ensure a successful NGW. Survey employees as to their needs and continually communicate progress in the NGW project.

7. In all moves a process must be in-place for both the macro and micro associated events. Have an employee move process, pre, during, and post move, to assure the move becomes a nonevent.

8. Review your NGW protocols for your personal compliance with the agreed upon rules. If there are no written protocols, suggest that one be developed.

Implementing PEP in Your Move

9. Clearly understand the issues, within your workplace, that influence the loss of information value within your organization.

10. Review your current information organizational process and make changes as necessary to eliminate wasting time looking for information.

11. Apply Chapter 2 in this book and Chapter 2 in my *Hi-Tech PEP* book, which offer effective organizational processes for both the paper and electronic worlds.

12. Becoming PaperSmart requires a plan. Determine your goals and the training necessary to become PaperSmart. Research what support organizations are available internally and externally.

13. Notebook users must establish an effective back-up system to ensure the ability to easily recreate files. Decide, based upon your new data activity, how often you must update your notebook, what off-line or network storage process you will use, and how often you will back-up. Back-ups should be done no less than once a week.

To Work More Effectively from Home

14. Plan your office hours and advise family members, friends, and associates.

15. Plan, on your electronic calendar, when you will spend time in the corporate office.

16. Review upcoming meetings and travel plans and schedule time to effectively plan these events.

17. Home officing requires an environment where work can be accomplished in an effective manner. If you are home officing, review your current (both physical and human) situation, the shortcomings in this environment, and the steps needed to be taken to create a value-added environment to assure productivity.

CHAPTER 8

Be a *Do It Now* Manager!

If you wait for people to come to you, you'll only get small problems. You must go and find them. The big problems are where people do not realize they have one in the first place.
—W. Edwards Deming

Chapter 8 Preview

In this chapter, you will learn how to:

- Successfully get others organized.
- Make the best use of your newfound time.
- Employ one of the most effective means of delegating work.
- Practice effective management with the principle of walkabout.

I once delivered the Personal Efficiency Program (PEP) at a manufacturing plant in England. The participants included managers, administrators, and shop supervisors. I had several PEP coaches with me to facilitate the program; in fact, my participation was limited to introducing the concept and getting a few participants started. One supervisor was particularly enthusiastic about the prospect of getting better organized. He wanted to know all about PEP and how he might use it. I told him, "If you think PEP is good for you, wait until you see what it can do for the people who work with you."

I suggested that the most effective use of his newfound discretionary time would be to move around the shop floor to visit with his people every day and to find out firsthand from them what they needed to get themselves better organized and produce what they needed to produce.

When I returned to the manufacturing plant a few months later, I was approached by the same supervisor. He excitedly described his experience with PEP. He asked if I had known about the strike that occurred in the plant the month before. I told him I had heard about it but didn't know the details. He asked, "Did you know that the whole factory went on strike except for my section?" He said that when senior managers looked into why his was the only section not going on strike, they found that the employees in his section had no complaints. They said that all of the things that they had felt were wrong had been dealt with and handled by the supervisor during the previous months.

The kinds of things this *Do It Now* manager did are described in this chapter.

MANAGEMENT BY WALKABOUT

One of the most important tools a manager has to get things done effectively and efficiently is a technique called management by walkabout (MBWA), or as some call it, visible management, or management by wandering around.

Through the process of MBWA, getting around to my people and seeing what they had to deal with and what problems they faced, I created the PEP program.

Years ago I worked as a manager in a business where the employees were under tremendous pressure to supply services, produce products, and get them out the door. I was responsible for some two hundred people. A typical day consisted of meeting with the senior management team to discuss internal issues and meeting with customers, then doing lots of paperwork, primarily to satisfy the reporting demands of the higher executive levels. My job was a study in crisis management. I seldom, if ever, was able to leave the office.

But then two things helped me change that. First, I got myself organized. I had help in establishing routines with my assistant and I began to deal more effectively with the paperwork I was responsible for. Second, I used the time resulting from my reorganization to get out of the office and practice management by walkabout. I spent nearly half the day every day getting out to visit with every single person I was responsible for. I would stop at their desks or work areas, sit down, and chat with them to find out how things were going. I soon realized that most of the people were working extremely hard, but they were not being very efficient or effective in their work. The general scene was one of disorder.

When I first started MBWA, people were suspicious. They wondered why I was there and what I was looking for. But this suspicion quickly went away when they found that I would come back regularly and that I showed a genuine interest in what they were doing. Soon they began to open up and address long-term productivity issues. I listened intently to what they had to say and tried to respond to their expressed needs.

If I didn't respond to a need, I felt very uncomfortable facing the person again. MBWA forced me to be effective in dealing with the issues that were brought up, especially those issues that I wholeheartedly agreed should be dealt with.

I discovered that most of the people I managed had no idea how to work effectively. It wasn't that they didn't work hard; in fact, they obviously worked much harder than they really needed to. That's when I discovered that if I could help them do something to improve how they did their work, I would get the most results from my efforts as a manager.

This was MBWA, with a twist. Yes, I listened; yes, I responded, but I also coached them how best to organize themselves and get on top of what they needed to do. I coached them on how to organize and improve their work processes. I helped them improve their organizing skills and apply them to their work environment. This was not just lip service: I visibly coached and facilitated the process. I would not only listen, I would look. After noticing a disorganized condition, I would try to discover the underlying causes. What I often discovered was that people could no longer see their actual working conditions.

For example, I might ask a man to clean out his desk. Once he had finished the task, I would look at the desk. And more often than not, I would find that things were overlooked or not even seen by him in the first place.

I have come to believe in black holes, or at least in the black hole phenomena in organizations in which you send something out and it seems to get lost, never to be seen again. Well, those black holes are usually in desk drawers and files. Things simply get shoved away without being dealt with.

Why aren't many important items dealt with? The reasons are many: bad working habits, procrastination, not knowing exactly what to do, poor planning, poor organization, crisis management, and many more. Interestingly enough, rarely do I find that bad intentions or lack of effort are the cause of production difficulties. Often people do not have the authority to handle the problems they face. Or they find things difficult to address, even though another person might find the same things very easy to deal with. Or they feel that every direction they turn, they run into a wall, so they give up trying.

Often I find that arbitrary rules, poor policies, and inefficient work processes create these negative feelings in people. Eliminating these rules and creating new standards almost always improve the morale and productivity of people. What seems like insurmountable and intractable problems to them are, in most cases, within the supervisor's ability to handle. For example, if someone on staff needed a computer to process her work better, I could authorize the purchase immediately, have procurement get it fast, and allow the person to get on with her work with the resource that she needed.

Through MBWA I discovered an extremely effective way to coach people in their jobs. I did this by going through their pending files with them. We would go through each piece of work, one by one, and have them process it then and there. In the pending files, I found procrastination, misunderstanding, and arbitrary rules that prevented people from doing the things they needed to get done. I would have never found these problems simply by asking because, as is often the case, if people had known what the problem was, they would have resolved it. I had to see the process and how they worked to notice that they didn't have the necessary tools, or that they experienced many disruptions, or what was making the work difficult to do.

Within a very short period of time in this management position, I experienced something I had never before experienced—visible results, evident not only to me, but to everybody. The office became much neater. Things were labeled. Common files became comprehensible and usable. People began to take pride in their surroundings. They began to work together to solve the problems that made their work harder to do. The more I concentrated on the basics of work, the more visible the results became.

The more time I spent out of my office with the people who did the work—discussing, looking, testing, resolving, eliminating blocks to production, coordinating—the more real production results we achieved and the easier it was to achieve them. This was a complete revelation to me then.

Having since seen how many other companies work, I know that MBWA is not used by executives and managers to the degree it could be. Countless times as a consultant I have been told by people that their boss has never been to their office. Most managers merely pay lip service to the MBWA concept.

I challenge you to use the time you gain through PEP to be out and about with your people and become a *Do It Now* manager. That is PEP's greatest payback. Let us look at why.

AN EXAMPLE OF MBWA

One of the most effective executives I have ever known ran a bank in Luxembourg. He consistently outperformed his peers, chalking up 20% to 25% return on equity, year after year, in good and bad times.

Neatness and orderliness were his mantras. He had a flat table desk with no drawers in an open office environment. In his view, drawers would only end up keeping the work hidden. He preferred to get the work done and the paper forwarded to where it belonged. He processed his work immediately. He delegated liberally. You would seldom find him at his desk because he spent most of his time around the seven floors of office space. He hated meetings—they were too often a waste of time—so would hold very few of them. Those that he had were held before or after banking hours and were therefore brief and to the point.

He hated clutter and would make this known when he saw it. The bank had a rather large turnover of personnel (being a foreign bank in Luxembourg to which personnel was regularly rotated from the home office for training and experience), so the repeated message for old and new staff was: be orderly; be quick; don't accumulate; get it done, now!

His role was to establish the objectives of the bank and devise strategies to meet those objectives and then put an organization there to execute these strategies. He was very good at it!

WHY MBWA WORKS

Many success factors come as a result of MBWA. Being out and about, you see and hear things you otherwise wouldn't see and hear. Being out and about prompts you to ask questions and improves your communication and listening skills. Most difficult problems don't go away at the first attempt to deal with them; but, by being out and about with your people, you get their input. You find yourself following up and addressing the problems and testing solutions.

Staff productivity problems are too often affected by things out of their control. To resolve these problems, people who work in other divisions may have to cooperate, even though they have their own priorities. As the manager, you are the only person who can bring these groups together and work out solutions. If you have been out and about, you know the real issues and can help push through solutions.

Another reason why MBWA works is simply because people receive much-needed attention. Remember reading about the study done in the late 1930s by a company called Western Electric? They conducted an experiment on improving productivity in the workplace. They found that if they turned the lights up on the factory floor, productivity went up. Then they tested to see what would happen when they turned the lights down on the factory floor. Interestingly, productivity went up again. One conclusion drawn from this study was this: When attention is placed on the needs of people, production increases, even if the things getting attention aren't the right things.

If you are out and about, attending to the issues and needs of the people producing the products, productivity will improve. If in the process of MBWA you concentrate on the right things, your rewards are that much better.

FACE-TO-FACE COMMUNICATION

Our pride often makes it tough to talk about our failings, especially when communicating with our bosses. What might be obvious to others may not be so visible to us. These blind spots create a division or gulf between management and the people doing the work. The best way to bridge the gap is to communicate one-on-one, face-to-face. When you are talking about the same issues on the same level in the same space, you communicate more effectively; MBWA creates these golden opportunities to communicate. You encourage open communication when you ask people how they work, what they are doing, and what things will make their lives and jobs easier. *Do It Now* management means being out there with people, asking questions and making observations that enable you to comprehend, to listen, to learn.

When I'm out and about in my work, I often ask PEP participants to give me a brief statement of the strategy of their operation. The senior executive of one PEP group was shocked to find that none of the participants in the group, except for himself, could state what the strategy of the operation was. When he and I discussed the matter later, he told me that he thought everyone knew about it. The company had published an annual report about it for all the world to read and in two staff meetings he had covered it in detail.

I didn't find any of this very surprising. In all the years I've been working with companies, only once or twice have I found that employees had any real clue of the strategies being worked on by the company. Too often the companies didn't have a strategy at all. And in companies with a strategy, the communication of it was poor at best.

If you have a message to get across, if you have a plan to get done, if you are trying to execute a strategy, or if you want to explain your vision of the future, there is no more effective method I know than meeting face-to-face with your people.

A *Do It Now* manager communicates the vision and strategy of a company continuously through his or her actions as well as words. If the company's strategy is to get the competitive edge through dramatic improvement in the quality of customer service, the *Do It Now* manager demonstrates this by actions on the front line with the people who are dealing with the customers and often with the customers themselves. All aspects of communication are greatly enhanced through MBWA.

FOLLOW-UP METHOD

Chapter 5 discusses the importance of follow-up and follow-through. With MBWA, you schedule follow-up and follow-through into your work process. Being out and about with your people is a natural way to follow-up and follow-through on the things that you want to get done.

DELEGATION

When I talk with executives about their failures to delegate, the most common reason I hear is how busy their people are and how overwhelmed they would be if they were given any more to do. This perception is often formed by seeing the person's desk piled with papers or by hearing how late he or she stays at the end of the day. MBWA gives you a much more accurate sense of how much work your people do. Moreover, you can see how the work might be spread out differently. My experience suggests that when a *Do It Now* manager is out and about, he or she ends up delegating much more and much more effectively.

WHAT DOES A *DO IT NOW* MANAGER DO?

A *Do It Now* manager provides the resources, encouragement, coaching, and training people need to produce what they need to produce, in as effective and efficient a way as possible. A *Do It Now* manager does this by visibly getting around on the front lines of the business.

CONCENTRATE ON THE PROCESS OF WORK

To be effective as a *Do It Now* manager, you should first and foremost focus on the process of the work. In my experience, sufficient pressure is placed on staff to produce, but rarely is sufficient pressure put on *how* the work is produced. As a *Do It Now* manager, if you help people to concentrate and focus on the process of work, you will ensure that their job continues to improve and things get easier for them. This focus gets them to resolve core issues and at the same time improves the quality of the product being produced.

Here is what you look for: Are the people well organized? Do they have files that are easy to use, for themselves as well as the people around them? Do they have the tools that they need to produce and are these tools operational? Are they employing good working routines? Do they plan? Do they avoid procrastination? Do they see where they fit into the grand scheme of things?

The most effective way to produce change is through small and incremental steps. There is no need for a *Do It Now* manager to overwhelm his or her personnel with too many things at once. Asking them to deal with and handle one small piece of the puzzle at a time and following up to see that it has been done is all that is usually needed. Again, it is very difficult facing your people once more after you may have promised to resolve some issue and failed to do so. The solution? Deal with it. Handle the issue. And until it is handled continue to keep on visiting the personnel and letting them know what it is that you are trying to do and what you are running into.

BUILDING TEAMS

In the course of employing visible management, it's not uncommon to discover that individual issues are impacted by members of the team. Also, it's common to find divisions of people within the organization. After all, this is how most organizations are structured. Visible management is an opportunity for you to get clarity on what individuals make up the team and the process of work. You are then better able to reorganize both the process and the team. Visible management is an effective tool in the reengineering process. You can greatly enhance team activity in the organization by eliminating the barriers between the team members. Without visible management, it is very difficult to isolate those arbitrary rules and barriers that can prevent the team from functioning properly.

DON'T BE TIED TO THE DESK

One senior manager, responsible for a division of nine hundred people in a large manufacturing firm, strongly felt that MBWA was one of the most important things he needed to do. But he said that he had no time to do it. He was constantly dragged into other problems, meetings, and crises. He felt tied to his desk.

The solution that he and I worked out was relatively simple. He would spend the whole morning out and about at different sites where his people were located and wouldn't even come to the corporate office until one o'clock in the afternoon. Interestingly enough, with a little bit of organization, screening of information that came to him, improved delegation, and elimination of waste of time, he was able to get out of the office earlier each day, and still put in the extra four or five hours getting around to his people.

Being "tied to the desk" is a common complaint from executives. Simply scheduling MBWA before sitting down at the desk works for some. A more permanent solution is to get rid of the desk completely. One manager did so and operated his business with a clipboard. Not having a desk forced him to get out and about with his people nearly full-time. When he had an important meeting, he would hold it in the office conference room.

In his book *Thriving on Chaos* (Alfred A. Knopf, Inc., 1987), Tom Peters tells a story of another manager who got rid of his desk and used "a small work area in two departments: a round table with three chairs and a file cabinet in an open area by the entrance door" (p. 428). This allowed him to be accessible and still work with his secretarial support and handle his mail efficiently. I like this idea. If you don't have a desk, you don't have a place to store extra papers and materials that you will never use, anyway.

START WITH YOURSELF

It is human nature to see the cause of one's difficulties "over there." But many improvements can be made within your own area at little or no cost. This experience is common when employing quality improvement processes in companies. If you go after the red herring—a new $9 million computer system when you don't have the money or it will take two years to install it—you will miss the hundreds of improvements you could make in the interim.

ELECTRONIC TOOLS TO ENHANCE MBWA

As a manager, you likely have a few layers of management between you and the front lines. Bypassing those can create problems. A solution is to bring them with you, electronically. One way to do MBWA is by using electronic tools. If you can't get around often enough to your people, electronic tools can help.

E-mail is one such tool. Inviting employees at all levels to communicate both problems and suggestions directly opens the lines of communication. Your physical presence in their areas periodically makes e-mail that much more effective.

For smaller businesses, networking software allows you to communicate directly through PCs without having to invest lots of money. Lotus Notes, one such software application, is easy to customize for your business. The customized databases can be accessed by anyone authorized in any geographical location with a telephone. Anyone in the organization can participate and contribute to important issues and questions put forward by yourself or others. Most telephone companies offer their own e-mail services, and as long as you have a PC and a modem it is possible to communicate.

MBWA IN AN ALTERNATIVE OFFICE

Management by walkabout assumes management and personnel work in the same location. But as you know, current industry trends are toward getting personnel as close to the customer as possible. For sales and service personnel, that usually means being out of the office in front of customers. Many people work out of the home, at least part of the time. Alternative office designs (open office architecture and facilities where personnel have no permanently assigned space or desks) make it difficult to know where people are at any given time. So what is a *Do It Now* manager to do? Work harder at it! Such work environments make it all the more important to put forth the effort and arrange to visit staff members wherever they may be working.

For many years IBT has provided a special PEP service to company sales forces (and in some cases remote service representatives) where we visit the home offices of remote personnel and help organize their home offices. The most consistent feedback to this very popular program is how valuable it is to have someone from the outside (not outside the company—outside the home) see their work environments. Not only can these outsiders advise on how to set up the office better and introduce routines to make it more pleasant and productive, but also they are in a position of influence so that things that need to be remedied can be remedied quickly and effectively. The function of a PEP consultant is really similar to the role a good MBWA manager can play.

A good manager will arrange to go on sales calls with his or her people and while doing so observe both sales competency and organizational systems to support sales. This might include, for example, how the person has organized his or her car or how easy or difficult it is to connect to the server and process e-mail.

Because so many staffers are now mobile, they are that much further out of the loop when it comes to current strategy or goals (or progress on the strategy or goals). The *Do It Now* manager needs to be that much more active relaying news on the company strategies and progress.

Technology such as mobile phones, remote access to e-mail, pagers, and so on all help. Having this technology in place and utilizing it is a first step. But in the case of meetings, there is a qualitative difference between speaking to someone through a telephone conference call and being able to see the eyes of the person sitting across from you as you discuss important issues. And these technology tools are no substitute for your eyeballs when it comes to seeing *how people work as they work,* though desktop videoconferencing may soon make this easier.

Remember, as a manager, your greatest insight will come from where the rubber meets the road.

CLOSING THOUGHTS ON MBWA

If you are a senior manager, you might think that you have a nearly impossible schedule as it is. Where are you to get additional time in the day to walk about? Sam Walton, the brilliant mind behind the building of Wal-Mart, the largest retail store chain in the world, spent about 80% of his time out and about in his stores. He reportedly traveled four days a week visiting the stores and spent one day in the office. With revenues topping $70 billion, you can be certain Sam could have kept himself occupied in an office. He chose to do otherwise. By being out and about, he solved many management problems directly and greatly reduced paperwork and other time-consuming activities such as devising policy, setting strategy, dealing with the budget, and contacting customers. Sam found that these roles are more effectively carried out with the input of those who have to do the work.

The question then is not how much time you have; rather, it is how you use it. Is it important to you to practice visible management? Is it important to you to know what is going on in the front lines?

The most effective use of management time is getting out and about with people every single day. If you concentrate on the process of work and make it easier for your people to produce, you will do much toward accomplishing the vision, strategy, and goals of the operation.

FOLLOW-UP FOR CHAPTER 8

1. Schedule a block of time in your day to get out and about to your areas of responsibility. The most effective time may be first thing in the morning. If so, don't even bother to come into the office until after you have made the rounds *visibly.*

2. Concentrate on the process of work and how it may be improved.

3. Communicate the vision. Know the strategy of your operation and communicate that strategy in actions and words. Help your people envision where your operation is going.

4. Deliver on what you promise. If you say you are going to do something for an employee, *do it.* If you find it's difficult or impossible, get back to the person and let the employee know where you stand. Do everything in your power to keep your word.

5. Focus on helping your employees improve teamwork when you are out and about.

CHAPTER 9

Organizing the Team to Act Now!

The more you give staff the opportunity to contribute to the problem-solving process, the easier it is going to be to improve your team efficiencies.

Chapter 9 Preview

In this chapter you will learn how to:

- Identify areas of team improvement.
- Establish common platforms and standards for a department.
- How to take advantage of the electronic tools you already have.
- How to delegate and manage tasks in a team.
- Common calendar use.
- Project planning—How to execute your team improvements.

You have been able to put into practice the steps laid out in the previous chapters and you are better organized and prepared to work. As a team leader you have taken to heart the *Do It Now Manager* function, getting about seeing your staff and improving how they perform. You may now be ready to move to a whole new level of team efficiency within your group.

One of our senior consultants in Europe worked with a large multinational company introducing the Personal Efficiency Program to one of their departments. After having gone through the PEP program and taken further steps to organize the department, the manager told our consultant that she had recently put her team through a course on team training. The purpose of the course was to get to know each other better and improve the way they worked together. The team members who also did PEP reported back that PEP gave them more efficient team training than the actual course they had taken. The team leader said the reasons for this were:

- They had managed to pinpoint the group problems in a simple, personal, educated, and entertaining manner.
- The PEP program and the way it was presented fit the tempo of the group and gave all participants the chance to contribute to the problem-solving process both during and between scheduled course times.
- The participants all learned about the others' work situations making it easier to understand the group as a whole instead of only seeing it from an individual and isolated point of view.

This is not an isolated success. It appears that when people go through the Personal Efficiency Program they become more aware of often overlooked processes and how these processes affect both the individual and team members.

Here is how you can make your team more effective, efficient, productive, and happier.

It's not just about getting faster and more advanced technological tools, it's about knowing what we have and learning how to use them effectively.
—STEVE EMMONS

SURVEYING FOR AREAS OF POTENTIAL IMPROVEMENT

IBT developed a template to check content and the amount of self-produced documents for one of our pharmaceutical company clients. The company, a Lotus Notes user, wanted to know how many documents were double-filed.

The survey form template was sent to the staff, filled in, and forwarded back to the team leader and IBT. The result was documentation to prove that the vast majority of documents received were double-filed, both as paper and electronically. Also, there was no common filing drive.

By surveying staff, you, too, can find useful information. What type of calendar system does the staff have? What type of calendar system do they *use*? Are people's files structured in such a way that it's intuitive for other people to find them? Do staff members print out e-mails as well as keep them in electronic form? Are documents located on individual C: drives or on the server personal drives that properly belong on the shared drive? Does the company have a groupware application that makes it easy to set up meetings? Do the employees use it? Have standards been established and documented so the staff knows how to perform in a common and proper way?

By putting together a simple electronic survey document with these questions and others of interest, forwarding them to the staff, and collecting responses within a reasonable period of time, you will soon be able to pinpoint the most obvious areas to address and improve.

Tip: If you are a Lotus Notes (LN) user you may be able to quickly identify how many attachments and duplicate files exist in your department with the use of Notes. One View we have found particularly useful with LN clients is "sorted all by size." You can see the name of the attachments in an e-mail and sort by the attachment name and how many duplicates of the attachments stored in LN show up.

TEAM = T – Together   E – Everyone
A – Achieves   M – More
—ANONYMOUS

ESTABLISHING COMMON PLATFORMS AND STANDARDS

A highly successful director of a private banking department at one of our clients in Luxembourg stated, "Teams work better when they have common tools." Another senior manager in a large pharmaceutical company phrased it this way: "I do actually take time to reflect. You can only do that if you feel you are organized and have control of information. With PEP we are able to establish a common platform to stand on."

Many companies struggle to get their work done simply because they have not taken the time to establish common standards. We find that many companies often have the tools. Microsoft Outlook or Lotus Notes are often available to the employees. But if you were to survey staff on their use, you would likely find that a few employees might use the Outlook calendar, some employees might use a paper calendar, and many might maintain both. Few employees will use these applications to manage their tasks. Most continue their task management with a piece of paper on their desks.

You can make a great deal of progress with your team efficiencies simply by encouraging staff to use the tools they have in a common way.

- Does your department file all documents on a shared server or do some of the people keep documents on their own C: or other server-based personal drive?
- Has a structure been defined for your shared drive and made known to all departmental personnel? Is the structure you created for your shared drive consistent with the common paper file system, so that people can find things just as quickly?
- Is there a storage limit to how many messages and documents you are permitted to keep? If so, do people know to put attachments on the shared drive and make links (shortcuts) to them rather than to have the attachments in your in box? Do clear instructions exist on the maintenance of files including erasing, renaming, and storing? Are these rules documented in a handbook or on the company intranet and available to all staff?
- Does your firm have a common calendar system? If so, is it in use? If in use, do rules exist on how the calendar information is posted? Are the rules available to staff?
- Are you using Outlook, Lotus Notes, or any other groupware application that facilitates the planning of meetings, vacations, and so on? Do you use it?

- Does the staff process their e-mail and paperwork in the same way? Do they have best practices rules and recommendations on how to work efficiently with e-mail?

Knowledge Management is the process through which organizations generate value from their intellectual and knowledge-based assets. Most often, generating value from such assets involves sharing them among employees, departments and even with other companies in an effort to devise best practices.
—MEGAN SANTOSUS AND JON SURMACZ

Knowledge Management

One of your most valuable assets is the knowledge of the team or group. To take advantage of this in-house knowledge you need structures so people can intuitively find that knowledge. Typically, companies have structures that have been designed and developed by many people over the years and they are normally impossible for new people to understand. If it is left up to individual staff to make up their own systems, you will never have true knowledge management.

We have worked with numerous companies to help them identify areas where standards and common platforms would benefit them. By rolling up our sleeves with the management team and the employees, we have been able to make major improvements in the performance of the team.

DOCUMENT CONTROL

One can recover up to 20% of the team's time simply by making it easy for team members to retrieve necessary information. The first step would be the traditional PEP approach to controlling the paper flow. Have staff purge the papers that are obviously unnecessary. Identify which of these papers belong in the departmental or common file system, and which belong in the individual's file system. We have learned that the better the common files are organized with someone who is trusted assigned responsibility, the less each person will save in their own files. Brainstorm for the types of file systems that best suit the individuals and the department and establish agreement on category names, color coding, and anything else that the department feels would be useful in making it easy to retrieve information.

Assuming that your company has a local area network (LAN) and a shared drive, invite your IT department into the process. Identify what shared drive is going to be used by the department. Using the categories you have established for the department's paper, create mirror categories within the shared server.

Establish rules for what gets saved and where these saved documents go. Assign an individual responsibility for maintaining shared drive files. With the help of your IT department have each person check their files and personal folders and move documents to the common drive. Make certain the server drive structure/categories are populated with all departmental information that belongs there.

Tip: Most companies limit the amount of disk space available for the individual. One way to conserve disk space is to have e-mail attachments moved to the shared drive and create links and/or shortcuts to these documents rather than to have the attachments stored on the C: or personal servers drive.

If company document retention procedures exist, be sure to follow them. If they do not exist, keep track of this whole process and devise rules for the future so that all staff are well aware of exactly what is kept where and why.

Tip: Staff need to be well aware of their own responsibilities to know what to save. It is critical that all employees have their own job functions and objectives clear, to know what the correct information to save is.

By cleaning out the paper files of the individuals and establishing common paper document files for the department, you will find that it is much easier to control the paper flow. At the same time, by establishing a subject-driven structure on your common server and designing rules and standards all staff follow, you will soon discover that the staff produce more quickly and with higher quality as a result of having information that they need at their fingertips.

Technology may occasionally look like the key driver. It's not. What matters is your willingness to invest in peer-to-peer collaboration in ways that your employees define as valuable, and in ways you never have before.
—BILL JENSEN

SHARED SOFTWARE

Shared software allows team members to communicate and share information and can be a wonderful tool to improve productivity.

Now that you have organized you and your departments' paper and electronic documents, information should be easier to find and retrieve. You can take team efficiencies to the next level by having the team members use applications such as Lotus Notes (the leading groupware application) and Microsoft Outlook, as well as many other fine applications on the market.

Since the vast majority of our clients work with either Outlook or Lotus Notes, I attempt to cover some of their functionality. I believe these applications can make a big difference in how your team gets things done.

Microsoft Outlook is not a groupware application per se. Lotus Notes is, but there are a number of functions that both Outlook and Lotus Notes have in common. Both provide solutions to:

- Electronic mail or messaging.
- Group calendaring and scheduling.
- Group conferencing.
- Meeting support.
- Information sharing.
- Tools to develop specific applications in these areas.

Lotus Notes has additional functionality including:

• *Discussion database*. This allows groups of people to electronically discuss a topic of common interest. They can participate at their convenience from anywhere and at any time. A record of this discussion is kept for reference. Only one copy of information exists (unlike multiple e-mail messages) so it is easier to update and takes up less space on the network.

• *Replication*. Lotus Notes updates databases that are located on multiple servers or computers. During replication database copies are compared for differences. New data is added to all copies on the database and obsolete information is removed. This feature allows users to work remotely without being directly connected to the network server.

• *Unstructured information*. Lotus Notes allows you to enter data freeform and it does not have specific structural requirements. An example would be a word processing document being unstructured data. Searching this data is sometimes difficult. Groupware's strong point is storing unstructured data. Text information can be searched for specific phrases and words.

• *Threaded discussions*. Discussion subjects are called items. After reading an item the user is prompted for a response, which is appended to the original item. Items and responses are searchable. Users are informed of new items or responses that have been added since they last read the discussion. New responses and items are presented in the order that they are added topic by topic, to stimulate an ongoing conversation with other participants.

• *The View*. A list of documents in a database is usually sorted or categorized to make finding documents easier. A database can have any number of views: by author, date, subject, and so forth.

There are many nifty features with both Outlook and Lotus Notes. Team members can access and share information such as common calendars and organize and execute projects, as well as manage and delegate tasks, and so forth.

Although the vast majority of our clients use Outlook and/or Lotus Notes, the word *use* may be a misnomer. The fact is that few of these applications features are actually used. My best guess is 75% of Outlook and Lotus Notes users use only the e-mail function.

Our clients have found they have had much to gain by simply getting their team members to utilize the tools that they already have. Reported benefits from the expanded use of shared software applications include:

• Use of the calendar function, both privately and as a shared calendar.
• Task management—keeping track of everything they need to do.

- Project planning—getting complex tasks with numbers of people involved, executed.
- Vastly improved delegation and follow-through of tasks. Outlook, Lotus Notes, and other groupware applications make it much easier to delegate and follow-through on.
- E-mail handling—filing capability and easy access to stored e-mails.
- Contact management.

Calendaring

If your company has either Outlook or similar shared software application, one of the most productive things you can do for your team is to get them to use the shared calendar function. One of our clients recently began working with Outlook's shared calendar. Prior to beginning this initiative, some of the staff used the electronic calendar while they *all* used a parallel paper system of writing down everything that they needed to do. The client staff all use Outlook calendar and it is open for everyone to see. Now that everybody uses the Outlook calendar, they can know when the people are free and book meetings far more efficiently.

Tip: It is important to block time for your own work in your personal calendar; otherwise the applications that attempt to find available time for a meeting will use your work time up!

By having permission to read others' calendars, team members can see what other team members are doing. The handwritten parallel system is gone. Clients are very satisfied and positive about the results of this effort.

Our clients have used this shared calendaring function to efficiently book meetings, conference rooms, and the use of automobiles, to make common resource plans, and to plan the time it takes for tasks or projects to be completed.

Your Personal Calendar

I highly recommend that each individual set up their calendar in either a five- or seven-days-at-a-glance view. That way you can more easily do and keep track of your Weekly Review and Action Plan (WRAP).

TASK MANAGEMENT

Both Lotus Notes and Outlook have excellent task management functionality. The problem is most people don't use them. This is a shame because our clients who have decided to use Outlook or Lotus Notes task management have reported wonderful results.

All tasks should be noted within the team's groupware application. In both Outlook and Notes it is possible to organize tasks in such a way that they can be viewed from many different perspectives.

Using categories within Outlook and Lotus Notes you can take complex activities and break them down into small components (project planning). You can schedule these tasks in the calendar as appropriate. You can also organize the tasks under categories such as the project name, the person involved, the department involved, the function involved, and so on.

There are different ways you can set up your Outlook view and see only the tasks and activities for the week. In Outlook, I have created a category called Weekly Plan. In this category go all the tasks that I am going to do in the upcoming week. I was able to customize my Outlook calendar section with tasks assigned to the Weekly Plan placed at the top of the Task column. That way I can take a look at all of my appointments, scheduled activities, and tasks for the week on one screen.

Another option for viewing all tasks for a specific week is by use of the date fields. Assign the Monday of the week as the start date and assign the Friday of the same week the due date. When you want to view only the tasks for the week, open the Task section of Outlook and choose the view: Next Seven Days. You can also view these next seven days tasks together with your calendar scheduled activities in Outlook Today. (See Figure 9.1.)

Because tasks can be assigned to many categories, it is possible for me to view those tasks in different ways. I can see everything that an employee needs to do under his/her name. I am also able to see the same delegated task under other assigned categories like Budgets. That way I can view all budget tasks regardless of whom they are assigned to. This is a useful function to keep track of all the things you need to do. But there is another function that you can use with these applications, which for a team leader or manager, is invaluable.

*People will not do things
unless they know it is being followed up on.*
—MANAGER (PRIVATE BANKING)

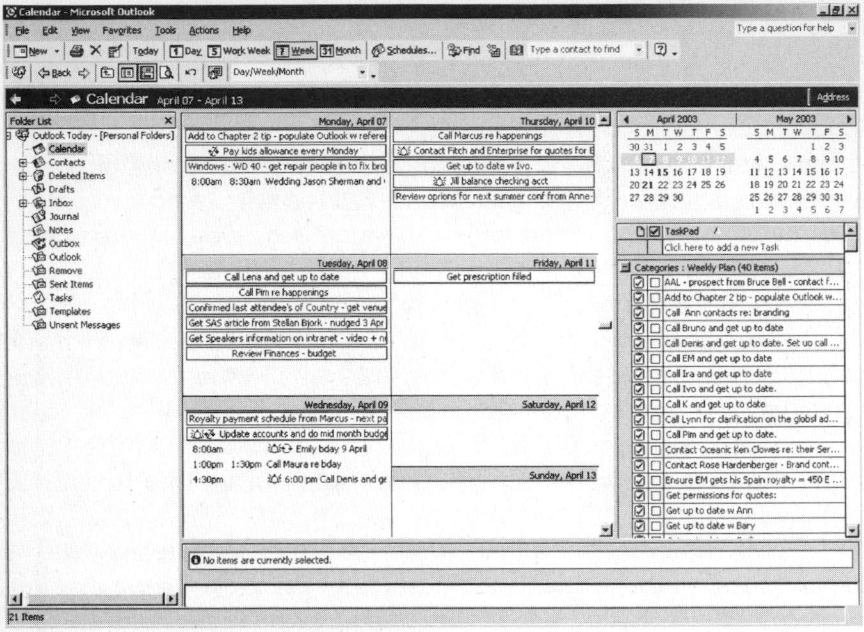

Figure 9.1   Sample seven day at a glance calendar with a weekly plan task list. All activities for the week are available at a glance.

Delegating Tasks

Outlook makes delegating tasks easy. Lotus Notes can be used for delegation and task management but is not as robust as Outlook unless the team is set up to use TeamRoom. (More on TeamRoom follows later in this section.)

An important first step for a team leader is to make certain that all team members understand the delegation system you're putting in place and how it functions. As mentioned in Chapter 2, there are some people who resent being told to do anything. How one goes about assigning tasks and following through influences how enthusiastically the person being delegated to is going to do the task, so it is important to establish ground rules with your people to begin with.

In Outlook it is possible to forward a task to an individual (the task goes automatically into his/her task list) and to have Outlook automatically remind the manager at the appropriate time of these open tasks. To delegate a task properly, you want to establish a starting date, a due date, and a reminder date. With Outlook your staff can report the percentage of the task that has so far been completed. All the team leader needs to do is open the task view, and by noting "% complete" he or she can quickly see whether a task is progressing or not without having to ask.

Tip: It is a rule of thumb that the earlier in the planning process overload is detected and tasks are delegated, the more effective you will be.

One of our banking clients assigned Categories to all of his personal and delegated tasks. He delegated tasks and ensured they were followed up on. (It so happens he had a personal assistant to help him do these follow-ups). He reported greatly improved task management. Outlook has become a very important tool in his arsenal to get things done.

You can view your open tasks in many different ways. If you go into the task section in Outlook, you can select how you want to view the tasks. It may be by category, by overdue tasks, by the responsible person, or even by tasks that need to be done in the next seven days. With both Outlook and Notes you can send tasks to others by e-mail.

One of my Australian colleagues developed another technique for managing delegated tasks in Outlook. He suggests you set up a separate sub-folder under tasks that is only used for delegated items (you delegate a new task by dragging and dropping from one of the e-mail folders). You can then categorize by the name of the person to whom the task has been delegated. When you then set the view command by category, each person's tasks are grouped together. These can be ordered by due date or any other metric.

In Lotus Notes you can create new To Do items for a group by using delivery options in your LN To Do items and assign them to the participants of the group. Save them in a category For Others and you can keep track of the delegated tasks. Lotus Notes will reply back acceptance of the task (unless the receiver initiates a different response).

One of our Lotus Notes clients has begun to use a LN function called TeamRoom to manage the group tasks. TeamRoom requires setup by the company IT department. The TeamRoom leader is the manager of the department. Group members read and fill in documents to populate TeamRoom with tasks and relevant information. The tasks are organized by categories and contain forms or fill-in documents in Word. It is possible to design overviews in many ways: by owner (person); by meetings (communication type); by category; and by due date; and also to make document links to reports on the specific topic.

TeamRoom is one of the many optional tools available within Notes. This is a very advanced and useful way of working with Notes.

Note: Any of these systems require the active agreement of the staff and must to be tested to iron out the bugs. Needless to say, success also depends upon people using their task list actively.

MANAGING COMPLEX ACTIVITIES—PROJECT PLANNING

Many of us are familiar with and probably use project planning software to manage our major projects. Unfortunately, too many of us overlook the fact that we have complex tasks that we may not have considered project planning material when in fact they should be. Sometimes these complex tasks sit on our To Do list for ages as elephant legs because we have not taken and broken these activities down into the smallest possible bites. To use project planning software to manage one of these complex tasks is like using a Ferrari to deliver milk. Both Outlook and Lotus Notes can be used for these daily task projects with the advantage of having all the information within the Outlook or Notes environment. (See Figure 9.2.)

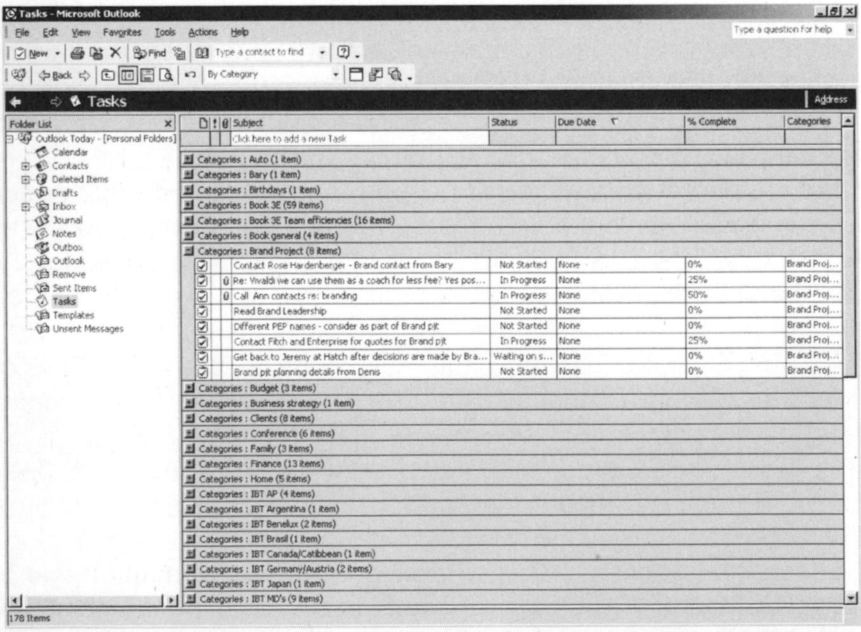

Figure 9.2   Sample project plan using Categories in Outlook.

As a team leader, plan your complex tasks within Outlook by creating a category for the task project. You can easily view all of the tasks involved with that particular project under its category. You can delegate tasks on the project and follow-up, as well as be able to easily see a list of all tasks the person has on his or her plate.

Lotus Notes' delegating function is not nearly as robust as Outlook's. It is possible to convert an e-mail into a task and it is also possible to forward a task by e-mail to an individual. But viewing the tasks from many different categories or even creating your own category (to name the task project) is problematic in Lotus Notes.

CONTACT LIST/ADDRESS BOOK

A common contact list, which often includes address book information, can be an important tool for the team. Depending on the application you are using, you typically can store important information about contacts and/or clients, including address information, e-mail information, and even details and notes about the client and/or contact that the team should have.

Microsoft Outlook Contact information can be viewed in many different ways. Furthermore, it is possible to quickly access all correspondence and activities surrounding a contact in Outlook. Simple keystrokes taking you into the Contact section and opening up the Activities tab will let you list out all of the correspondence, e-mails, and notes that you might have had with that contact and posted in the Outlook environment. Lotus Notes has similar functionality, as do most shared software applications.

One of our clients felt that this function was so important they assigned an assistant responsibility for posting new contacts and maintaining the Contact information.

Tip: Save time posting contact information. Encourage your contacts to send you a vCard (the Internet standard for creating and sharing virtual business cards). You can scan the information from physical business cards into the contact list.

Outside vendors have Lotus Notes and Microsoft Outlook add-on applications that allow you to improve the software functionality, track important client activities, and are particularly useful for sales forces.

COMPANY INTRANET

Most of our company clients have an intranet as well as a common groupware and/or Outlook application. Intranets are a very useful tool for storage of company general information as well as for easy access for users.

In our experience, intranets can sometimes be a mess. They are typically organized by the IT department, which does not necessarily know how department files are organized. Clients tend to put too much information onto the first level of entry of the intranet, the result being that the user often is confused. We find that having the client follow the same structure on their intranet as the shared drive and other departmental files makes it much easier and more intuitive for the user to be able to access intranet information they need.

Many of our clients use their intranet to organize not only information but meetings, to post common calendars, and to manage shared resources like conference rooms. Depending on the version of Outlook and the client's use of an intranet, it is possible to share the use of a calendar and/or publish it on the intranet. The user can call into the mail server and open the calendar in the functional mailbox in Outlook or the calendar in the group database in Notes. Depending on the rights, they can read and write the information there so that everyone using the central calendar will be kept updated.

This same function can be accomplished by granting access to one's personal calendar so that others can read it. In Notes, when they replicate their laptop data on a daily basis with the central server, everyone has the latest information.

Our clients have used the intranet to post important information people can access and comment on, such as objectives for the new year as well as common projects the user may need to access.

Several of our Outlook and Notes clients have connected calendar information to the company switchboard. The switchboard has a screen, the user types in the name of the individual, and his or her calendar shows up automatically. This way, the switchboard knows exactly where everyone is and what they're doing and can direct calls from clients and others accordingly. Making contact information as well as calendar information available to the switchboard and/or possibly an assistant, makes it much easier for everyone concerned to get things done.

DON'T OVERLOOK LOW-TECH SOLUTIONS

One of the more obvious low-tech solutions that benefit the team is the establishment of common departmental paper files. But this just scratches the surface of the potential low-tech solutions available to a team leader.

Proactive Attitude to Work

The purpose of getting the team organized is so that they can act now! People tend to act on tasks if they are easy to do so. If it is easy to find and retrieve information, people can act on it. Enabling team members to do things now is one of the most important benefits in getting team members organized.

Attitudes can be shaped in other ways. One client reported that the organizational changes described in this chapter were smooth and quick and that common work habits were working very well. The thought process of the group became "We Will" instead of "I Will." Another client reported major progress toward a more proactive attitude toward work. This same client had a clean desk policy and the group was able to achieve this. Implementation of work planning and making better use of Outlook functionality contributed to a better overview of the work to be done and created more tranquility within the department. We find that when you put attention on helping people to perform their task in a more organized way, they respond with a more positive attitude toward their work.

Up to now I have been discussing team members within a specific group. One of our clients, a large automobile manufacturer, found that not only was there improvement in the homogenous team, but those who had participated either in PEP or in these initiatives in other departments, ended up becoming as they described "more like a network" of support across divisional barriers.

Support Staff

Several part-time Human Resources department personal assistants (PAs) worked for one of our multinational banking clients. These PAs had their own group of people to service and support. If one of the staff from the group had a problem and needed an answer right away, the statement, "Sorry, my colleague is back again in a few days" or "I don't know if she already made progress on that" was unacceptable.

Every assistant had to find her way through the files of the other two PAs to answer all of the questions that might arise. This was always a problem for them. Our IBT consultant implemented a personal file system (the same for all three), with the same categories and labels and in the same place in the desk. Each file had a task list in front that could be read to determine what was done and what was planned. The rule was established that every file was put back in its place at the end of the day, even if the task was not complete. All the PAs had to do when they needed to find something in another assistant's desk was go to the other assistant's desk and open the files that they were very familiar with. This one simple action dramatically improved the performance of the group.

The banking client then took this a step further. Their department paper files were color-coded so that not only were the files organized in a common way, but the colors also enabled people to more quickly determine functions and thereby find files even more quickly.

INITIATING PROJECT GROUPS

The more you give staff the opportunity to contribute to the problem-solving process, the easier it will be to improve your team efficiencies.

Accomplishing the team efficiencies as described in this chapter will be a complex affair. Your best resource will be your staff. Their contributions to the resolution of these problems will ensure both success and maintenance of the new processes you are putting in place.

The best tool to accomplish your goals will be project-by-project improvement. Assign staff workgroups to tackle the different improvements uncovered by survey. Have the workgroups brainstorm for solutions. Ensure that they carefully identify (or take into consideration) the team's goals and objectives when deciding upon actions to be taken. After all, the purpose of getting organized is the accomplishment of the team's goals and objectives.

Create and manage projects to implement these improvements.

- Assign someone responsible for each project.
- Identify the goal of each project.
- Detail out the tasks to accomplish the project goals.

- Note task start date and due date and key deadlines to meet, as well as identify who will execute the tasks for the individual projects.
- Execute and follow-through.
- Replan as necessary until project goals are accomplished.

This is your road to success.

One of our clients did this exact thing. The client initiated two workgroups; one to standardize a project workplace and one to determine how to file contracts that were problematic for them. The results were startling. The first workgroup found that they could develop similar structures and work flow for the following processes:

- Official orders (public offers).
- Change orders.
- Order confirmation.
- Structure of project binders.
- Database for suppliers.

The second workgroup found the best way to file and structure contracts. By knowing exactly how they wanted to set up these improvements they were able to initiate project groups to implement the workgroup suggestions.

According to the client, our biggest contribution might have been to open questions on issues that were so hot that nobody had wanted to discuss them before. PEP put the issues on the table.

What has worked for us with our clients is:

- Identify areas of improvement.
- Assign workgroups to brainstorm solutions to the issues.
- Create projects and project teams to execute the solutions to those issues.
- Prioritize the implementation of the projects.
- Execute, execute, execute.

Team leaders have much to do. Get started now!

FOLLOW-UP FOR CHAPTER 9

1. Survey staff for areas of improvement. How does staff keep track of tasks? What type of calendar system does the staff have and use? How are the staff's files structured? How does staff handle documents? These and many other questions can be asked to identify where time is being wasted and how things can be improved.

2. Establish workgroups to brainstorm for solutions to the most obvious areas to be addressed in Number 1.

3. Identify areas of improvement based upon the workgroup discussions, and formulate project teams to address the highest priority issues.

4. Execute the projects.

5. Replan as necessary to ensure goals are met.

CHAPTER 10

Maintain It Now

*The time to repair the roof
is when the sun is shining.*
—JOHN F. KENNEDY

Chapter 10 Preview

In this chapter, you will learn:

- A task is done when you have put everything back in better condition than when you picked it up.
- The less you keep, the less you have to maintain.
- The purpose of good maintenance is to make it easy to produce next time.
- You should add tasks to each weekly plan that will create improvements in your work situation.

An associate once told me of a young man whose parents gave him a new car when he turned 18, to celebrate both his high school graduation and his first real job. Although the young man made a point of having his car washed once a week, he never changed the oil in the car. Naturally, when this simple, routine maintenance step was skipped repeatedly, the car's engine parts began to grate and grind against one another. Eventually, the entire engine locked up. The result was a burned-out engine and a useless car, all because ordinary maintenance hadn't been done.

Beyond the loss in monetary terms, what struck me was the foolishness involved and the fact that it needn't have happened at all. Here was a fellow who had neglected the most basic and practical of car maintenance procedures, ignoring routines that should have guaranteed a smoothly operating car for years to come.

As I mulled over this story, I thought, perhaps the parents never taught their son the importance of changing the car's oil. My hunch, though, is that they simply *assumed* that he knew how important it was and that he was changing the oil regularly. It's such a basic, integral part of car maintenance, it may not have crossed their minds that he might not be changing the oil.

People have a very low awareness of maintenance in their administrative work. Executives, when cornered to explain their lack of action on the subject, say they "expect" their people to know these things because "they're professionals." If they think about it at all, they assume someone else is working on it, so they do not demand it be done.

We know the consequence for that young man. The consequence for you of not getting and keeping yourself and your people organized is far more severe than a locked-up engine.

ENTROPY

Entropy can be defined as a measure or degree of disorder toward the breakdown of any system. In physics this is the second law of thermodynamics. It is a natural law of the universe that systems will tend to evolve from order to disorder and with this disorder there is increased complexity. Want a simple life? Make orderliness part of your everyday work process!

If you hope and expect to work in an orderly environment you must recognize the natural tendency for the environment to move in the direction of disorder and *you must work to maintain that order.*

Try neglecting your garden for a while and you will soon see the effect of entropy.

You will have hopefully made many changes by now as a result of the book and PEP processes. Maybe your desk is cleaner, your files are organized a bit better, and things are where they are supposed to be. You have a better system in place. You can be assured, because of the law of entropy, any system you have put in place will tend toward breakdown unless you consistently work toward orderly maintenance of the system.

So, what is the trick? Make maintenance part of your work cycle.

MAINTENANCE AND THE WORK CYCLE

I learned a lesson about maintenance from an old-timer who worked for IBM. He would travel to customer sites and repair their mainframe computers. He would often have younger technicians with him on these jobs. He was the butt of jokes because he had "peculiar" clothes and work habits. He used to wear overalls with dozens of pockets in them. In his pockets were all the different tools he needed or might need. If he saw something to be repaired, even if it hadn't been part of the original repair order, he'd repair it. If he saw a drop of oil on the ground he took out his cloth and cleaned it up, then and there. As he used a tool he cleaned it and put it back in the appropriate pocket. If a tool broke, he had a requisition form in his pocket that he filled out right then to replace the tool. His colleagues would attack the job not bothering to clean up as they went and inevitably when the end of the day came the old-timer was done and ready to go before the others. This was his way of working. He maintained an organized state.

Simply stated, maintenance is part of the work cycle. Think of it this way: Each piece of work, each task, has a beginning, middle, and end. Part of the task beginning must include organizing (planning, preparing for, setting up) for the task. In the middle is the act of doing the task. Finally, along with task completion, the ending must include maintenance points, including "put things back where they belong," and "improve the condition of everything you touch" (including files, tools, and so forth).

Maintenance routines should be thought of in the same way. The easiest way to do this is to incorporate basic maintenance routines into your work cycles, in exactly the same planned way you change the oil in your car. In the same automatic way you slide in behind the wheel, insert the car key, and start the engine, you know that the car's oil must be changed on a routine basis if your car is to be in top shape. Why should you expect work to be any different?

For example, how might you handle the job of answering a letter from a regular client? You should start with the client's file, so you have the client's past history of association with your company at hand. You can then refer quickly, easily, and accurately to any pertinent facts. You can verify the spelling of names based on materials sent to you from the original sources. You should be able to cite dates, based on copies of invoices or order forms. You would have copies of all earlier letters to refer to. You'll likely discover resources you didn't know existed.

The point is, by going to the client's file, you don't risk embarrassing yourself (and your company) by being uninformed. What you know influences what goes into the letter, and the quality and content of the letter is likely to be greatly improved.

Assuming you're using a paperwork process, when you complete a letter and get ready to put it into your out box, what do you do with the client's file? You take one or two minutes to put it into order. Sort letters into chronological order, with the most current letter on top. Eliminate duplicate letters. If there are loose business cards in the file, staple them to the folder itself so they don't fall out of the file and become lost. Or file them in the Rolodex. Two minutes, tops! And when you put the file back, it will be in better shape and more current than it was when you picked it up. That's maintenance.

This maintenance routine applies to your computer files as well. If the composed letter is in the client's directory, quickly glance through the rest of the directory, purge any unneeded documents and organize what's left. A colleague of mine found 1,800 messages in someone's groupware database. No one can use that much information or keep up with it. His client simply didn't organize (or more likely, didn't delete) as he went along. Time is not the issue. The issue is making organization part of the work process.

MAKE IT EASY

The purpose of maintenance is to make it easy for people to produce. If the copy machine runs out of paper while you're making copies, fill the machine to a functional level. Don't put a dozen sheets in the tray so you can finish your job and leave the next person to run out of paper. Don't leave your files in such a hopeless state that no one, yourself included, can hope to make sense of them. Instead, turn everything you touch into a tool for increased efficiency and productivity.

Maintenance means organizing yourself in a way that makes forward movement easy. If you empty your stapler, refill it. If you reach in your drawer and you're out of staples, go to supply now and get a box of staples. Fill your stapler and get on with your work. Don't leave small details hanging unsettled, so they trip you up at a later time. Few things are as frustrating when trying to take a telephone message as reaching for a pen and not finding one or going through half a dozen before you find one that actually works. If a pen is out of ink, throw it away; today most pens are meant to be disposable.

SHOULD YOU BE MAINTAINING IT IN THE FIRST PLACE?

For maintenance to continue, it has to consume as little of your time and effort as possible. Otherwise, being human, you're going to find yourself putting it off "until it's more convenient," or you're "not quite so tired," or "when you have the time" or whatever excuse you may find not to do it. Therefore, you want maintenance to be both efficient and painless.

If you've been thorough in purging your files, you'll have little (or at the least much less) to maintain. If you discover that you are spending time maintaining something you seldom if ever use, you have to question its worth to you. Start questioning why you're maintaining it. If it's something you can honestly do without, do without!

MAINTENANCE AND *DO IT NOW*

If you have taken to heart the concept of *Do It Now* you will have ample opportunity to reinforce it with maintenance. Why? Because maintenance isn't always the most "important" or most "urgent" thing to do. There will always be reasons to postpone a maintenance action. But if the words *Do It Now* pop into your head when you first recognize some maintenance action, you will act. If you see some tool that needs repair, you will *Do It Now*. If a supply runs out you will fill it immediately. *Do It Now* becomes the habit and it extends itself to maintenance.

MAKE MAINTENANCE A HABIT

Just as you automatically brush and floss your teeth in the morning it's best and easiest to establish nonthinking, efficient maintenance routines in your work. As covered in Chapter 3, batching and scheduling the processing of your paperwork and e-mail daily keeps your day-to-day work flow under control. A weekly organizing time can be incorporated into your weekly planning process to maintain your organized state. Bring your filing up to date. Back up your hard drive. Check on your supplies.

Just as you've scheduled a time each day to empty your in tray, you should schedule a time for the big jobs that are so tempting to put off, such as purging your files of any unnecessary clutter they may have accumulated. I have often found people do this sort of complete cleaning of the office at the end of the year, usually between Christmas and New Year's when it seems everything slows down in the office. They use the time to get rid of the old year's papers, set up the next year's files, purge what they haven't used lately, get rid of the stacks of magazines they saved to read, and generally clean up. While this is better than not doing it at all, it is, in my experience, not enough. Purging and cleaning on a quarterly basis seems to work best. Schedule it in your calendar, say half a day. Close the door and get to work reorganizing, purging, going through all of your books, reference files, archives, and such.

Figure 10.1 shows a schedule for maintaining your system.

THE 21-DAY CHALLENGE

An IBT Australian colleague, Sharon McGann, has enjoyed a great deal of success with her students applying what she has dubbed her 21-Day Challenge. At the very beginning of the PEP process, Sharon asks each of her students to select one habit to work on and change for the better. The challenge is to work on the habit every day for 21 days. The catch is if you miss a day, then you go back to the beginning; you must keep at it for 21 consecutive days!

Progress is monitored and discussed by Sharon and her student throughout the whole PEP process (which might last several months). This habit-changing process becomes the student's personal model of what occurs while trying to develop one new habit. This understanding is then used as a basis for further action plans and other habit changes.

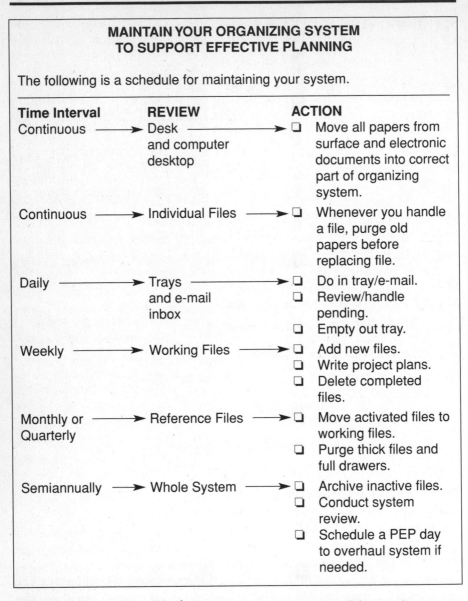

Figure 10.1 Schedule for maintaining your organizing systems.

Are you up to the challenge? What work habit would you most like to change? Devise a strategy to change the habit, to substitute a new habit for this unwanted one. And every day for 21 days straight, carry out your habit-changing plan. If you fail one day, begin again from day one. Keep track of your experiences and feelings during this process.

Understanding better how you respond to this challenge will make the next challenge that much easier to meet.

MAINTENANCE OF COMMON FILES

One hard-won lesson learned helping clients maintain their common file organization is if everyone is responsible for the files, no one will take responsibility.

As a team leader, it is up to you to assign *named individuals* responsibility for the department common files. The responsibilities can be divided up—one person for the shared drive files, another for the shared paper files, and so forth. All team members know who is responsible for what.

The same can be said for other common tools. If a common calendar is kept to track team schedules or where people are, it is important that one person be made responsible for its maintenance.

MAINTENANCE AND TRAVEL

I'm on the road most of the time. I travel overseas monthly and in the United States once or twice a month. By choice, our office has no assistant. We organize ourselves and cover for each other. The idea of how to do this came from a small company in Sweden and has served us well since.

We have had to use electronic tools as well as services from the telephone company to keep in touch. We make it a practice of calling the office every day and processing what has come in, over the telephone. We have had to organize ourselves to do this. Whoever is in the office keeps all incoming correspondence at hand under each person's name. As one of us calls in all of the correspondence is quickly gone through. Normally we respond to this correspondence immediately by telephone from where we are. You can believe this is a fast process because telephone costs are high and we don't care to waste money. If a fax needs to be sent, the person in the office sends it. If there is junk mail we throw it away. Some items can only be dealt with when we return, but they turn out to be much less than would otherwise be there. This system has worked very well in all companies where it has been introduced.

One executive never schedules a meeting for exactly when he returns. He always allows himself a few open hours upon return to wrap up everything from his trip (summary of activities, receipts, any offers he may have to prepare as a result of the trip) and get caught up with all that has accumulated while he was away.

We once worked with a company that had sales representatives working out of their homes. They organized their week so they would do their sales calls Monday through Thursday and spend Friday in the office getting the administration in order and setting up the new week. The reps regularly complained that one day was not enough in the office; they had to work on the weekend to keep up. However, one rep always managed to get his work done in the five-day period. How he did it was simple. He had envelopes addressed to the regional office, corporate office, his boss, accounting, and home office in his briefcase. As something came up to be forwarded to one of those places he would put it immediately in the appropriate envelope. He would process his receipts daily and they would go into the accounting envelope. By the time he was on his way home on Thursday all he would have to do was mail the envelopes. Meanwhile he called in and handled his phone messages several times a day and dealt with all of them immediately. When we put this system in with the other sales reps the problem disappeared.

PREVENTIVE MAINTENANCE

Not only must you focus on maintaining a well-organized state, you must consider the actions you can take to prevent future organizational problems. For example, when you complete this year's tax return, set up a file for the new year. As tax-related information arrives during the year, file it immediately. If you plan ahead, and start the tax preparation process early, collecting the necessary information during the year, you won't panic around March and April when it's due.

You can also identify peak periods during the year and organize yourself to deal effectively with those periods. Early preparation can lessen the burden when those peak periods arrive.

MAINTENANCE AND CONTINUOUS IMPROVEMENT

Even after all the times I used the word "maintenance" in this chapter, it is not precisely what you should be concentrating on. Yes, an end product is to prevent you from backsliding into old, nonproductive habits. It isn't enough, however, to PEP yourself up and then concentrate only on keeping things that way. You also have to work to make things better. You should work conscientiously and deliberately to improve how you do your work. In today's fast-paced, competitive environment it isn't enough to do better and stay that way. You must continue to excel. Even if you've made considerable progress, your real goal should be continuous improvement in everything you do.

I've mentioned that people seldom include tasks on their To Do lists that are geared toward improving how they complete their work. It isn't that people aren't thinking about these things. In fact, with quality and reengineering drives under way in most companies, many people are thinking about exactly these things but not in relation to their day-to-day work. Instead, they think of continuous improvement in terms of maintaining the plant's no-defects product record for a year.

Every week I make it a point to ask myself the question, "What will I do in the next week to improve my work situation?" There have to be several tasks on my weekly plan that will make my work life easier, make me more effective, increase my knowledge, or in some way change the way it is to a better way.

I might add a task to read two chapters from a software application I'm interested in expanding my use of. I have seen people choose tasks from their personal improvement goals and schedule them into their work calendars. I encourage people to add those spontaneous ideas that come up and act on them. "Learn how to use that new printer" might be one. We all have a thousand and one things we would like to do or get to make things better. Well, do them!

Include these objectives in your weekly plan. Schedule them. You will discover that you tend to figure out how to get them done in the least amount of time. Because the task is there, you act on it. Better yet, gradually and continuously your office is not only keeping its new image and efficiency, it is improving it.

You are making change part of your everyday life. And you are the one directing the change.

PERIODIC CATCH-UP

Some people don't feel the need to maintain their organization minute-by-minute. They may not care to. They have successfully kept pace with their workload by periodically catching up on their organization. If in the middle of a project or peak period they will keep up as best they can, at the end of it they can spend the time they need to get themselves back in order. Here are a few important things to consider if you decide to work this way: Do not allow more than a couple of weeks to go by before you get reorganized. You should be very thorough about your cleanup. Keep very good reminder systems in place so important things don't fall between the cracks.

MINIMUM MAINTENANCE

Once you're organized, the minimum maintenance you should do (which is better than nothing) is to clean off your desk each day before you go home.

WHAT TO DO WHEN IT ALL GOES TO POT

So okay, you have purged your desk and office and it looks like the cockpit of an F-16 aircraft. You are organized like never before. You finally got into a routine that keeps your day-to-day flow of paper, messages, information, e-mail, and so forth under control. You plan your work each Friday. You bought a notebook computer and have begun to learn an organizing software, and you feel pretty good about yourself. You are cruising along and bang—you run into a brick wall! You are called to Tokyo to replace a colleague for six weeks. Or a big customer puts your account up for review and you need to prepare a presentation to salvage it, so for two weeks straight, 16 hours a day, you are dealing with that. Or you go on vacation and come back to backlogs and a mess all over again. Something like this will happen to you. And let me tell you, you'd better be clever with how you respond.

In my experience, people do not fall back into their *new* ways. No, chances are they slide back into old habits. And face it, you managed to cope using your old ways, right? It has probably been a real struggle to get organized. To have to do the Personal Efficiency Program (PEP) all over again! It was a good try, but you're just not the organized type. Believe me, I have heard all of these. Don't despair or give up. There is an easy and painless way to deal with this. Have a *Do It Now* day. Put a sign on your door saying you are off for the day, pile all of your papers on your desk, and go through the process again. It is much easier and takes far less time than the first time you did it. Maybe a few hours and your paperwork will be under control again.

To make this *Do It Now* day easier, try to keep up with your daily flow of information, anyway. If you are having to spend your days getting the presentation prepared, take an hour of that time and blast through what has come in the day before. Delegate liberally, then and there. Be decisive (even ruthless) about what you are not going to do. Use (and maintain) your tickler system to get papers off the desk and in their proper place. Take advantage of the circumstances to see how efficient you can be, and when you are back to normal keep that same pace!

It may never get this bad for you. But the work flow usually shifts at times and you may find yourself beginning to drown. One client, a director of one of the largest industrial firms in the world, described it this way:

When work builds up and momentarily gets on top of me, I know what to do to deal with it because I have learned the necessary procedures.

You now have learned the procedures, too.

Maintenance means recognizing the inherent cycle within every piece of work you do, from preparing yourself to do the work to putting everything back where it belongs after the work is completed, and guaranteeing that everything is in as good or better condition than when you first picked it up. Maintenance means organizing yourself while you work.

The most important thing to maintain is change for the better.

FOLLOW-UP FOR CHAPTER 10

1. Recognize maintenance as the most basic and practical of work routines, and you'll be guaranteed a smoothly operating system for years to come. Make it a point to practice basic, practical maintenance routines that will guarantee the hard work you've put in to "get PEPped" will pay off for years to come.

2. Make your maintenance routines automatic, exactly in the same planned way you change the oil in your car. It's worth your time and effort to establish nonthinking, daily routines to maintain yourself and to maintain an organized state. Failure to maintain the system will result in an inability to work at all.

3. Have systems in place that will prevent you from falling back into old ways. Have routines that trigger continuous personal improvement and help you maintain those systems as a matter of course. Schedule this maintenance into your week.

4. Remember to think of work to be done in terms of work cycles. Each piece of work has a beginning, middle, and end. The task beginning includes preparing and setting up for the task. In the middle is the act of doing the task. Along with task completion, the ending includes maintenance points, including putting things back where they belong, and improving the condition of everything you touch, including files, tools, and so forth.

5. Realize that the advent of the computer means paper files aren't the only things that require maintenance. We now have computer files, and e-mail, as well. Maintaining your hard drive means having backup systems and using them regularly, so your electronically stored data isn't at the mercy of a sudden power failure.

6. Identify all common files of the team/department. Assign individual responsibility for the maintenance of these files.

7. Set a weekly organizing time to keep your long-term flow of work under control. Spend time each week planning for the coming week and maintaining your organized state. Get your filing up-to-date. Back up your hard drive. Check on your supplies. Use a quarterly, annual, or other schedule for maintenance to keep your maintenance on track and up-to-date.

8. If you discover you're spending time maintaining something you seldom use, seriously question its worth to you. If the reason you're maintaining something doesn't make sense to you, let that be a red flag to you. Ask why you're maintaining it. If it's something you can honestly do without, do without!

9. Organize yourself while you work. Make maintenance a part of the planning process and you'll be including it from step one to step done. Plan for success. Establish good habits. Make maintenance a non-thinking habit, and you'll find it's an easy step on your road to success.

10. Don't get comfortable! Your real goal should be continuous improvement in everything you do. PEP is a tool, or a framework, to allow you to accomplish it.

EPILOGUE

Just One New Habit

What characterizes a well-adjusted person is not chiefly the particular habits he holds, but rather the deftness with which he modifies them or responds to changing circumstances. He is set to change, in contrast to the more rigid, dogmatic, self-defensive individual who is set to sit tight.
—WENDEL JOHNSON

You may find very little profound thought in these pages, but there is a great deal of experience.

In essence, we have discussed the way you have conditioned yourself to approach your work: your habits. Most people will tell you (and I daresay too many of us believe) that it is very difficult to change habits. It isn't easy. But it can get better. It is possible to adopt new ways of doing things, to develop new habits in your life. You may have experienced walking into a new restaurant out of curiosity or by accident, and having found that you like it, you may make it a point to return again and again.

It all begins by adopting one new habit, that of taking action. *Do It Now* when the idea crosses your mind to test out a new method for doing your work. Try driving to work on a different route when the idea strikes you.

The bad habit isn't necessarily being messy. The bad habit includes constantly neglecting the habit's correction—never doing a thing about it. Break that cycle and act on it now rather than postponing. You will find you'll have it licked in no time. It's up to you to act on your ideas as they occur. You will discover you can indeed be the master of your habits.

Meeting Improvements Checklist

MEETING PREPARATIONS

1. The need for the meeting is clear. _____
2. Appropriate persons are attending. _____
3. A meeting location was reserved. _____
4. Needed material has been ordered and is available. _____
5. Meeting invitations have been sent out on time. _____
6. The invitation contains the following:

   • Purpose for the meeting. _____
   • Agenda points to be discussed. _____
   • Location of meeting. _____
   • Start and end times. _____
   • Preparations to be done by the participants. _____

CHAIRPERSON

1. Leads the meeting. _____
2. Keeps to the schedule. _____
3. Encourages participation. _____
4. Allows participants to complete their communications. _____

5. Ensures no straying from the subject. _____
6. Summarizes meeting points. _____
7. Ensures decisions are made (who? what? when?). _____

ASSISTANT

1. Writes minutes. _____
2. Notes who, what, and when for all actions. _____
3. Distributes minutes within acceptable time. _____

PARTICIPANTS

1. Always arrive on time. _____
2. Listen and attempt to understand others. _____
3. Do not interrupt. _____
4. Ensure an open and creative atmosphere. _____
5. Communicate clearly, and are businesslike and to the point. _____
6. Distribute documentation. _____

APPENDIX B

Time Stealers

MEETING TIME STEALERS

- Reason for meeting not clear.
- Wrong participants.
- Too many meetings.
- No agenda.
- Poorly written or no minutes.
- Useless conversations/discussions.
- No feedback.
- No decisions.
- Too little or no follow-up.
- Weak chairperson.
- Meetings not starting on time.
- Too many interruptions from outside.
- Failure to stick to the agenda.
- Not ending on time.
- Taking more time than estimated.
- No restricted time per item.
- Poor preparation by chair.
- Poor preparation by participants.
- No structure in meetings.
- Poor or no deliberation.
- Too long a distance and travel time to meeting location.

PHONE TIME STEALERS

- No plans for privacy.
- Unstructured conversations.

- Wish to be involved in too many things.
- Inability to keep conversations short.
- No realistic time estimated.
- Lack of priorities.
- No assistant's filter.

POOR DELEGATION

- Insecurity (i.e., fear of failing).
- Lack of trust in others.
- Too much control.
- Bad or no guidelines.
- Delegation of formal responsibilities without real authority.
- Fear that a colleague can do the job better than you.
- Preference for action over management.
- Stressed-out fellow workers.

IRRESOLUTE MANAGER

- Overlap of function descriptions with another's.
- Equivocal guidelines.
- Lack of self-discipline.
- Would rather do than think.
- No function description.
- Unclear priorities.

POOR COMMUNICATIONS

- Lack of awareness that colleagues need information.
- Language problems.
- Use of the wrong media.
- Bad timing.
- Listener not open to new ideas.
- Delay in answering.
- Too much information.
- Too much communication.

- Unclear communication.
- Poor information management.
- Poor communication management.
- Unreliable information.
- Irrelevant information.
- Incomplete information.

POOR DECISION MAKING

- Irresoluteness/delays.
- Lack of trust in decision process.
- Fear of the consequences of mistakes.
- No realistic time limits.
- Postponement of unpleasant and difficult tasks.
- Ignorance of the consequences of decisions.
- Lack of (strategic) vision.
- Lack of awareness of departmental objectives.
- Unclear targets.

LACK OF SYSTEMATIC WORKING

- Lack of priorities.
- Too many issues at the same time.
- No planning.
- All problems handled as if having the same priority.
- Too little too late.
- Too much in too short a time.
- No time for preparation.
- Interruptions.
- Inability to say no.
- Desire to be helpful despite impact on core work.
- Need to feel important and be involved with everything.
- Reluctance to be blunt with others.
- Need to be part of it all.
- Need to feel challenged or involved in something different/new.
- Inability to finish things.
- Lack of time limits.
- No respect for other person's time.

- Lack of insight.
- Inability to find the data in the mess easily.
- Stress.
- Lack of discipline.
- Lack of time to plan.
- Lack of planning.
- Time/capacity shortage.
- Interruptions by unexpected visitors.
- No plans to avoid unexpected visitors.
- Door always open.
- Personnel continuously coming in asking for approval.
- Inability to end a visit.
- Failure to say no to clients.
- Too many routine things and papers.
- Lack of priorities.
- Not delegating work, feeling you can do it quicker and better yourself.
- Everything dumped on desk.
- Lack of personal organization.
- Lack of short- and long-term goals.

COMPUTER MALFUNCTIONS

- Computer goes down and cannot access files.
- Internet connection is slow.
- Download of information is slow.
- E-mail attachments are in software application you do not have.
- You cannot find the information you need on an Internet search.
- Computer freezes and loses information.
- Peripherals (printers, modems, etc.) stop working.
- Computer crashes and you lose your information.

I am grateful to Time Manager International A/S for permission to use their material in the compilation of this time wasters list.

APPENDIX C

Recommended Reading

Becker, Franklin and Fritz Steele. *Workplace by Design*. San Francisco: Jossey-Bass Publishers, 1995.

Bettger, Frank. *How I Raised Myself from Failure to Success in Selling*. New York: Simon & Schuster, 1947.

Bittel, Lester R. *Right on Time*. New York: McGraw-Hill, 1991.

Bliss, Edwin C. *Getting Things Done: The ABC's of Time Management*. New York: Scribner, 1976.

Bruce, Andy and Ken Langdon. *Do It Now*. New York: DK Publishing, Inc., 2001.

Covey, Stephen R. *The Seven Habits of Highly Effective People*. New York: Simon & Schuster, Inc., 1989.

Drucker, Peter F. *The Effective Executive*. New York: Harper & Row, 1966.

Dyszel, Bill. *Microsoft Outlook 2002 for Dummies*. Hoboken: John Wiley & Sons, 2001.

Ellis, Albert and William J. Knaus. *Overcoming Procrastination*. New York: Signet, 1979.

Gookin, Dan. *PC's for Dummies*. Foster City: IDG Books, 1996.

Haberman, Scot Andrew Falciani and Scott Haberman. *Mastering Lotus Notes R5*. San Francisco: Sybex, 1999.

Hafner, Katie and Matthew Lyon. *Where Wizards Stay Up Late: the Origins of the Internet*. New York: Simon & Schuster, 1996.

Hedrick, Lucy H. *365 Ways to Save Time*. New York: Hearst Books, 1992.

Hill, Napoleon. *Think and Grow Rich*. New York: Fawcett Crest, 1960.

Hobbs, Charles. *Time Power*. New York: Harper & Row, 1987.

Jenks, James M. and John Kelly. *Don't Do. Delegate!* New York: Ballantine Books, 1985.

Jensen, Bill. *Work 2.0: Rewriting the Contract.* Perseus Publishing, 2002.

Knaus, William. *Do It Now: How to Stop Procrastinating.* New York: Prentice-Hall Press, 1979.

Kraynak, Joe. *The Complete Idiot's Guide to Computer Terms.* Indianapolis: Alpha Books / Macmillan Computer Publishing, 1994.

LeBoeuf, Michael. *Working Smart: How to Accomplish More in Half the Time.* New York: Warner Books, 1979.

Lehmkuhl, Dorothy and Dolores Cotter Lamping. *Organizing for the Creative Person.* New York: Crown Trade Paperbacks, 1993.

Londergan, Stephen and Pat Freeland (Author). *Lotus Notes 5 for Dummies.* Hoboken: John Wiley & Sons, 1st edition (May 1999).

Mackenzie, R. Alec. *The Time Trap.* New York: McGraw-Hill, 1972.

Mayer, Jeffrey J. *Time Management for Dummies.* Foster City, CA: IDG Books, 1995.

McCay, James T. *The Management of Time.* Englewood Cliffs, NJ: Prentice-Hall, 1959.

McGee-Cooper and Ann and Duane Trammell. *Time Management for Unmanageable People.* New York: Bantam Books, 1993.

Morris, Larry. *E-Mail and Messaging.* Indianapolis: New Riders Publishing, 1994.

Negroponte, Nicholas. *Being Digital.* New York: Vintage Books, 1995.

Nelson, Stephen L. *The World Wide Web for Busy People.* Berkeley: Osborne/McGraw-Hill, 1996.

Peters, Thomas J. and Robert H. Waterman, Jr. *In Search of Excellence.* New York: Harper & Row, 1982.

Petrick, Jane Allen. *Beyond Time Management.* Palm Beach, Florida: Informed Decisions International, Inc., 1998.

Schlenger, Sunny and Roberta Roesch. *How to be Organized in Spite of Yourself.* New York: New American Library, 1989.

Senge, Peter M. *The Fifth Discipline.* New York: Doubleday/Currency, 1990.

Seymour, Jim. *Jim Seymour's PC Productivity Bible.* New York: Brady/Simon & Schuster, 1991.

Winston, Stephanie. *Getting Organized.* New York: Warner Books, 1978.

INDEX

About the Institute for Business Technology

The Bridge between Human Behavior and Technology

Should you wish to download free copies of any of the forms found throughout this book, copies of the Appendixes (Meeting Improvements Checklist and Time Stealers), please see our company web site at www.ibt-pep.com, or write or call:

> The Institute for Business Technology International Inc.
> P.O. Box 1057
> Boca Raton, FL 33429, USA
> Telephone (1) 561-3670467
> Fax (1) 561-3670469
> E-mail ibtint@ibt-pep.com

If you would like more information about the Personal Efficiency Program or if you would like to speak with a PEP representative, contact one of the following Institute for Business Technology offices:

IBT Argentina
Besares 2268
(1429) Ciudad de Buenos Aires,
Argentina
Telephone (54) 11 4702–5211
Fax (54) 11 4702–5211 (same as
    voice number)
E-mail egonilski@arnet.com.ar

IBT Asia Pacific
Level 10
56 Berry Street
North Sydney NSW 2060
Australia
Telephone (61) 2 99553333
Fax (61) 2 99555480
E-mail ibtanz@ibt-group.com.au
Web site www.australia.ibt-pep.com

IBT Australia
Level 10
56 Berry Street
North Sydney NSW 2060, Australia
Telephone (61) 2-99553333
Fax (61) 2-99555480
E-mail ibtanz@ozemail.com.au

IBT Austria
Reichsratsstrabe 5
1010 Wien, Austria
Telephone (43) 14039904
Fax (43) 14035213
E-mail office@ibt-pep.at
Web site www.ibt-pep.at

IBT Benelux
P.O. Box 688
1180 AR Amstelveen,
Burgemeester Haspelslaan 31
1181 NB Amstelveen,
Netherlands
Telephone (31) 206473752
Fax (31) 206477633
E-mail ibt@ibt-nl.demon.nl
Web site www.belux.ibt-pep.com

IBT Canada/Caribbean
78 Donegani, Suite 210
Pointe Claire
Quebec H9R 2V4, Canada
Telephone (1) 514 426 2325
Fax (1) 514 426 4986
E-mail pep@ibtcda.ca

IBT Consulting (M) Sdn. Bhd.
P.O. Box 127
14007 Bukit Mertajam
Penang, Malaysia
Telephone 604–5371843
Mobile 019–4773570
Fax 604–5386708
E-mail mbahari@tm.net.my

IBT Do Brasil
VMF Com. e Representação Ltda
Rua Dr. Carlos Augusto de Campos,
170-133
04750-060 São Paulo-SP, Brasil
Telephone 55 11-5548 33 89
E-mail Brasil@ibt-pep.com

IBT France
Case Postale 339, CH-1224
Chene-Bougeries
Geneva, Switzerland
Telephone (41) 228691100
Fax (41) 228691101
E-mail ibt@ibt.fr
Web site http://fr.ibt-pep.com

IBT Germany
Wilhelmstr 43
58332 Schwelm, Germany
Telephone (49) 233693900
Fax (49) 2336939030
E-mail info@ibt-pep.de
Web site www.ibt-pep.de

IBT South Korea
c/o HI-PRO Consulting
Samdo officetel 601
12-1 Yoido-dong
Youngdeungpo-ku
Seoul, South Korea 150-010
Telephone (82) 2 761 1080
Fax (82) 2 761 1082
E-mail hipro@chollian.net

IBT Luxembourg
87 Bd. Robert Shuman
L 8340 OLM
Luxembourg
Telephone (352) 308997
Fax (352) 305228
E-mail info@ibtconsult.com
Web site www.belux.ibt-pep.com

IBT Mexico
1651 Scooter Lane
Fallbrook, CA 92028, USA
Telephone (1) 760-731-1400
Fax (1) 760-731-1414
E-mail bary.sherman@ibt-pep.com

IBT New Zealand
Level 5, 27 Gillies Ave.
Newmarket, New Zealand
Telephone 64 9 529 1740
Fax 64 9 529 1741
E-mail k.anda@xtra.co.nz
Web site www.nz.ibt-pep.com

IBT Norway
Vardevn. 13A
N-1440 Drobak, Norway
Telephone (47) 64936210
Fax (47) 64936219
E-mail johan@ibtgruppen.no
Web site www.ibtgruppen.no

IBT Poland
Ul.Orzechowska 4/1
02-068 Warsaw, Poland
Telephone +48-22-875 0321
Fax +48-22-875 0322
GSM +48-695 590 7595
E-mail pim@jmenter.com.pl
Web site www.ibt-polska.com

IBT Scandinavia A/S
Lyngsoe Alle 3
2970 Hoersholm, Denmark
Telephone (45) 4925 1494
E-mail info@ibt-scandinavia.com
Web site www.ibt-scandivania.com

IBT Spain
IBT Consulting
C/Espronceda, 19 bajo A
28003 Madrid, Spain
Telephone +34-91 536 04 02
Fax +34-91 554 30 03
GSM +34-609 11 92 61
E-mail anne-marie.hansson
    @ibtconsult.com
Web site www.es.ibt-pep.com

IBT Sweden
Kraketorpsgatan 20
431 53 Molndal, Sweden
Telephone (46) 31-7061950
Fax (46) 31-877990
E-mail info@ibt.se
Web site www.ibt-pep.se

IBT Switzerland/France
Case Postale 339
CH-1224, Chene-Bougeries
Geneva, Switzerland
Telephone (41) 228691100
Fax (41) 228691101
E-mail ibt@ibt-pep.ch
Web site www.ibt-pep.ch

IBT United Kingdom
P.O. Box 95
Dorking, Surrey
RH4 3FR, England
Telephone (44) 1306887944
Fax (44) 1306884161
E-mail help@ibtonline.co.uk
Web site www.ibtonline.co.uk

IBT USA
1651 Scooter Lane
Fallbrook, CA 92028, USA
Telephone (1) 760-731-1400
Fax (1) 760-731-1414
E-mail bary.sherman@ibt-pep.com